SPACE
ENCYCLOPEDIA

 Om Books International

Reprinted in 2020

Corporate & Editorial Office
A-12, Sector 64, Noida 201 301,
Uttar Pradesh, India,
Phone: +91 120 477 4100
Email: editorial@ombooks.com,
Website: www.ombooksinternational.com

© Om Books International 2016

ISBN: 978-93-84625-95-5

Printed in China

10 9 8 7 6

Sales Office
107, Ansari Road, Darya Ganj,
New Delhi 110 002, India
Phone: +91 11 4000 9000
Email: sales@ombooks.com

SPACE
ENCYCLOPEDIA

Om
KIDZ
An imprint of Om Books International

Contents

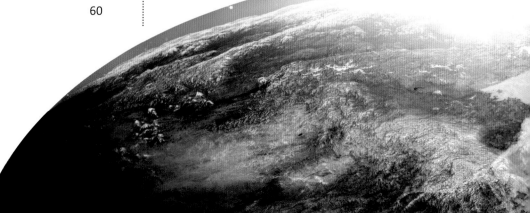

What is Space?

Space begins where Earth's atmosphere ends. There was a time when space was believed to be completely empty. However, this is not true. The vast gaps between the stars and the planets are filled with huge amounts of gases and dust. Even the emptiest parts of space contain at least a few hundred atoms or molecules per cubic metre.

● Space is black

There is neither air to breathe nor light to scatter in space, making it difficult for humans to survive. Space is black and not blue like our sky. This is because the amount of oxygen molecules is comparatively less in space. It mainly consists of vacuum and the molecules present are not sufficiently close because of which sound does not get transmitted.

● How big is it?

No one really knows how big space is. Long distances in space are measured in "light-year", which represents the distance that light takes to travel in a year. This is roughly about 9.3 trillion km.

● Marvels of space

Besides vacuum, space consists of planets, stars, several hundred galaxies, matter, dust, gases and so on. Just like we have winds, there are solar winds that occur in space. Let us look at all the amazing things that exist high up in the heavens that leave us awestruck every time we explore it.

Space – Introduction

Outer space is the empty void that exists between various celestial bodies, including Earth. Space is not completely empty. It consists of hard vacuum with low density of particles, mostly plasma of hydrogen and helium, as well as some electromagnetic radiation, magnetic fields, neutrinos, dust and cosmic rays.

Density and temperature

The baseline temperature in space is 2.7 Kelvin (K). We know this based on the background radiation from the Big Bang. There is a fourth state of matter called plasma, which is neither solid, liquid or gaseous. Plasma accounts for most of the baryonic or ordinary matter in space. It has a density of less than one hydrogen atom per cubic metre and a temperature of millions of Kelvin. It lies in the space between the galaxies. The local concentrations of plasma have condensed into stars and galaxies.

Dark matter

Observations have provided evidence that 90 per cent of the mass in most galaxies is in an unknown form called "dark matter". Dark matter interacts with other matter through gravitational forces, but not electromagnetic forces. Current data indicates that the majority of the mass-energy in the observable universe is a poorly understood vacuum energy of space. Astronomers, over time, have labelled this as "dark energy". Intergalactic space occupies the maximum volume of the universe.

Even space has laws

The Outer Space Treaty established the framework for international space law. This treaty was passed by the United Nations General Assembly in 1967. The treaty prevents any claims of national sovereignty and allows all the states to freely explore outer space. The 1979 Moon Treaty made the surfaces of objects like planets and the orbital space around these bodies, the jurisdiction of the international community covered by the Space Law.

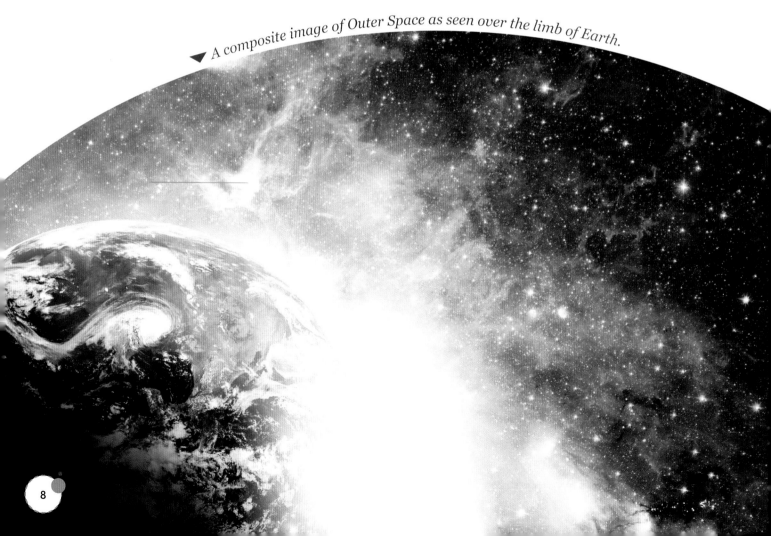

▶ A composite image of Outer Space as seen over the limb of Earth.

Despite the drafting of the UN resolutions for the peaceful use of outer space, anti-satellite weapons have been tested in Earth's orbit. Current legislation only prohibits weapons of mass destruction, like nuclear weaponry and atomic bombs being placed into outer space.

Space exploration

Humans began the physical exploration of space during the twentieth century. The advent of high-altitude balloon flights followed by manned rocket launches facilitated this exploration. Yuri Gagarin of the Soviet Union first achieved Earth's orbit in 1961. Unmanned spacecrafts have reached all the known planets in the solar system since then. The high cost of getting into space means that manned spaceflights have been limited to the lower Earth orbit and the moon. Voyager 1 became the first human-made spacecraft to enter the interstellar space, leaving the solar system in August 2012.

An expensive affair

The current economic burden prevents us from becoming a spacefaring civilisation. Certain proposed concepts for doing this involve non-

An image of a satellite orbiting Earth.

rocket space launchers such as rockoon, skyhook, a rocket sled and an air launch.

Other concepts include momentum exchange tethers that make use of centrifugal acceleration and ionic propulsion.

Space elevators are also one of the proposed means of conducting space travel without the use of expensive resources. A space elevator extends into the space attached to the surface of Earth with the help of a ribbon-like structure.

These proposed concepts look promising when it comes to reducing the financial implications of space travel and exploration as they aim at saving on fuel, energy, and loss of equipment and human lives.

Bust of Neil Armstrong, the first man to land on the moon.

Outer Space Environment

Outer space is a void that lies beyond the uppermost ranges of the atmosphere of Earth and between all other objects in the universe. Although it is considered to be a void, outer space can be thought of as an environment in itself. Radiation and objects pass freely through it. A human or another living being in the outer space environment without any protection would not survive even for a few moments.

Total vacuum

The basic environmental characteristic of outer space is the vacuum or the nearly total absence of gas molecules. The gravitational attraction of large bodies, such as planets and stars, pull the gas molecules close to their surfaces, which leaves the space between them practically empty. Stray gas molecules are usually found between these bodies. Their density is so low that they can be thought of as being unreal.

Effect of pressure in outer space

On Earth, the atmosphere applies pressure in all directions. At sea level, it is 101 kilopascals but in space, it is almost zero. With no external pressure, the air within a human's lungs, without any kind of protective shield, would immediately rush out into the vacuum.

Effect of pressure in space on humans

The sudden absence of external pressure that balances the internal pressure of the body would damage delicate tissues such as the eardrums and the capillaries. The body would swell, causing tissue damage and lack of oxygen supply to the brain. This would result in unconsciousness in under 10 seconds. Dissolved gases in the body fluids would expand, causing the skin to stretch much like a pumped up balloon. Bubbles would form in the bloodstream making it ineffective as a transporter of oxygen and nutrients to the body's cells.

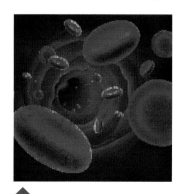

▲ *A human blood vessel.*

Temperature in space

The temperatures in outer space are hazardous. The objects that receive sunlight in space and are at Earth's distance from the Sun, can scale to over 120 °C while those on the shaded side can be as low as -100 °C. Because of the space environment, a comfortable temperature range cannot be sustained, posing a grave problem.

Other environmental factors

There are other environmental factors in space such as microgravity, radiation of electrically charged particles from the Sun, ultraviolet radiation and meteoroids. Meteoroids are small bits of rock and metal left over from the formation of the solar system about trillions of years ago and from comets and asteroids collisions. They are small but travel at very high velocities and can easily seep into the human skin. Debris from previous space missions is also very dangerous. A tiny paint chip travelling at thousands of kilometres per hour can do significant damage.

Planets and stars in space surrounded by nebulae. ▶

OUR UNIVERSE

The night sky has trillions and trillions of stars. Many of these are visible to the naked eye on a clear night. We can also see some of the planets that orbit our Sun as well as the moon. All these objects are a part of our universe.

However, they aren't the only part of our universe. The stars and planets that we can detect are only a tiny part of everything that's out there. The observable universe is a sphere that is a little over 90 billion light years in diameter. The rest of it is invisible to us because the originating light, post the Big Bang, hasn't even reached us yet.

The Big Bang

The Big Bang Theory is a widely accepted explanation for the existence of our universe. It states that the universe began as a singularity from a hot, dense state and rapidly expanded (not exploded as the name suggests) over nearly 13.8 billion years to the state that we are in at present, and continues to expand. This model was proposed by Russian mathematician Aleksandr Friedmann and Belgian astronomer Georges Lemaître during the 1920s.

An infographic explaining the Big Bang and the following events:

9 billion years later
Formation of the solar system and Earth.

300 million years later
Stars and galaxies begin to form.

380,000 years later
Electrons and nuclei combined into atoms.

First seconds after Big Bang
Birth of subatomic particles.

Expanding and cooling universe

Approximately 13.8 million years ago
Big Bang

Beginning of time and the dawn of light

According to this theory, the universe expanded from a highly compressed state (extremely high temperature and density). The cosmos contained a multitude of fundamental particles such as electrons, neutrons and so on. The free electrons made it impossible for any light to pass through, thus rendering our universe in darkness. There was also a huge amount of dark energy, a mysterious force that is thought to be the driving force behind our universe's current acceleration.

FUN FACT

American physicists Arno Penzias and Robert Wilson discovered the Cosmic Microwave Background Radiation quite accidentally in 1965. Along with evidence and fact, the scientists haven't yet been able to find any objects pre-dating the Big Bang. Hence, this theory has been accepted only as of now.

Falling temperatures and the afterglow

As the universe expanded, it cooled down rapidly. The temperature dropped from an extremely hot 5.5 billion degrees to a lot less. This caused the elementary particles to combine or degrade. Specifically, the protons decayed and the free electrons combined with the nuclei. A million years later, this light started passing through the universe. This primary light, or the "afterglow", is known as the Cosmic Microwave Background Radiation (CMBR).

An artist's rendition of the afterglow of the bang starting to leak into the universe.

Before the Big Bang

The question of what the beginning of the universe was like has been debated and pondered for over millennia. Today, it is widely accepted that the universe began at some point — it hadn't always been this way. This brings us to an even more important question; what existed before it?

Supernatural theories

Many attribute the creation of the universe to a supernatural being, i.e., a God or several Gods. It is stated that in the beginning, the only entity that existed was "The Being". The rest of the creation was a void. And then, "The Being" brought the entire universe into existence.

The scientific perspective

Modern scientists mostly agree that the universe began around 14 billion years ago with the Big Bang. What preceded the Big Bang is hotly argued amongst the scientists. Until the twentieth century, most scientists did not even agree that the universe had a beginning, so this debate is a fairly recent one.

However, all scientists agree upon one thing that existed before the universe began: chaos, or rather, statistical chaos. This is a scientific way of saying that we have no way of knowing for certain. All the laws of physics that hold true now and have held true since the last 14 billion years would have broken down at this beginning.

The bigger picture

One of the most popular theories is that our universe is a child universe, that our universe broke away from a parent universe during the Big Bang. If you consider the universe to consist of everything, it's difficult to understand how it could have come from something even bigger. If our planet is a part of a solar system, which is a part of a galaxy, which is a part of a universe, which is a part of a parent universe, can you imagine how vast infinity is?

However, the idea of something existing "before" the Big Bang is flawed. Before the Big Bang, the concept of time didn't exist. Therefore, the idea of something coming "before" couldn't exist either.

▶ *The birth of the universe was as a flash of light breaking through. Pictured here is an artist's imagination of this beginning.*

Other Theories of our Universe

The Big Bang is the most popular theory in existence today. However, there are and probably always will be other theories competing with this one. Some of the originally proposed theories have already been discarded. A theory is discarded if what has been observed of the universe does not match the predictions of the said theory.

Some of the more common theories are explained below:

Oscillation Model Theory – It states that the universe is a cyclic process.

Steady State Theory – Here, it is believed that the universe has no beginning or end. Matter is being continuously created. The theory is not prevalent at the moment.

Hawking-Turok Theory – This theory states that the universe was instantaneously created from a tiny particle like a pea. What this particle was made from is yet to be explored, but that is how it began.

Eternal Inflation Theory – The assumption here is that there are an infinite number of universes. Our universe is just one among them. There was a rapid expansion following the Big Bang. According to this theory, the rapid expansion never really stopped. It just continued in other universes. Thus, this inflation is "eternal".

FUN FACT

Among the varied theories about the universe, one states that the universe is nothing but a hologram. It's a flat, two-dimensional image that is projected onto a sphere by a vast computer.

Oscillation Model Theory

This theorises that the universe is a cyclic process. It started with a Big Bang and will continue till the universe expands to its maximum size. At this point, there will be a rapid contraction, called the "big crunch", until the universe contracts back to a single point. This singularity would then explode again, restarting the cycle. These oscillating cycles are a result of the collision of "branes". The branes are thought of as multi-dimensional membranes with something called a higher-dimensional volume. The mathematical model for these is quite complex.

▲ *An artist's rendering of an oscillating universe.*

The Steady State Theory

This theory is now an obsolete, expanding universe model. It was proposed as an alternative to the Big Bang theory. In this theory, new matter is continuously created as the universe expands.

Majority of cosmologists, astrophysicists and astronomers now reject this theory. The observational evidence points to a cosmology with a finite age of the universe.

This theory does not predict any age or a distinct point of origin. The idea was originally proposed by Sir James Jeans during the 1920s.

▶ *Sir James Jeans.*

This theory asserts that although the universe is expanding, it does not change its appearance over time; therefore, the universe has no beginning or end.

Steven Weinberg explained its failure as, "The steady state model does not appear to agree with the observed dL versus z relation or with the source counts... In a sense, the disagreement is a credit to the model. Alone among all cosmologies, the steady-state model makes such definite predictions that it can be disproved even with the limited observational evidence at our disposal". Thus, it was credited as a good example of cosmic theory, although it is incorrect.

Neil Turok and Stephen Hawking, authors of the Hawking-Turok theory

Eternal Inflation Theory

Our universe is just one among the many universes that exist. According to this theory, the rapid expansion, following the Big Bang, never really stopped. It just continued in other universes. Thus, this inflation is "eternal". In theories of eternal inflation, the phase of the inflation of our universe's expansion will never end. This is true for only some regions of our universe. As these regions expand very quickly, most of the volume of our universe at any given time is inflating.

This image is an artist's rendering of what different universes being born rapidly would look like. This collection of multiple universes is known as a multiverse.

The Hawking-Turok Theory

This theory co-exists with the Big Bang. Rather than explaining the Big Bang itself, it tries to explain that the Big Bang needed an impetus. This impetus was provided by a particle that they describe as an "instanton". The instanton is a hypothetical particle that has the mass of a pea but is much, much smaller in size. As a result of this basic assumption, the theory is also called the "universe from a pea" theory.

This cone is supposed to represent the space-time continuum. The direction of the arrow shows how it progresses. It starts as time moves up along the height of the cone while space moves around the width of the cone. The continuum is then a cone with its tip pointing downwards. As a result, at the tip, both space and time meet at a single point. This point is known as the "singularity".

Wormholes

A wormhole is a passage through the space-time continuum that could create a quicker route for long journeys across the universe. This is true only in theory. The existence of wormholes is predicted on the basis of the theory of general relativity. They could be dangerous and in case of a sudden collapse, extreme radiation and unsafe contact with exotic matter could occur.

Wormholes and the theory of general relativity

Lorentzian wormholes, also known as "Schwarzschild wormholes" or "Einstein-Rosen bridges" connect the spaces that can be modelled as vacuum resolutions of Einstein's field equations, through merging models of black and white holes. Physicists Albert Einstein and Nathan Rosen used the theory of general relativity in 1935 to suggest that "bridges" may exist that connect two different points in space and time, creating a shortcut, reducing the travelling time and distance, but only in theory.

What do wormholes look like?

They have two, possibly spheroidal, mouths that are connected by a throat, which could be straight or winding. Astrophysicist Stephen Hawking suggests that wormholes may exist in "quantum foam", the smallest environment in the universe, where extremely small tunnels continuously open and close, temporarily connecting different places and time.

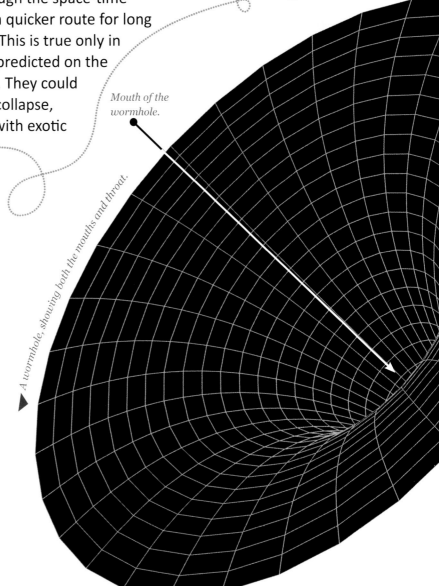

Mouth of the wormhole.

A wormhole, showing both the mouths and throat.

Problems of wormholes

Size: It is predicted that ancient wormholes exist on microscopic levels, which are about 10^{-33} cm wide. However, with the expansion of the universe, there is a possibility that some may have stretched to larger sizes.

Stability: The Einstein-Rosen wormholes would not be helpful for travel because they collapse quickly. However, recent research suggests that a wormhole containing "exotic" matter could remain open and unchanged for longer periods.

Exotic matter: Exotic matter contains negative energy density and huge negative pressure. If a wormhole contained adequate exotic matter, it could be used as a means of sending information or travellers through space.

FUN FACT

Wormholes are so tiny that humans couldn't use them, but with new technologies, scientists could possibly capture and enlarge them so that they could be useful to us.

Time travel

Besides connecting two separate regions within the universe, a wormhole could also connect two different universes. Some scientists speculate that if one mouth of a wormhole is positioned in a certain manner, time travel would become possible. However, Stephen Hawking argued against this. Though adding exotic matter to a wormhole may stabilise it to the extent that humans could travel safely through it, there is a possibility that the addition of "regular" matter could destabilise it as well.

Throat of the wormhole.

Too small for time travel

Wormholes such as these might prove to be too small and brief for human time travel. The question being, would we one day learn how to capture, stabilise and broaden them? According to Hawking, this is surely possible provided that we are prepared for some feedback. If we were to artificially prolong the life of a tunnel through folded space-time, then there is a possibility that a radiation feedback loop may occur; this would destroy the time tunnel like an audio feedback can ruin a speaker.

A tunnel in space

In space, masses that place pressure on different parts of the universe could combine eventually to create a kind of tunnel. This tunnel would, in theory, join two separate times and allow passage between them. It is also possible that some sudden physical or quantum property could avert such a wormhole from occurring.

Speedy travel

Wormholes allow superluminal or faster-than-light travel by ensuring that the speed of light is not exceeded locally at any time. While travelling through a wormhole, subluminal or slower-than-light speeds are used. If two points are connected by a wormhole, then the time taken to cross it would be less than the time taken by a light beam to travel through space outside the wormhole. However, a light beam travelling through the wormhole would always be faster than the traveller. To understand this phenomenon better, we can use the analogy that running from one place to another may take longer than driving the same distance.

Mouth of the wormhole.

Will the Universe End?

There are several theories that predict the end of the universe. However, if it will actually occur is uncertain. Scientists have been researching this and have come up with three theories as to how our universe could come to an end. There are three schools of thought that consider the universe to be open, flat or closed.

Open universe

Studies suggest that the universe will expand forever. As it expands, the matter it contains will spread and become thinner and thinner. The galaxies will exhaust their resources to make new stars. The existing stars will slowly fade. Instead of a fiery structure, the galaxies will transform into coffins filled with dust and dead stars. Then, the universe will become dark, cold and eventually, lifeless.

Flat universe

In this scenario, the universe will consume all the energy from the Big Bang and after it has consumed all the energy, thereby exhausting it, the universe will come to a stop. This is a contrast to the open universe theory because it will take an infinite amount of time for the universe to reach the equilibrium point of the consumption of energy.

Closed universe

Astronomers believe that a closed universe will reduce its pace until it reaches its maximum size. Then, it will recoil, collapsing on itself. Simultaneously, the universe will become denser and hotter until it ends in a hot and dense singularity. A closed universe will lead to what is called a "big crunch", which is the opposite of the Big Bang. However, scientists are still researching the end of our universe.

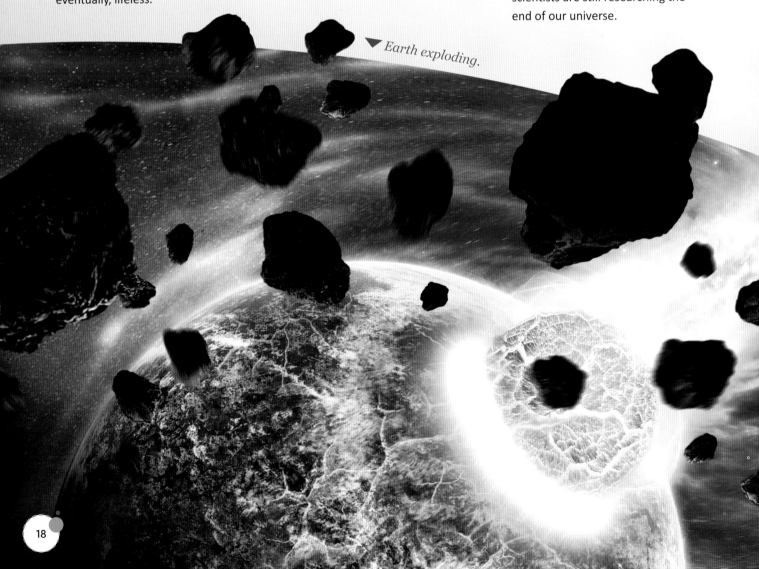

▼ *Earth exploding.*

A multiverse is a portmanteau of the words "multiple" and "universe".

The big crunch

This is based on Einstein's theory of general relativity. This theory suggests that the universe's expansion will stop at a certain point and it will begin to collapse into itself, pulling everything with it until it is transformed into the biggest black hole.

For scientists to predict the possibility of a big crunch with certainty, they will have to determine certain properties of the universe. One of them is its density. It is believed that if the density is larger than a certain value, known as the "critical density", a collapse is possible.

Multiverse

The multiverse theory states that there will be no real end to the universe. It states that when our universe was created, there were multiple more universes created and that they are all at different stages of their existence. When our universe ends, there will be other universes that will still go on and newer universes that will be created.

False vacuum

A false vacuum is a vacuum where the entropy is great but has not yet reached its maximum state. As a result, there is still a lower energy state that can be reached and some usable energy left in this false vacuum. This theory believes that every time we reach such a false vacuum, the universe decays to reach a true vacuum and begins multiple new universes in the process.

The big bounce

This is a theorised scientific model related to the beginning of the known universe. According to one version of the Big Bang theory of cosmology, in the beginning, the universe had infinite density. This seems to be at odds with everything else in physics. The big bounce is also a cyclic theory. It consists of multiple repetitions of the Big Bang followed by big crunches. The main difference is the absence of the "brane membranes" that dilate and bleed entropy out of the universe.

Our Universe Today

Our universe is huge and includes those things that we can see and know about as well as those that we cannot. The planets, stars and galaxies comprise only a small part of it. The part of the universe that we can see is called the observable universe. It is currently about 91 billion light years in diameter. The size of the entire universe is unknown and may be infinite. There are probably more than a 100 billion galaxies in the observable universe. Currently, our universe is made up of the following elements:

Energetic universe

There is a lot of energy in our universe. This energy helps us to understand and learn about its infiniteness. There are both positive and negative energies present. However, light energy allows us to see the objects in our universe. The energy present in celestial objects helps us to get a better understanding of it. Another form of energy that exists in the universe is that of the X-rays.

Distant quasar

Quasars are extremely bright, distant galaxies powered by supermassive black holes at their centres. Their light may help us probe the period when the first stars and galaxies were forming. Quasars are studied through telescopes both on Earth and in space.

◄ An x-ray image of NGC 4258/M106, a galaxy with extra arms, a supermassive black hole and a light illustration of glowing gas.

Galaxy group

Studies suggest that galaxies exist in groups. Galaxies that are a part of such groups frequently interact and even merge together in a vibrant cosmic merging of interacting gravity.

Star cluster

When the stars are born, they grow from large clouds of gas. As a result, they form in groups or clusters. After the remnant gas is heated and blown away, the stars come together due to gravity.

Star birth

Stars are born when clouds of gases and dust collapse. Due to this, their density and temperature increases. The temperature and density are highest at the centre of the cloud, where a new star eventually develops. The object that is formed at the centre of a collapsing cloud and which later grow into a star is called a "protostar".

Planet

Planets form one aspect of our universe. There are 15 planets in our solar system. However, of these, only eight planets orbit the Sun. Interestingly, evidence shows that there are several other planets in other galaxies.

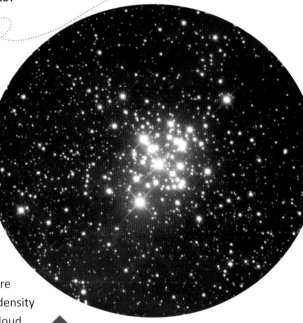

▲ *The Jewel box is a star cluster in our universe.*

Small world

Besides the galaxies, stars and planets, there also exist objects that float around in space. These objects include comets, asteroids, meteors as well as moons of other planets.

Unknown universe

Scientists suggest that our universe is composed as follows: Approximately 68 per cent dark energy, 27 per cent dark matter and 5 per cent normal matter. Studies about dark energy continue to astonish scientists as very little is known as of yet.

OUR GALAXY

▲ *Earth and our galaxy. This image shows Earth at night with trillions of stars that form our galaxy.*

A galaxy is a massive, gravitationally bound system consisting of stars, stellar remnants and interstellar mediums of gas, dust and dark matter. The word "galaxy" is derived from the Greek word "galaxias", meaning "milky", referring to the Milky Way.

Galaxies contain multiple planets, star systems, star clusters and many types of interstellar clouds. An interstellar medium of gas, dust and cosmic rays all lie between these objects. Many galaxies are believed to have supermassive black holes at their centre.

There are more than 170 billion galaxies in the universe. Most are 1,000 to 100,000 parsecs in diameter. The majority of the galaxies are organised into galaxy groups and clusters, which in turn usually form larger superclusters. At the largest scale, these associations are arranged into sheets and filaments or even walls that are surrounded by massive voids.

Types of Galaxies

The current estimate suggests that there are between 100 to 200 billion galaxies in the universe. Each one of these has hundreds of billions of stars. A recent German supercomputer simulation has pegged that number to be even higher than 500 billion. In short, there could be a galaxy out there for every star in the Milky Way. The Hubble Space Telescope is used to explore space and learn more about it. This telescope gives us an estimation of the number of galaxies that actually exist. There are various types of galaxies in the universe.

Elliptical galaxy

This is the most abundant type of galaxy found in the universe. However, because of their age and dimness, they are outshone by younger, brighter collections of stars. These galaxies do not have the swirling arms of their more well-known siblings, the spiral galaxies. In contrast, they are more rounded and in the shape of an ellipse, a stretched-out circle. Some stellar collections are more stretched than others. Elliptical galaxies are denoted by the letter E. They are also given a number from 0 to 7. An E0 galaxy looks like a circle while an E7 galaxy is elongated and thin. These galaxies have an extensive range of sizes. The largest elliptical galaxies can be over a million light years in diameter. The smallest dwarf elliptical galaxies are less than one-tenth the size of the Milky Way. These galaxies have very little gas and dust.

Spiral galaxy

Most of the bright galaxies in the neighbourhood of the Milky Way are spiral galaxies, although irregular galaxies are the most common. Spirals have the smallest range of masses and sizes. These objects can contain between 10,000,000,000 and 400,000,000,000 times the mass of our Sun, and their diameters range from 16,300 to 163,000 light years. Our own Milky Way is close to the upper value. All spiral galaxy labels begin with the letter S, followed by a lower case letter a, b or c.

Barred spiral galaxy

A barred spiral galaxy is one with a bar through the centre. Around two-thirds of the spiral galaxies have a bar-like region of stars at the centre. Their spiral arms emerge from the two ends of the bar that guide gases and dust towards the central bulge. The flow of this matter results in many barred spirals to have active nuclei. New stars are born as a result of gases and dust from these galaxies.

▶ *More than 60 per cent of the known galaxies are elliptical.*

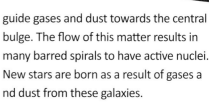

▲ *Messier 109 is a barred spiral galaxy.*

▲ Spiral galaxies are named after the spiral shape formed by their stars.

About 20 per ▶ cent of all galaxies are irregulars.

▼ Lenticular galaxy in space surrounded by thick dust lanes.

Lenticular galaxy

Lenticular galaxies share characteristics of both spiral and irregular galaxies. Like spiral galaxies, they have a central bulge and a flat disc-like shape. Like irregular galaxies, they are populated by old stars. The Sombrero galaxy, also called M104 or NGC 4594, is one of these. It is about 28 million light years from our planet in the constellation Virgo. It gets its name because it resembles a Mexican hat – sombrero. The dark dust lane forms the hat's rim and the galaxy's bulging core forms its crown.

Irregular galaxy

Irregular galaxies do not have many common features. Many of them are the result of galaxy collisions or near misses. One type of irregular galaxy is called the "starburst galaxy". Starburst galaxies are extremely bright as many new stars are born within a short period. These galaxies are usually found in groups or clusters, where collisions and near-misses between galaxies are common. In case of a few irregular galaxies, the astronomers cannot figure out why they look so strange. These galaxies are denoted by the letters "Irr".

Elements of our Galaxy

A galaxy is an extensive collection of stars, glowing nebulae, gas and dust united by gravity. Scientists believe that a black hole, which is the remains of a massive star, is situated at the centre of many galaxies. The galaxy that contains our solar system is called the Milky Way. There are several elements that form our galaxy.

Galaxy dust

The space between the stars is filled with gas and tiny pieces of solid particles or dust. Most of this gas and dust result from the death of stars, which either exploded or blew off their outer layers, returning their material to space. From this material, new stars are born. Mostly, this gas and dust can be detected using infrared light.

Star nursery

Stars are formed within clouds of hydrogen gas. A part of the cloud then forms a dense ball of gas. More gas is attracted because of gravity, thereby compressing the ball into a tighter and hotter mass. As a result, a nuclear fusion is triggered, which converts hydrogen into helium and radiates energy as a very bright star.

▲ *An image of the well-known Carina nebula caught by an European telescope, unveiling the previously hidden features of an exquisite star nursery.*

▲ *Dust usually obscures the view of the stars and the planets.*

Spiral arms

The Milky Way has spiral arms coming out of its central bulge. These arms are made up of young, bright, blue stars and older, white stars as well as dust and gas. There are stars that lie between these spiral arms; however, they are not as bright. These stars slowly orbit the central bulge following their own path. They take several hundred million years to complete their orbit.

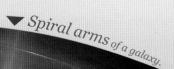

▼ *Spiral arms of a galaxy.*

Hot blue star

Stars get their colour depending on their temperature. The coolest stars appear red, while the hottest ones are blue. For a star, its temperature is determined by its mass. Blue stars have at least three times the mass of the Sun or even more. Interestingly, whether a star has 10 times the mass of the Sun or 150 solar masses, it appears blue to our eyes.

▲ *Stars display different colours in space. They get their colours due to their temperature and mass.*

Solar system

Our solar system was formed about 4.6 billion years ago. It includes the eight planets and their natural satellites, dwarf planets such as Pluto and Ceres, asteroids, comets and meteoroids. The Sun contains almost all the mass present in the solar system and exerts a tremendous gravitational pull on the celestial bodies.

▲ *The Solar System*

Central bulge

A galaxy contains stars, gas and dust. In a spiral galaxy such as the Milky Way, the stars, gas and dust are organised into a "bulge" and "disc", containing "spiral arms" and a "halo". The bulge is a round structure primarily made of old stars, gas and dust. The outer parts of the bulge are difficult to distinguish from the halo. The bulge of the Milky Way is roughly 10,000 light years across.

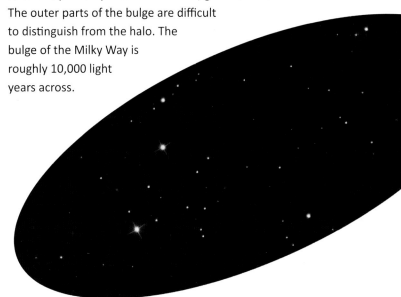

Black hole

Black holes are huge but surprisingly cover only a small region. Because of their mass, they have an extremely powerful gravitational force. Nothing can escape them; even light is trapped by a black hole. Black holes have three layers: the outer and inner event horizon, and the singularity. The event horizon of a black hole is the boundary around the mouth of the black hole, where light loses its ability to escape. The singularity lies at the centre of the black hole. It is a one-dimensional point that contains infinite mass in a considerably small space.

▲ *Black hole in one of the Nebulas.*

Dark matter

Dark matter is a kind of matter that cannot be seen using telescopes. However, it accounts for most of the matter in the universe. The existence and properties of dark matter are inferred from its gravitational effect on visible matter, radiation and the large-scale structure of the universe. Dark matter accounts for 23 per cent of the universe.

Colliding Galaxies

Several galaxies are members of a group or a cluster. As groups and clusters contain many galaxies that are close together, galaxies tend to collide with each other. In fact, the Milky Way galaxy is colliding with the Sagittarius Dwarf galaxy right now. Galaxy collisions are common, but stars in each galaxy are so far apart that star collisions are extremely rare. Even if galaxies do not actually collide, they can still cause harm to each other.

When galaxies interact

When two galaxies pass close to each other, the gravity that they exert can cause both of them to bend out of shape. Both crashes and near misses between the galaxies are referred to as "interactions".

What happens when they collide?

When two galaxies interact, the clouds of gas inside each galaxy may compress. Compressing the clouds can cause them to collapse under their own gravity, transforming them into stars. This process can lead to a burst of star formation in the interacting galaxies. A new generation of stars may form in a galaxy where the normal star formation may have stopped long ago. Galaxy collisions takes place over hundreds of millions of years, so we cannot see them occur. The various types of galaxies are given as follows:

Cartwheel galaxy

The cartwheel galaxy is also known as "ESO 350-40". This galaxy is a lenticular and ring galaxy. It is about 500 million light years away in the constellation of Sculptor. It is an estimated 150,000 light years across. It also has a mass of about $2.9 - 4.8 \times 10^9$ solar masses. Scientists have observed that it rotates at 217 km per second. It was discovered in 1941 by a Swiss astronomer, Fritz Zwicky. Zwicky considered his discovery to be "one of the most complicated structures awaiting its explanation on the basis of stellar dynamics". It is slightly larger than the Milky Way.

Black Eye galaxy

The Black Eye galaxy, also known as Messier 64 (M64), Evil Eye galaxy or Sleeping Beauty galaxy, is a famous spiral galaxy that is located in the constellation Coma Berenices. It lies at a distance of 24 million light years from Earth. It is known for the enormous light-absorbing dust band in front of its central region, which has earned the galaxy the names "black eye" or "evil eye". Because of the dust band, the stars in the galaxy's bright core are blurry. This galaxy is a popular target for amateur astronomers because its bright nucleus can be observed even through a small telescope. Messier 64 is also notable for being composed of two counter-rotating discs, almost equal in mass. The inner disc contains spectacular dust clouds and lanes.

▼ Cartwheel galaxy.

▼ Messier 64 (M64) or the Black eye galaxy.

▼ Mice galaxies right before their collision.

All the stars in this galaxy rotate in the same direction as the gas in M64's core region, i.e., clockwise, while the gas in the outer regions rotates in an anti-clockwise direction.

Mice galaxies

These galaxies, which are also known as NGC 4676, are a pair of interacting galaxies that are located around 300 million light years away towards the constellation Coma Berenices. These galaxies get their name because the long streams of stars, gas and dust thrown off of each other as a result of their interaction resemble the tails of a pair of mice. These galaxies will eventually merge to form a single galaxy. The tails are the remains of their spiral arms.

ARP 272

ARP 272 is a pair of colliding galaxies, which consists of two spiral galaxies, NGC 6050 and IC 1179. It is around 450 million light years from Earth in the constellation Hercules. The galaxies are a part of the Hercules Cluster, which is a part of the Great Wall — one of the largest known structures in our universe. The two galaxies in ARP 272 are in physical contact through their spiral arms.

Antennae galaxies

The Antennae Galaxies, also known as NGC 4038/NGC 4039, are a pair of interacting galaxies in the constellation Corvus. They are currently going through a starburst phase. Here, the collision of clouds of gas and dust, with knotted magnetic fields, causes rapid star formation. They were discovered in 1785 by William Herschel. These galaxies are locked in a fatal embrace. Once normal, calm spiral galaxies like the Milky Way, the pair has spent the past few hundred million years bickering with each other. This clash is so fierce that stars have been ripped from their host galaxies to form a streaming arc between the two. In wide-field images of these galaxies, the reason behind their name is clarified — far-flung stars and streamers of gas stretch into space, which create long tidal tails suggestive of antennae. These two galaxies are known as the Antennae Galaxies because the two long tails of the stars, gas and dust ejected from them due to the collision resemble an insect's antennae. The nuclei of these two galaxies will eventually join to become one giant galaxy.

UGC 8335

UGC 8335 is an interacting pair of spiral galaxies that resembles two ice skaters. It is located in the constellation of Ursa Major, the Great Bear, around 400 million light years from Earth. The interaction has united the galaxies through a bridge of material and has pulled together two curved tails of gas and stars from the outer parts of their bodies. Both galaxies show dust lanes in their centres. It ranks 238th in the Arp's Atlas of Peculiar Galaxies.

FUN FACT

Did you know that the Sun travels around a galaxy once every 200 million years – a journey of 100,000 light years?

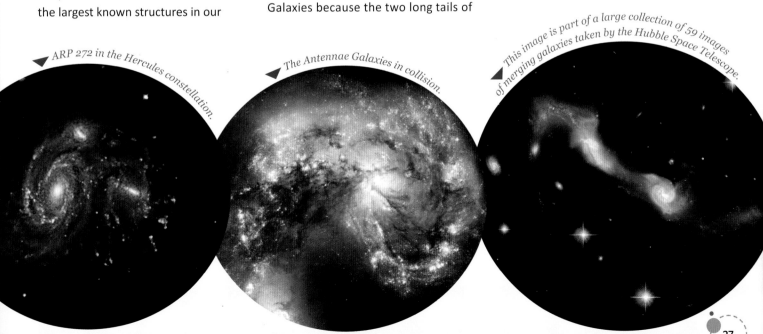

ARP 272 in the Hercules constellation.

The Antennae Galaxies in collision.

This image is part of a large collection of 59 images of merging galaxies taken by the Hubble Space Telescope.

Active Galaxies

From a normal galaxy, most of the light is emitted from the stars that are evenly distributed throughout the galaxy. However, there are some galaxies that emit intense light from their nuclei (the centre). If these same galaxies are viewed in the X-ray, ultraviolet, infrared and radio wavelengths, they seem to be giving off significant amounts of energy from their nucleus. Such galaxies are called active galaxies. They represent a very small percentage of all galaxies. There are four main types of active galaxies, which are given as follows:

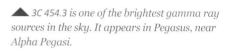

▲ *3C 454.3 is one of the brightest gamma ray sources in the sky. It appears in Pegasus, near Alpha Pegasi.*

Radio galaxy

A radio galaxy serves as a strong source of electromagnetic radiation or radio waves. Their discovery provides proof that the universe can expand, contradicting the steady state theory, suggesting that the universe would remain steady. Compared to ordinary galaxies, a radio galaxy emits as much as a thousand to a million times more energy per unit time. The giant elliptical galaxy M87 in the Virgo cluster is an example of a nearby radio galaxy.

Quasar

Quasars are the farthest objects that can be seen from our galaxy, and are extremely bright masses of energy and light. Quasar is short for "quasi-stellar radio source" or "quasi-stellar object". They are the brightest objects in our universe, although when seen through a telescope they do not appear that bright. This is because quasars are extremely far away. They emit radio waves, X-rays and light waves. They appear as faint red stars to us. Some are believed to produce 10 – 100 times more energy than our entire galaxy and is only as big as our solar system.

Blazar

A blazar is a dense energy source fuelled by supermassive black holes. They are considered to be one of the most dangerous phenomena in space. These extragalactic objects were first seen and discovered around 1972, because of the technology of "A Very Long Baseline Interferometry". The name was coined by astronomer Ed Spiegel in 1978. They are usually divided into two, the BL Lacertae objects (BL Lac) and Optically Violent Variable (OVV) quasars. There are also a few intermediate blazars, which have the properties of both the BL Lac and the OVV. They emit high-energy plasma jets as quick as the speed of light. They are a type of compact quasars.

They are characterised by their high speed and energy. They are also extremely powerful.

Seyfert galaxy

Almost all Seyfert galaxies are spiral galaxies and are named after the American astronomer Carl Seyfert, who identified them in 1943. They are among the most intensively studied objects in astronomy because they are thought to be nearby, low-luminosity versions of the same phenomenon as observed in quasars. They have cores that emit as much energy at all wavelengths as the total radiation output of our own Milky Way. However, they do not contain well-defined radio lobes. A striking feature of these galaxies is that their luminosity can change rapidly. In the constellation Pegasus, NGC 7742 is known to be a Seyfert galaxy. It is about 72 million light years away. It resembles a fried egg, with a very bright nucleus that is visible at all wavelengths. It is ringed by blue-tinted stars forming regions and faintly visible spiral arms. The yolk — its yellow centre — is about 3,000 light years across.

◀ *The power of a quasar originates from supermassive black holes that are believed to exist at the core of all galaxies.*

THE MILKY WAY

▲ Spiral galaxy NGC 6744 is believed to resemble the Milky Way a lot.

The Milky Way was formed shortly after the Big Bang as one of the denser areas of mass distribution in the universe. Compare this to a pudding with lumps in it, the lumps being the stuff the universe emerged from. Some of these denser areas were globular clusters, which contain older stars.

These stars form the stellar halo. Within a few billion years of the formation of the first stars, the Milky Way had accumulated so much mass that it started spinning quickly. Due to the conservation of the amount of rotation, the gaseous interstellar medium collapsed from a near-spherical shape and changed to a flat disc. Thus, the newer stars, including the Sun, formed in this spiral disc.

The galaxy formation process has not stopped as our universe is constantly evolving. The Milky Way has already swallowed several galaxies and is expected to collide with the nearest galaxy Andromeda in a few billion years.

Parts of the Milky Way

The Milky Way consists of three basic components: (1) the disc that contains the spiral arms (2) the halo (3) the nucleus or the central bulge. The halo and the nucleus are collectively referred to as the spherical components of the galaxy.

Bulge

The bulge is a round structure made primarily of old stars, gas and dust. The outer parts of the bulge are difficult to distinguish from the halo. The bulge of the Milky Way is roughly 10,000 light years across.

Halo

It primarily contains single old stars and clusters of old stars. It also contains dark matter, which is the material that we cannot see. The Milky Way's halo may be over 130,000 light years across.

Disc

The disc is a flattened region that covers the bulge in a spiral galaxy. It is shaped like a pancake. The Milky Way's disc is 100,000 light years across and 1,000 light years thick. It consists of mostly young stars, gas and dust, which are concentrated in its spiral arms. Some old stars are also present.

Spiral arms

The spiral arms are curved extensions. They begin at the bulge of a spiral galaxy, appearing like a "pinwheel". The spiral arms contain a lot of gas and dust as well as young blue stars. They are found only in spiral galaxies.

Stars, gas and dust

Stars come in a variety of types. Blue stars, which are very hot, tend to have shorter lifespans than red cooler stars. The regions of galaxies where stars are currently forming are bluer than the regions where there has been no recent star formation. Spiral galaxies have a lot of gas and dust, whereas elliptical galaxies contain very little of it.

Centre of the Milky Way

The galactic centre is the rotational centre of the Milky Way. It is located about 27,000 light years from Earth. There is believed to be a supermassive black hole (SBMH) at the centre of the Milky Way, known as Sagittarius A* (Sgr A*). Besides the Sgr A*, there are massive star clusters, such as the Arches, Quintuplet and the GC star cluster.

Supermassive black hole

A SMBH is the largest type of black hole, in the range of many hundreds thousands to billions of solar masses. The SMBH is found in the centre of almost all massive galaxies.

In and around the SMBH

The accretion of gas around the black hole, typically in the shape of a disc, works as a major fuel for the SMBH. The central region around the Sagittarius A* contains thousands of other stars. More than 100 OB and Wolf – Rayet stars have been identified by scientists so far. However, the existence of young stars is baffling to scientists. This is because black holes are supposed to emit tidal forces, which in turn should have prevented any star formation activities. But the young stars exist in spite of this.

Chandra X-ray observatory image of Sagittarius A*, the radio source corresponding to the supermassive black hole of the Milky Way galaxy.

A vector of the supermassive black hole at the centre of the Milky Way.

Sagittarius A*

It is a bright and very compact astronomical radio source at the centre of the Milky Way, near the border of the constellations Sagittarius and Scorpius. Sgr A* was discovered on 13th and 15th February, 1974, by astronomers Bruce Balick and Robert Brown using the baseline interferometer of the National Radio Astronomy Observatory. The name Sgr A* was coined by Brown because the radio source was "exciting", and excited states of atoms are denoted with asterisks.

FUN FACT

Did you know that Sagittarius A is a larger astronomical feature that comprises the Sagittarius A*?

Spiral Staircase and the Arms of the Milky Way

There are three main types of galaxies; ellipticals, spirals and irregulars. This classification is based on the shape of the galaxy. The spiral-type galaxies have spiral arms that are similar to the shape of a spiral staircase. The spiral structure has been a mystery to astrophysicists since many years. The most common theory today is that a spiral structure can be regarded as a density wave, which revolves in the galactic disc similar to waves spread in the ocean.

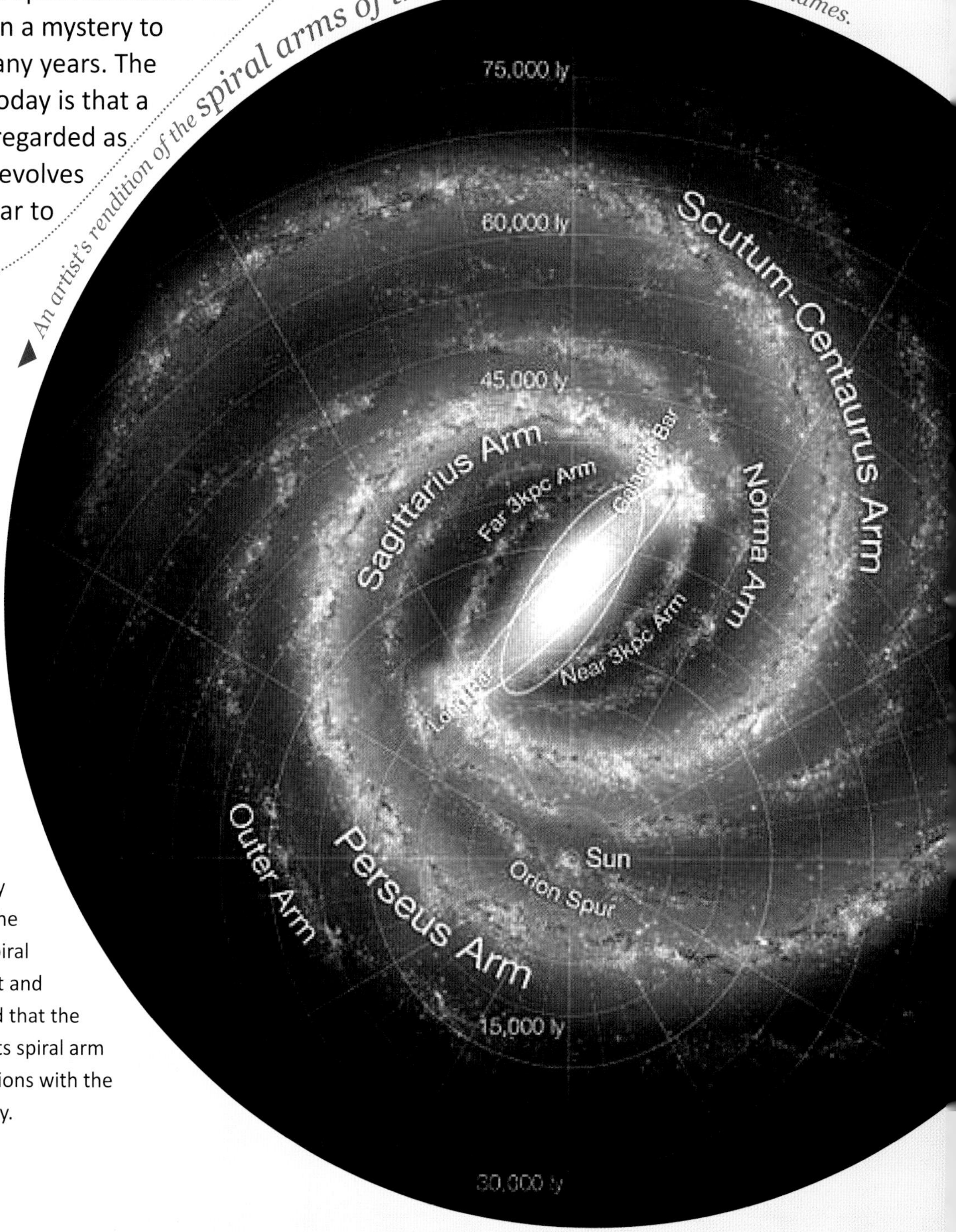

Movement of arms

Like stars, the spiral arms also rotate around the centre, but unlike the stars, they do so with constant angular velocity, which means that stars pass in and out of spiral arms.

As the gas in the interstellar medium passes into the density wave, it becomes denser, and this leads to the formation of new stars. The hottest and brightest stars have short lifetimes so that they are born and die very close to the density wave. This is why the spiral arms are traced by the brightest and youngest stars. It was suggested that the Milky Way may have obtained its spiral arm structure due to repeated collisions with the Sagittarius Dwarf Elliptical galaxy.

An artist's rendition of the spiral arms of the Milky Way along with their names.

75,000 ly

60,000 ly

45,000 ly

Scutum-Centaurus Arm

Sagittarius Arm

Far 3kpc Arm

Galactic Bar

Norma Arm

Near 3kpc Arm

Long Bar

Outer Arm

Perseus Arm

Sun

Orion Spur

15,000 ly

30,000 ly

Formation of arms

Our Milky Way is a barred as well as a spiral galaxy. This means that our galaxy probably has two major spiral arms, plus a central bar. However, there is also the possibility that our galaxy contains four arms or there may be only two arms, or our galaxy could even have two main arms and two extra arms. This point is still being debated and a conclusion is yet to be reached. The spiral arms are named after the location in which we view them in the sky, which is given as follows:

- Perseus arm (considered one of the two primary spiral arms)
  - Outer arm or Norma
    - Scutum-Centaurus arm (considered as one of the two primary spiral arms)
      - Carina-Sagittarius arm
      - Orion-Cygnus arm/Orion spur (which contains the Sun and our solar system)

Description of the arms

The Perseus arm is the arm that is just outside the Sun's location in the galaxy. It is about 700 to 1000 parsecs from us. Beyond the Perseus arm, there may be a more distant arm, but they become less distinct in the outer galaxy zone. On the inside of the Sun's orbit lies the Sagittarius – Scutum arm. On the inside of the Sagittarius – Scutum arm, we can find the Centaurus – Carina arm. This is at a distance of approximately 3000 parsecs from the centre.

Spiral patterns

It is thought that the Milky Way contains two different spiral patterns. The first one is the inner one. This is formed by the Sagittarius arm, which is the one that rotates fast. The second one is the outer one. This is formed by the Carina and Perseus arms, which is the one that has a rotation velocity, which is slower and whose arms are also tightly wound.

Sun's location in our galaxy

Surprisingly, we're not located in one of the Milky Way's two primary spiral arms. Contrary to popular belief, our solar system is actually located in one of the minor arms. The arm that we are located in is called the Orion arm or the Orion spur. The Orion spur lies between the Perseus arm and the Carina – Sagittarius arm of the Milky Way.

The Sun is located at a distance that is nearly two-thirds of the radius of the disc from its centre. The Orion spur merges with the Perseus spiral arm towards the constellation named Cygnus.

Importance of spiral arms

Besides being the primary sites of star formation, the spiral arms are important in determining many factors within the galaxy. These factors are its density, temperature and chemical composition (i.e., the amount of carbon, hydrogen, oxygen, etc.) of the interstellar gas, as well as the dynamics of the stars and the gases within the galaxy.

A barred, spiral galaxy, like our Milky Way.

FUN FACT

According to studies, as spirals burn through their gas and dust and their star formation decreases, they lose their spiral shape and move on to the next stage of galactic evolution – elliptical galaxies.

Milky Way's Halo

The galactic disc of the Milky Way is surrounded by a spheroidal halo of old stars and globular clusters, most of which lies within 100,000 light years of the galactic centre. Globular clusters date back to 15 billion years and are the oldest components of the galaxy.

Constituents of the halo

The halo is spherical in shape and contains little gas, dust or star formation. It extends beyond the disc.

The clusters found in the halo are globular clusters and therefore, are stellar remnants, low mass stars or other low mass objects. Halo stars are not the first generation of stars because they contain elements heavier than hydrogen and helium.

The halo stars pass through the disc and the nucleus of the galaxy, but spend the majority of their time far above or below the plane of the galaxy.

Gaseous halo

In addition to the stellar halo, there is a gaseous halo with a large amount of hot gas. The halo extends for hundreds of thousands of light years, much further than the stellar halo and close to the distance of the Large and Small Magellanic Clouds. The mass of this hot halo is nearly equivalent to the mass of the Milky Way itself. The temperature of this halo gas is between one million and 2.5 million K.

Accumulation of stars

Halo stars may be acquired from small galaxies, which fall into and merge with the spiral galaxy, for example, the Sagittarius Dwarf Spheroidal galaxy is in the process of merging with the Milky Way. Observations show that some stars in the halo of the Milky Way have been acquired from it.

FUN FACT

Did you know that the swirling gases around a black hole transform it into an electrical generator, making it spout jets of electricity billions of kilometres into space?

Beyond the Milky Way

"Who are we? We find that we live on an insignificant planet of a humdrum star lost in a galaxy tucked away in some forgotten corner of a universe in which there are far more galaxies than people". – Carl Sagan

▲ *One could say that our sky is a window to the universe. In the image above, everything we can see is a part of our Milky Way galaxy. It is vast, beautiful and full of hundreds of billions of stars, planets and much, much more.*

The wonders of our galaxy

If one is to look beyond our galaxy with current telescopes, astronomers have observed middle-aged and mature galaxies. Using the Hubble Space Telescope provided the most detailed view of the early universe. Almost 1500

◄ *Coddington's nebula is a dwarf irregular galaxy in Ursa Major.*

galaxies were observed at various stages of evolution, some even old enough to date back to when the universe was only a billion years old.

Strange objects in space

Many recognisable shapes were seen in space, which appear red due to the light emitted from older, mature stars. An example is the crystal blue spiral galaxies that are brilliantly illuminated by virtue of the glow of their hot, young stars. Amongst these, also noted were strange, tadpole like objects that were apparently merging galaxies, also known as "train wrecks". In addition, multiple faint dwarf galaxies were observed.

What is missing?

We need more information on how far away these galaxies are from us, how these galaxies cluster and clump together, how quickly they're moving either towards, or away from both us and each other, and how massive they really are.

Some of these objects may date back to the first generation of galaxies and stars. Did these cosmic shards and fragments evolve into today's recognisable galaxies? Are they as small as they appear, but bright from great bursts of star formation? Or, are they massive, with much of their stellar population hidden by clouds of dust?

Galactic Neighbours

Our Milky Way galaxy is not alone in its cosmic neighbourhood. It belongs to the Local Group, which is a set of about 30 galaxies that are united due to their reciprocal gravitational attraction. The Local Group is dominated by two massive galaxies; the Milky Way and Andromeda galaxies, a close analogue of our galaxy that is about 2.5 million light years away. Let's take a look at our closest galactic neighbours.

1. Andromeda

Most people believe that the Andromeda galaxy is our closest neighbour. However, Andromeda is the closest spiral galaxy and not the closest galaxy.

3. Large Magellanic Cloud

The Large Magellanic Cloud (LMC) is a nearby galaxy, and a satellite of the Milky Way.

The Large Magellanic Cloud is recognised as a disrupted barred spiral galaxy.

This is a real image of M31 "Andromeda galaxy" taken with a 10-inch astrograph telescope.

2. Triangulum

It is a spiral galaxy approximately three million light years from Earth in the constellation Triangulum.

This is sometimes informally referred to as the Pinwheel galaxy.

FUN FACT

Did you know that if you fell into a black hole, you would stretch like spaghetti?

5. Barnard's galaxy

Barnard's galaxy, also known as NGC 6822, IC 4895 or Caldwell 57, is a barred irregular galaxy approximately 1.6 million light years away in the constellation Sagittarius.

7. Sagittarius Dwarf

The Sagittarius Dwarf elliptical galaxy is a small, elliptical, loop-shaped, satellite galaxy of our Milky Way that lies about 70,000 light years away from Earth in the constellation of Sagittarius.

Star formation in NGC 602, a part of the wing region of the Small Magellanic Cloud. Magellanic Clouds have long been included in the folklore of native inhabitants of south sea islanders and indigenous Australians.

Palomar 12 was first suspected to have been captured from the Sagittarius Dwarf galaxy about 1.7 Ga ago in 2000.

4. Small Magellanic Cloud

The Small Magellanic Cloud (SMC) is one of our closest neighbours.

This dwarf galaxy is about a tenth of the Milky Way's size and contains only 10 million stars.

6. Sextans A

Also known as UGCA 205, it is a tiny dwarf irregular galaxy. It spans about 5000 light years across.

Irregular galaxy Sextans A.

Andromeda

The Andromeda galaxy (M31) is a spiral galaxy that is approximately 2.5 million light years from Earth in the Andromeda constellation. It is the nearest spiral galaxy to Milky Way. It gets its name from the area of the sky in which it appears in the Andromeda constellation and is the largest galaxy in the Local Group.

Star formation

M31 was formed out of the collision of two smaller galaxies between five and nine billion years ago. According to scientists, Andromeda was born roughly 10 billion years ago from the merger of many smaller proto-galaxies. The rate of star formation in the Milky Way is much higher, with M31 producing only about one solar mass per year compared to three to five solar masses for the Milky Way. The rate of supernovae in the Milky Way is also twice that of M31. M31 contains one trillion (10^{12}) stars, at least twice the number of stars in the Milky Way galaxy.

Barred spiral galaxy

The galaxy is a barred spiral galaxy, with the Andromeda galaxy's bar viewed almost directly along its long axis. The spiral arms are outlined by a series of H II regions, described as resembling "beads on a string". Studies show two spiral arms that appear to be tightly wound, although they are more widely spaced than in our galaxy.

Andromeda's nucleus

M31 is known to harbour a dense and compact star cluster at its very centre. The luminosity of the nucleus is in excess of the most luminous globular clusters.

There are approximately 460 globular clusters associated with the Andromeda galaxy. The most massive of these clusters, Globular One, has the greatest luminosity in the Local Group with several million stars.

Satellites

The Andromeda galaxy has satellite galaxies, consisting of 14 known dwarf galaxies. The best known and readily observed satellite galaxies are M32 and M110.

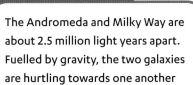

FUN FACT

The Andromeda and Milky Way are about 2.5 million light years apart. Fuelled by gravity, the two galaxies are hurtling towards one another at a speed of 402,000 km per hour!

The Andromeda galaxy.

Andromeda-Milky Way Collision

The Andromeda – Milky Way collision is a galactic collision predicted to occur in about 4 billion years between the two largest galaxies in the Local Group — the Milky Way and Andromeda galaxies.

▲ *A representation of Earth in the Milky Way and Andromeda approaching it.*

Stellar collisions

While the Andromeda galaxy contains about one trillion stars and the Milky Way contains about 300 billion, the chance of even two stars colliding is negligible because of the huge distances between the stars.

Black hole collisions

The Milky Way and Andromeda galaxies each contain a central supermassive black hole that will converge near the centre of the newly formed galaxy. When they come within one light year of one another, they will emit gravitational waves that will radiate further orbital energy until they completely merge. Gas taken up by the combined black hole will likely create a luminous quasar or an active galactic nucleus.

Fate of the solar system

Based on current calculations, scientists predict a 50 per cent chance that in a merged galaxy the solar system will be swept out three times farther from the galactic core than its current distance. There's also a 12 per cent chance that the solar system will be ejected from the new galaxy sometime during the collision. However, there would be no adverse effect on the system and the chances of any disturbance to the Sun or planets may be unlikely. Without intervention, by the time the two galaxies collide, the surface of Earth will have already become far too hot for liquid water to exist, thereby ending all terrestrial life.

Merger remnant

According to simulations, this post-collision object will look like a giant elliptical galaxy, but with fewer stars than the current elliptical galaxies. It is, however, possible that it could result in the formation of a large disc galaxy.

An artist's representation showing the collision of Andromeda and Milky Way.

FUN FACT

In billions of years, the Milky Way galaxy and Andromeda galaxy will collide into one super galaxy.

Large Magellanic Cloud

The Large Magellanic Cloud (LMC) is a nearby galaxy, and a satellite of the Milky Way. At a distance of slightly less than approximately 157,000 light years, it is the third closest galaxy to the Milky Way. The dwarf galaxy looks like a faint cloud in Southern Hemisphere skies. It lies on the border of the constellations Dorado and Mensa.

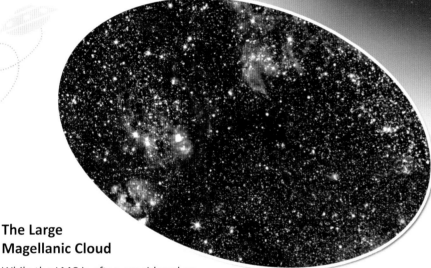

Tarantula Nebula, in LMC, the most active star-forming region in the Local Group.

The Large Magellanic Cloud

While the LMC is often considered an irregular-type galaxy, the LMC has a prominent central bar and spiral arm. The central bar seems to be warped so that the east and west ends are closer to the Milky Way than the middle. The LMC's irregular appearance is possibly the result of tidal interactions with both the Milky Way and the SMC.

It has a mass equivalent to approximately 10 billion times the mass of the Sun (10^{10} solar masses), making it roughly 1/100th as massive as the Milky Way and a diameter of about 14,000 light years.

Features of the LMC

Like many irregular galaxies, the LMC is rich in gas and dust, and it is currently undergoing vigorous star formation activity. The LMC is full of a wide range of galactic objects and phenomena that make it aptly known as an "astronomical treasure-house" described by American astronomer Robert Burnham Jr.

Surveys of the galaxy have found roughly 60 globular clusters, 400 planetary nebulae and 700 open clusters, along with hundreds of thousands of giant and supergiant stars. Supernova 1987a — the nearest supernova in recent years — was also located in the LMC.

Bridging the gap

There is a bridge of gas connecting SMC with the LMC, which is evidence of tidal interaction between the galaxies. The Magellanic Clouds have a common envelope of neutral hydrogen indicating that they have been gravitationally bound for a long time. This bridge of gas is a star-forming site.

FUN FACT

The most massive star in the universe is thought to be R136a1, located in the LMC.

Small Magellanic Cloud

The Small Magellanic Cloud (SMC) is an irregular-type galaxy that is roughly 200,000 light years from our Milky Way galaxy and is one of its closest neighbours. It is also one of the most distant objects that we can see with the naked eye. It forms a pair with the LMC and together these are known as the Magellanic Clouds. They were named after the navigator Ferdinand Magellan.

SMC is located in the constellation of Tucana and appears as a hazy, light patch in the night sky.

Mini Magellanic Cloud (MMC)

It is speculated that the SMC may be split in two, with a smaller section of this galaxy behind the main part of the SMC (as seen from Earth), and separated by about 30,000 light years. This smaller remnant is the Mini Magellanic Cloud.

The SMC has been detected as a foggy image when seen through the telescope in the lighter patch of the night sky. This cloud is located in the Tucana constellation.

Formation of the SMC

The SMC, along with the LMC, is classified as an irregular galaxy, i.e., a galaxy with an ill defined shape, rich in gas and dust. A close study of the Magellanic Clouds indicates that they were both once barred spiral galaxies. It contains a central bar structure. Over time, however, the gravitational interactions with the Milky Way distorted the galaxy, creating an irregular-type galaxy.

Properties of the SMC

It is approximately 7000 light years in diameter and contains about seven billion solar masses. While it is about half the size of the LMC, it contains nearly as many stars, meaning that it has a higher stellar density. However, the star formation rate is currently lower for the SMC. This is probably because it has less free gas than LMC, and therefore had periods of more rapid formation in the past.

FUN FACT

In some native stories, the LMC/ SMC are camps of an old man and an old woman—with other sky people bringing them food from the river, the Milky Way.

Barnard's Galaxy

It is a dwarf irregular galaxy about 1.6 million light years away and perhaps one-tenth our galaxy's size. Barnard's galaxy or NGC 6822 lies in the constellation Sagittarius and is a member of the Local Group. It is thus named as it was discovered by E. E. Barnard in 1884, with a six-inch refractor telescope. It is one of the galaxies that is closer to our own. With regard to structure and composition, it is similar to the SMC. It is about 7000 light years in diameter.

Region of star formation

The reddish nebulae reveal regions of active star formation, where young, hot stars heat up nearby gas clouds. The bubble is a nebula with a clutch of massive, hot stars at its centre that is sending waves of matter smashing into the surrounding interstellar material, generating a glowing structure, which looks like a ring from our perspective. Other similar ripples of heated matter thrown out by young stars are dotted across Barnard's galaxy.

Irregular dwarf galaxies like Barnard's get their bloblike forms due to close encounters with other galaxies. Gravity's attraction can significantly change the shapes of the passing or colliding galaxies, pulling and throwing stars, and forming irregularly shaped dwarf galaxies such as NGC 6822.

Star clusters in the galaxy

In the 1920s, Edwin Hubble found three star clusters in Barnard's galaxy that he believed were all very old objects similar to globular clusters in the Milky Way. However, images taken by the Hubble Space Telescope have shown that the three clusters belong to completely different ages. The stars in the cluster called Hubble VII were formed about 15 billion years ago, and are about the same age as our own galaxy and the universe itself. It seems that our galaxy formed most of its big clusters in the first couple of billion years after the Big Bang. Barnard's galaxy began generating new massive star clusters all along. The largest currently active star formation region in NGC 6822 is Hubble X. The nearly circular bright cloud at the core of Hubble-X measures about 110 light years across and contains a central cluster, less than four million years old, of many thousands of young stars.

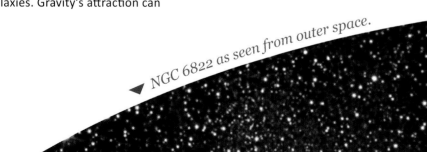

NGC 6822 as seen from outer space.

Sagittarius Dwarf

The Sagittarius Dwarf Elliptical galaxy or Sag DEG, Sgr dE or the Sagittarius Dwarf Spheroidal galaxy, is a small elliptical loop-shaped satellite galaxy of our Milky Way. It lies about 70,000 light years away from Earth in the constellation Sagittarius, while it is currently moving away from us at approximately 140 km per second. It is roughly 10,000 light years across and is home to four known globular clusters, including Messier 54. It had been credited with shaping the Milky Way's spiral arms.

Orbit around the Milky Way

It has orbited the Milky Way for a period of 550 to 750 million years about 10 times during its billions of years of existence, at a distance of about 50,000 light years from the galactic centre. During these orbits, it struck our galaxy some 1.9 billion years ago. It then looped over the galactic "north pole" and struck again about 900 million years later. Currently, it is moving back, on course for a third clash with the southern face of the Milky Way disc, which would occur in 10 million years or so.

How did the Milky Way get its arms?

Sagittarius Dwarf pays a high price though, as it is repeatedly pulled inward by the Milky Way's extreme gravity. It is being ripped apart by the blows, sending huge amounts of its stars and dark matter into the new arms. Its mass at the beginning was about 100 billion times that of our Sun, but has decreased by a factor of two or three. When all that dark matter first collided into the Milky Way, 80 to 90 per cent of it was detached. That first impact led

to instabilities that were enormous, that quickly formed the spiral arms of our galaxy. Impacts between galaxies and their friends are believed to be widespread in the cosmos, and many of the spiral galaxies were probably formed in this way.

FUN FACT

One interesting theory about the formation of the Sagittarius Dwarf has it arising from debris pulled from the LMC after a collision of the Magellanic Clouds with each other or the Milky Way.

▶ The Sagittarius Dwarf galaxy as seen from Earth.

Sextans A

Sextans A also known as UGCA 205, is a tiny dwarf irregular galaxy. It is about 5000 light years across. At 4.3 million light years away from Earth, Sextans A is one of most distant members of the Local Group, and is notable for its peculiar square shape. Massive short-lived stars exploded in supernovae, causing new star formation, producing further supernovae, resulting in an expanding shell. Young, blue stars now highlight areas and shell edges, which appear roughly square to observers from Earth.

▶ *Sextans A as seen from space.*

Observing Sextans A

Many dwarf irregular galaxies are surrounded by neutral hydrogen gas that extends far beyond where the galaxy's starlight fades away. Observations with radio telescopes have confirmed that Sextans A is no exception. The origin of this hydrogen gas and its effect on star formation are still unsolved puzzles. Yutaka Komiyama from Subaru Telescope, the observer of Sextans A, is now working on a solution using the Suprime-Cam data.

Sextans A is notable for its peculiar square shape.

Shape and star formation

Irregular galaxies do not have a regular symmetric shape like spiral or elliptical galaxies. These galaxies containing only 100 million to a billion stars are the most common type of irregular galaxy. One main characteristic of such galaxies, besides their shape, is continuous star formation. Sextans A has a mass comparable to only 100 million stars, one thousandth of the Milky Way, but contains a comparatively large amount of gas and dust, the raw ingredients for stars and planets. In the centre of Sextans A is a high concentration of neutral hydrogen gas that helps new stars develop.

The mysterious galaxy

When this galaxy was discovered, it created quite a buzz because it had a huge number of stars and also had an odd square shape. What is more mysterious is the fact that it seems like the Sextans was hit by something that set off a reaction of massive short-lived stars. These exploded into supernovae creating more supernovae but the reason for it is still unclear.

FUN FACT

The bright yellow star that we can see in the image does not belong to the Sextans A at all. This star is a part of our galaxy and can be seen in this image as the picture has been framed in that way.

Triangulum

The Triangulum galaxy is the third-largest member of the Local Group. It is one of the most distant and permanent objects that can be viewed by the naked eye. It is the smallest spiral galaxy in the Local Group. It is believed to be a satellite of the Andromeda galaxy due to their interactions, velocities and proximity to each other in the night sky.

This detailed image boasts M33's blue star clusters and pinkish star forming regions that outlines the galaxy's loosely wound spiral arms.

Visibility of Triangulum

Under exceptionally good viewing conditions, this galaxy can be seen with the naked eye. Being a spread out object, its visibility is strongly affected by small amounts of light pollution. It ranges from easily visible by direct vision in dark skies to a difficult prevented vision object in rural or suburban skies.

How was it discovered?

It was discovered by Italian astronomer Giovanni Battista Hodierna before 1654. In his work *Desystemate orbis cometici; deque admirandis coeli caracteribus – About the systematics of the cometary orbit, and about the admirable objects of the sky*, he listed it as a cloud-like nebulosity or obscuration and gave the cryptic description, "near the Triangle hinc inde", meaning "a pair of triangles". The galaxy was independently discovered by Charles Messier on the night of 25th – 26th August, 1764. It was published in his *Catalog of Nebulae and Star Clusters* as object number 33; hence, the name M33. Triangulum may be home to 40 billion stars, compared to 400 billion for the Milky Way, and one trillion stars for Andromeda.

Future of Triangulum

The fate of the Triangulum galaxy is unclear, but seems to be linked to its larger neighbour, the Andromeda galaxy. Suggested future scenarios include being torn apart and absorbed by Andromeda, fuelling the latter with hydrogen to form new stars; eventually exhausting all its gas, and thus the ability to form new stars, not permitting it to participate in the collision between the Milky Way and M31, which is most likely to end up orbiting the merger product of the latter two galaxies and fusing with it much later. Two other possibilities are a collision with the Milky Way before Andromeda arrives or an ejection from the Local Group.

Nebula

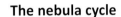

The literal translation of nebula is "cloud". But we know that a nebula is much more than a cloud. What exactly is it? A nebula is an interstellar cloud of dust, hydrogen, helium and other ionised gases. It is formed when portions of the interstellar medium collapse and clump together due to the gravitational attraction of the particles that comprise them. Nebulae contain the elements from which stars and solar systems are built.

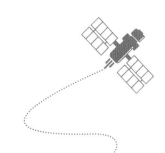

The nebula cycle

Interestingly, nebulae are not just the starting points of star formation. Ironically, they can also be the end points.

This could be thought of as the nebula – star – nebula cycle. Stars that evolve into red giants can lose their outer layers during pulsations in their outer layers, known as their atmospheres. It is this released matter that forms a planetary nebula. The planetary nebula is just one of four major types of nebulae. The other three are H II regions, supernova remnant and dark nebula.

Composition

They show swirls of light. Stars with different elements inside these nebulae cause them to glow with beautiful red, blue and green hues. Most nebulae are composed of approximately 90 per cent hydrogen, 10 per cent helium and 0.1 per cent heavy elements such as carbon, nitrogen, magnesium, potassium, calcium and iron. Some of the prominent nebulae are the Crab, Eagle, Orion, Pelican, Ring and Rosette Nebulae.

FUN FACT

In 1764, William Herschel mistakenly described the nebulae as "planetary" when he thought that the celestial body at the centre was a planet.

▶ *Images showing the varied rich colours of Nebulae, like the Crab, Eagle, Orion, Pelican, Ring and Rosette Nebulae.*

Star Cluster

Many stars tend to gather around each other, drawn by their gravitational fields. These groups of stars are called "star clusters". A globular cluster is one that consists of a spherical collection of stars. These orbit a galactic core. Their spherical shapes and the relatively high stellar densities towards their centres are due to the high gravity that they experience. Globular clusters are fairly common — the Milky Way has around 150 to 158 of these.

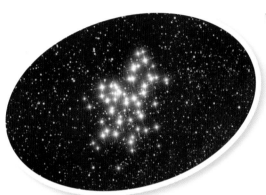  

Butterfly cluster

The Butterfly cluster, also known as Messier 6, or M6, is an open star cluster in the constellation of Scorpius. It gets its name due to its butterfly-like shape.

Giovanni Battista Hodierna was the first to record it in 1654. It is 1600 light years away, 12 light years in diameter and estimated to be 95 million years old. It is best seen during June, July and August from the Southern Hemisphere.

Pleiades

This star cluster is also known as the "Seven Sisters" and "Messier 45". It is a remarkable object in the night sky with a prominent place in ancient mythology. The cluster contains hundreds of stars, of which only a handful are commonly visible to the naked eye. The stars in the Pleiades were formed together around 100 million years ago, making them 1/50th the age of our Sun. They lie 425 light years away.

Binary stars

Albireo is located in the constellation Cygnus. It appears as a single point of light to the naked eye, but a telescope shows it to be a binary star. Binary stars are two stars bound together by their mutual gravitational attraction. These stars take thousands of years to orbit around each other. Alberio is 380 light years away. More than half of the existing ones live in binary systems. The Sun is unusual as it is solitary.

Globular cluster

It is a large group of old stars that are closely packed in a symmetrical manner. They get their name because of their uneven spherical appearance. They are the largest, most massive star clusters. Though several globular clusters are visible to the naked eye as hazy patches of light, they were heeded only after the telescope was invented.

Close pair

If two stars orbit each other at large distances, they evolve independently and are called a "wide pair". If the two stars are close enough to transfer matter via tidal forces, they are called a "close" or "contact pair". A team of astronomers discovered a close pair of white dwarf stars — tiny, extremely dense stellar remnants — that have a total mass about 1.8 times that of the Sun. When these two stars merge in the future, they will create a thermonuclear explosion leading to a Type Ia supernova.

Gas and Dust

Stars are born in the densest regions of the interstellar medium, or ISM, called molecular clouds. ISM is the name given to the gas and dust that exists between the stars in a galaxy. It is 99 per cent gas and one per cent dust, by mass. Molecular clouds are perfect star-forming regions, because the combination of these atoms into molecules is possible in very dense regions. Let us take a look at the various star formations that occur in the heavens above.

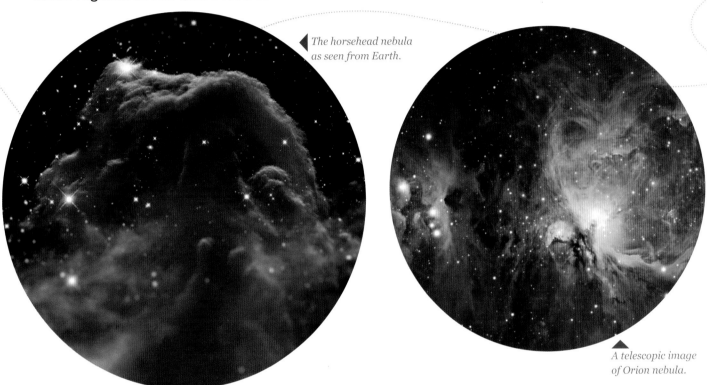

The horsehead nebula as seen from Earth.

A telescopic image of Orion nebula.

Horsehead nebula

The horsehead nebula is a dark nebula in the Orion constellation. It is also known as Barnard 33 (B33), as it was first photographed by American astronomer Edward Barnard. The nebula is situated south of the Alnitak star and is a part of the larger Orion molecular cloud complex. The Horsehead Nebula is approximately 1200 light years from Earth.

It is easily identifiable

It is easily identifiable because of its swirling cloud of dark dust and gases, which bears some resemblance to a horse's head. The pinkish glow is due to hydrogen gas ionised by the Sigma Orionis star that is nearby. The magnetic fields separate the gases, rendering the nebula into glowing streaks.

Orion nebula

It is the most noticeable of all constellations. The three stars of Orion's belt jump out at you midway between Orion's two brightest stars, Betelgeuse and Rigel, the two brightest stars in the sky. Once you find the belt stars, you can also locate the Orion Nebula, which is also known as M42, a stellar nursery where new stars are born. The higher the constellation Orion is in the sky, the easier it is to see it. It is due south and highest in the sky at midnight during mid-December. The stars return to the same place some four minutes earlier each night, or two hours earlier each month.

When is it visible

Look for Orion to be highest up around 10 pm during mid-January and 8 pm during mid-February. It is around 30 to 40 light years in diameter, giving birth to perhaps a thousand stars. A young open star cluster, whose stars were born at the same time from a portion of the nebula and are still loosely bound by gravity, can be seen within the nebula. It is sometimes called the Orion nebula star cluster. In 2012, an international team of astronomers suggested that this cluster in the Orion nebula may have a black hole at its centre.

Research from 2007 suggests that a stellar supernova could have already blown the pillars out of formation 6000 years ago. Because light takes time to travel, it may be another thousand years before we can see the end of these pillars.

The ETA Carina Nebula NGC 3372.

Pillars of creation

One of the images taken by Jeff Hester and Paul Scowen using the Hubble Space Telescope in 1995 became famous as the "Pillars of Creation", depicting a large region of star formation. The small dark areas are believed to be proto-stars. These columns are composed of interstellar hydrogen gas and dust, which act as incubators for new stars. Astronomers have found dense pockets of gas, aptly called "Evaporating Gaseous Globules" (EGGs) at the top of these pillars, where stars are believed to be formed.

ETA Carina nebula

ETA Carina nebula is also called the Carina Nebula or the Great nebula in Carina, a spectacular diffuse nebula in the constellation Carina. It is one of the largest and brightest in the sky. It is almost 7500 light years away. The ETA Carina nebula or NGC 3372 is one of the largest HII regions in the entire Milky Way. It is four times larger than the Orion nebula, which itself is part of the Orion molecular cloud complex. The only reason that the Carina nebula is not well known is because it cannot be seen from most of the northern hemisphere. It was discovered by Abbé Nicolas Louis de Lacaille during his two-year journey to the Cape of Good Hope during 1751 – 52. In addition to ETA Carina, the nebula contains several stars that are among the hottest and most massive known, each about 10 times as hot and 100 times as massive as our Sun.

New born star

The IRS 4 is a rare newborn star that is actually around half the age of the human race. It is 100,000 years old, with the surrounding material called Sharpless 2-106. The IRS 4 acts as an emission nebula as it emits light after being ionised, while dust far from IRS 4 reflects light from the central star. Therefore, it acts as a reflection nebula.

FUN FACT

As Earth rotates, the stars come back to the same place in the night sky every 23 hours, 56 minutes and 4.09 seconds. This is a sidereal day, or star day.

IRS 4 is one of the rare stars that is actually younger than the human race.

The Solar System

A solar system refers to a star and all the objects that travel in the orbit around it. Our solar system consists of the Sun, our star, eight planets and their natural satellites (such as our moon); dwarf planets; asteroids and comets. It was formed approximately 4.6 billion years ago from the gravitational collapse of a giant molecular cloud.

The inner planets

The four smaller inner planets, Mercury, Venus, Earth and Mars, also called the terrestrial planets, are chiefly composed of rock and metal. Venus, Earth and Mars, also called the terrestrial planets, are chiefly composed of rock and metal.

Inner planets

Mercury   Venus   Earth   Mars

Jupiter

The Sun contains 99.86 per cent of the system's known mass and gravitationally dominates it. The Sun's four largest orbiting bodies, the giant planets, account for 99 per cent of the remaining mass, with Jupiter and Saturn together comprising more than 90 per cent. Hence, the solid objects of the solar system (including the terrestrial planets, moons, asteroids and comets) together comprise 0.0001 per cent of the solar system's total mass. In comparison to Earth, whether we consider the weight or the size, the Sun is enormous. The Sun's mass is about 333,000 times that of Earth's. If we were to take a hollow ball the size of the Sun, we would need about 1,300,000 Earths to be able to fill that ball up. There are sunspots on the Sun that are the size of Earth.

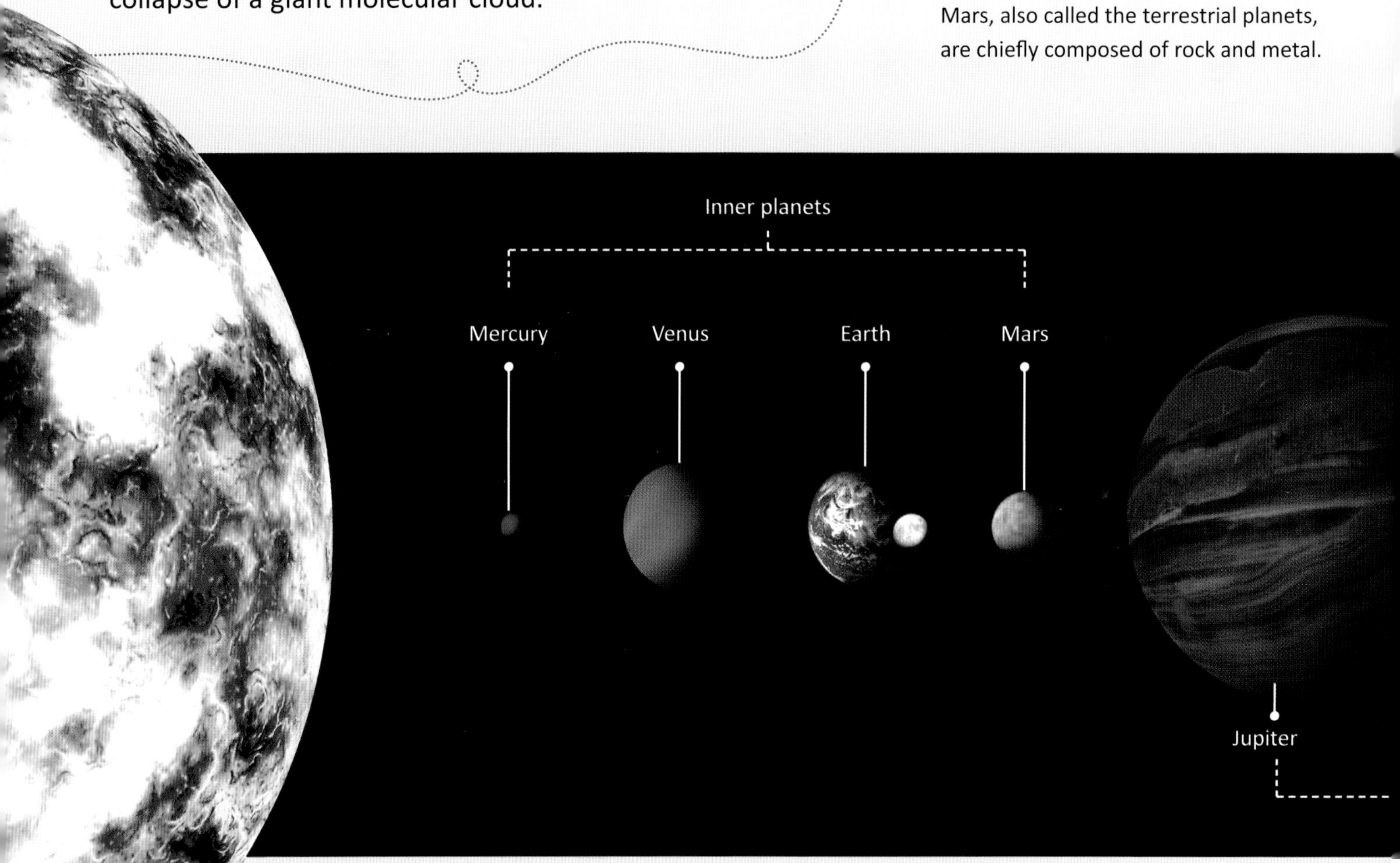

Image of the solar system and its planets as they stand from the Sun. This image shows the inner and outer planets.

If Earth were to be placed on the diameter of the Sun, we would need 109 Earths to cover the entire diameter. This is approximately the same as the distance between Earth and the Sun.

The outer planets

The four outer planets, the giant planets, are substantially bigger than the terrestrials. Each of these planets are encircled by planetary rings of dust and other small objects. This dust is made up of space dust and ice, which remain around these planets due to gravity.

The two outermost planets, Uranus and Neptune, are largely composed of substances with relatively high melting points compared with hydrogen and helium, called ices, such as water, ammonia and methane. These two planets are known as "Ice Giants".

Did you know that Saturn is not entirely solid? It is made up of gas, mostly liquid hydrogen and helium. It is only in the planet's very small core that rock is present.

Ice giants

Saturn   Uranus   Neptune

Outer planets

The solar system also contains regions populated by smaller objects. The asteroid belt, which lies between Mars and Jupiter, mostly contains objects, like the terrestrial planets, of rock and metal. Beyond Neptune's orbit lies the Kuiper belt and scattered disc, as well as linked populations of trans-Neptunian objects composed mostly of ices.

Within these populations, there are several objects that may be adequately large to have been rounded by their own gravity. Such objects are referred to as dwarf planets. Known dwarf planets include the asteroid Ceres and trans-Neptunian objects Pluto and Eris.

The Sun

 The Sun is the star at the centre of the solar system. It is almost spherical and consists of hot plasma interwoven with magnetic fields. It has a diameter of about 1,392,684 km. There is only a 10 km difference between its polar and equatorial diameters. This means that it is the next best thing to a perfect sphere, considering how big it is.

Distance from the Sun to Earth

Because Earth travels on an elliptical orbit around the Sun, the distance between the two bodies varies from 147 to 152 million km. The distance between Earth and the Sun is called an Astronomical Unit (AU).

Revolution around the Milky Way

The Sun is 24,000 – 26,000 light years from the galactic centre and it takes 225 – 250 million years to revolve around the centre of the Milky Way.

Elements of the Sun

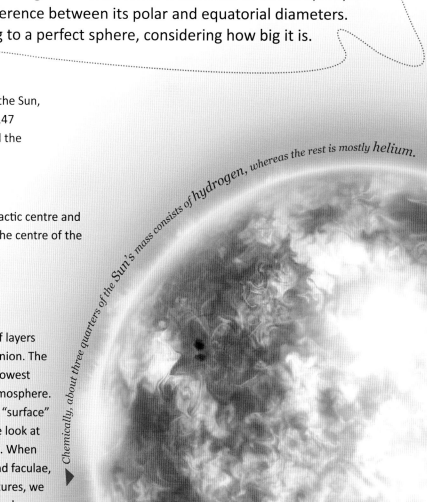

Chemically, about three quarters of the Sun's mass consists of hydrogen, whereas the rest is mostly helium.

1. Granulation

The Sun is made up of layers of material, like an onion. The photosphere is the lowest layer of the solar atmosphere. It is simply the solar "surface" that we see when we look at the Sun in visible light. When we observe sunspots and faculae, small bright cloud-like features, we are viewing them in the photosphere. The Sun's surface, like that of a boiling pot, is constantly changing. Solar granulation refers to the cell structure, or bubbly appearance, of the photosphere. The Sun's boiling nature allows heat from the core to be brought up through the convection zone and into the photosphere, just like heat from the bottom of a pan ends up heating the entire contents along with the air above it.

2. Spicules

Spicule

Sound Wave

Magnetic fields

A spicule is a jet of dense gas ejected from the Sun's chromosphere. Spicules have strong magnetic fields. They extend up to 10,000 km and although they fall back to the Sun, they are thought to contribute to the solar wind by feeding material into the corona. Approximately 100,000 spicules are active on the Sun's surface at a given time. They rise from the lower chromosphere at about 20 km per second to a height of several thousand kilometres. Within 10 – 15 minutes, they disperse or collapse.

3. Sunspots

Sunspots are regions on the solar surface that seem dark as they are cooler than the surrounding photosphere, around 1500 K. They only appear dark in a relative sense. If a sunspot is removed from the bright background of the Sun, it would glow rather bright. The largest sunspots observed had diameters of about 50,000 km, which makes them so large that they can be seen with the naked eye. Sunspots often come in groups with as many as 100 in a group. Interestingly, sunspot groups with more than 10 are quite rare. They develop and persist for periods ranging from hours to months and are carried around the surface of the Sun by its rotation.

Sunspots viewed against their natural light.

4. Solar flares

A solar flare is an abrupt brightening in the solar corona. These flares develop in a matter of few minutes, or even seconds, and may last several hours. They occur above the surface in the corona, and energy deposited at the surface raises a superhot cloud, about 100 million °C, which is a strong, long-lasting source of X-rays. Smaller flares do not show all these characteristics. Flares are brighter than the whole Sun in X-rays and in ultraviolet light. On 17th March, 2015, a storm on the Sun was so strong that it was strongly felt even on Earth.

Solar flares rarely occur during the three or four years of sunspot.

5. Corona

Corona is the outermost region of the Sun's atmosphere. It is made up of plasma (hot ionised gas). Its temperature is approximately two million Kelvins and has a very low density. It continually varies in size and shape as it is affected by the Sun's magnetic field. It shines only about half as brightly as the moon. It is not easily visible to the unaided eye, because its light is overwhelmed by the luminosity of the solar surface. The moon blocks the light from the photosphere, permitting one to observe the corona during a total solar eclipse. It can also be studied under non-eclipse conditions using a special telescopic instrument called a "coronagraph". Corona is Latin for a crown or wreath. The Sun's aurora is the shape of a crown when seen during an eclipse or through a coronagraph. This is why it is called a corona.

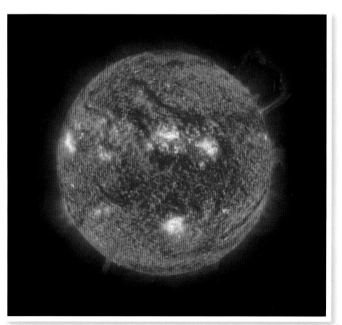

FUN FACT

Interestingly, the Sun loses five million tons of material every second. This is because there are many nuclear fusions that take place on the surface of the Sun. This is when two atoms fuse together to form one atom and release immense heat.

How did we get our Sun?

The Sun is one of more than 100 billion stars in the Milky Way. For a star, it is relatively young, part of a generation of stars known as Population I, which are relatively rich in elements heavier than helium. It is often said that the Sun is an "ordinary" star as there are many others similar to it. But there are many smaller stars than larger ones. The median size of stars in our galaxy is probably less than half the mass of the Sun.

How was our Sun formed?

The Sun was formed about 4.57 billion years ago from the partial collapse of a giant molecular cloud that consisted mostly of hydrogen and helium. Studies show that one or more supernovae must have occurred near the area where the Sun was formed. A shock wave from a nearby supernova could have triggered the formation of the Sun by compressing the matter within the molecular cloud and causing certain areas to collapse under their own gravity. Most of the matter gathered at the centre, whereas the rest flattened into an orbiting disc, later forming the solar system. Gravity and pressure within the core generated a lot of heat as it accumulated more matter from the surrounding disc, eventually triggering nuclear fusion.

Sun with fiery explosions and swirling turbulence.

How hot is the Sun?

When viewed from space, the Sun's colour is white; when low in the sky, atmospheric scattering makes it look yellow, red, orange or magenta. In the spectral class label, it is G2V; G2 indicates its surface temperature (5505 °C) and V denotes that the Sun is a main sequence star and generates its energy by the nuclear fusion of hydrogen nuclei into helium. In its core, the Sun fuses about 620 million metric tonnes of hydrogen each second.

The Sun has sufficient nuclear fuel to stay as it currently is for another five billion years.

Fate of the Sun

Eventually, the Sun will swell to become a red giant. Then, it will shed its outer layers and the remaining core will collapse to become a white dwarf. Slowly, this will fade and enter its final phase as a dim, cool object known as a black dwarf.

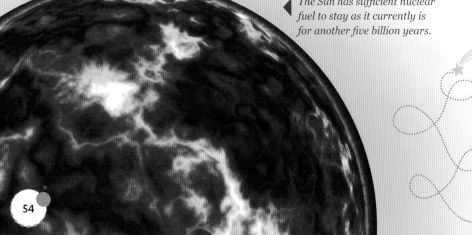

FUN FACT

If a hollow Sun was filled up with spherical Earths, then around 960,000 would fit within it.

Source of Energy

The more recent discoveries of coal, petroleum and natural gas are modern extensions of this trend. These fossil fuels are the leftovers of ancient plant and animal matter, formed using energy from sunlight, and then trapped within Earth for millions of years. Because the stored energy in these fossil fuels has accumulated over many millions of years, they have allowed modern humans to massively increase the production and consumption of primary energy.

Solar power

Solar power is the conversion of sunlight into electricity, either directly using photovoltaics (PV) or indirectly using concentrated solar power (CSP).

Growth of plants

Sunlight is a major source of energy for the plants. Plants convert sunlight into food using chlorophyll. This is known as photosynthesis. Our entire food web begins with plants. Hence, the Sun's energy essentially powers all the living organisms on Earth.

Effects of ultraviolet radiation

The ultraviolet radiation in sunlight has both positive and negative health effects, as it is both a principal source of vitamin D_3 and a mutagen.

FUN FACT

Every second, 1370 joules of the Sun's energy reach every Sun-facing square metre of Earth!

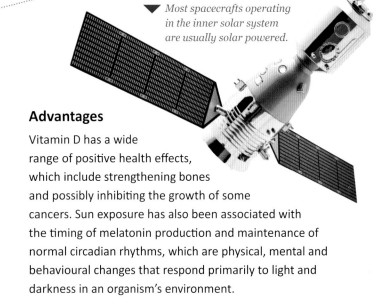

Most spacecrafts operating in the inner solar system are usually solar powered.

Advantages

Vitamin D has a wide range of positive health effects, which include strengthening bones and possibly inhibiting the growth of some cancers. Sun exposure has also been associated with the timing of melatonin production and maintenance of normal circadian rhythms, which are physical, mental and behavioural changes that respond primarily to light and darkness in an organism's environment.

Disadvantages

Long-term sunlight exposure is known to be associated with the development of skin cancer, skin aging, immune suppression and eye diseases such as cataracts and muscular degeneration. Short-term overexposure is the cause of sunburn and snow blindness.

Solar panels used to generate electricity on a large scale.

Solar Cycles

The solar cycle is a periodic change in the Sun's activity and appearance; visible changes occur in the number of sunspots, flares and other manifestations. Sunspots are magnetic storms on the Sun's surface.

Solar flares and CMEs

Solar flares are intense blooms of radiation that come from the release of the magnetic energy associated with sunspots. Coronal mass ejections (CMEs) are bursts of solar material that shoot off the Sun's surface. Other solar events include solar wind streams that come from the coronal holes on the Sun and solar energetic particles that are primarily released by CMEs.

What is a solar cycle?

The number of sunspots increase and decrease over time in a regular, approximately 11-year cycle, called the solar or sunspot cycle. The exact length of the cycle can vary. More sunspots mean increased solar activity — flares and CMEs. The highest number of sunspots in any given cycle is designated "solar maximum", while the lowest number is designated "solar minimum". The Sun is currently in an active phase of its 11-year solar cycle. The current cycle, called Solar Cycle 24, began in 2008. We are over five years into Cycle 24.

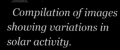

Compilation of images showing variations in solar activity.

Terrestrial organisms

During a solar minimum, the decrease in ultraviolet light received from the Sun leads to a decrease in the concentration of ozone, allowing increased Ultraviolet beams to penetrate through Earth's surface.

Terrestrial climate

Both long- and short-term variations in solar activity are hypothesised to affect global climate, but it has proven extremely challenging to directly quantify the link between solar variation and Earth's climate.

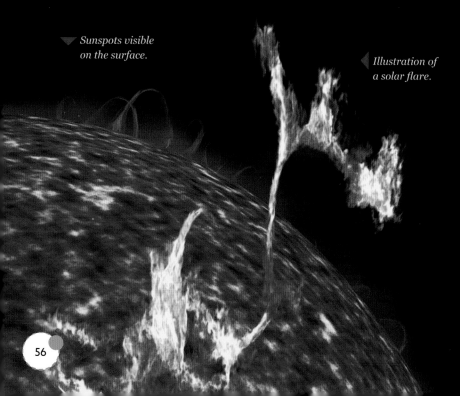

Sunspots visible on the surface.

Illustration of a solar flare.

FUN FACT

Did you know that "South" sunspots become "North" sunspots during the next solar cycle?

Sun Gazing

There are several right ways and many wrong ways to view the Sun; the danger being, prolonged, direct exposure can cause permanent damage to the retina, leading to loss of vision or blindness. To observe the Sun safely, one needs to filter out more than 99 per cent of the Sun's light before it reaches the eyes.

Projecting the Sun

The simplest, safest method of looking at the Sun is to look at its image projected onto a piece of paper. This technique is particularly useful during solar eclipses: the projected image will show all the phases of the eclipse, as if looking at the Sun itself.

A hole created in a natural cave to enable the safe viewing of the Sun.

Pinhole Projection Method

In a room with a Sun-facing window, without lights, sunlight enters through a small hole punched in a card near the top of the window. Another card is placed behind this card, in the shade, on which the Sun's image is projected.

Solar projection

Small telescopes are especially suited to the solar-projection method.

Whether projecting with binoculars or a telescope, using a sunshade to block ambient light from falling on the projection surface helps improve the view.

Viewing devices

Binoculars and telescopes concentrate the Sun's blazing light. It's even more crucial to use filters. The easiest and cheapest option is to use a sheet of solar-filter material specially made for telescope use.

These filters show the Sun's visible surface, the photosphere, in its natural "white" light, though the disc could look pale yellow, orange or blue, depending on the filter type. These let one gaze at the Sun for hours without any risk.

Lastly, there are specialised solar equipment that allow one to observe the Sun at very narrow wavelengths.

Observing the Sun through a telescope and a special filter to reduce sunlight. ▶

FUN FACT

In some religions, people practise staring directly into the Sun for a period of time, known as "Sun gazing". It is also done as a part of a spiritual practice.

Solar Eclipse

A solar eclipse is a natural event that occurs on Earth when the moon moves in its orbit between the Sun and Earth. This is also known as an occultation. It happens at new moon, when the Sun and moon are in conjunction with each other. If the moon was only slightly closer to Earth and orbited in the same plane, and its orbit was circular, we would see eclipses each month.

The lunar orbit

It is elliptical and tilted with respect to Earth's orbit, so we can only see up to five eclipses per year. Depending on the geometry of the Sun, moon and Earth, the Sun can be blocked either totally or partially. During an eclipse, the moon's shadow (which is divided into two parts: the dark umbra and the lighter penumbra) moves across Earth's surface.

Types of solar eclipses

An annular eclipse occurs when the Sun and moon are exactly in line, but the apparent size of the moon is smaller than the Sun. Hence, the Sun appears as a very bright ring, or annulus, surrounding the dark disc of the moon. A hybrid eclipse (also called annular/total eclipse) shifts between a total and annular eclipse. At certain points on the surface of Earth it appears as a total eclipse, whereas at other points it appears as annular. Hybrid eclipses are comparatively rare.

A partial eclipse occurs when the Sun and moon are not exactly in line and the moon only partially obscures the Sun. This phenomenon can usually be seen from a large part of Earth outside the track of an annular or total eclipse. However, some eclipses can only be seen as a partial eclipse, because the umbra passes above Earth's Polar Regions and never intersects its surface.

A total eclipse occurs when the dark silhouette of the moon completely obscures the intensely bright light of the Sun, allowing the much fainter solar corona to be visible. During any one eclipse, totality occurs at best only in a narrow track on the surface of Earth.

A total eclipse of the Sun. The sun has been covered by the moon.

The moon covers the Sun. This is visible as a total eclipse in some parts of Earth and partial eclipse in other. Some parts of Earth will not see an eclipse at all.

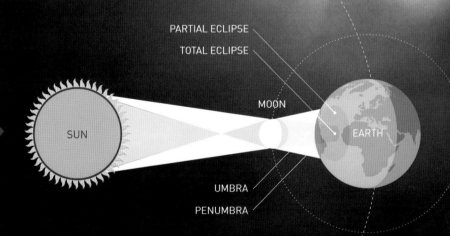

PARTIAL ECLIPSE

TOTAL ECLIPSE

MOON

SUN

EARTH

UMBRA

PENUMBRA

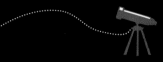

Occurrence and cycles

Total solar eclipses are rare events. Although they occur somewhere on Earth every 18 months on average, it is estimated that they recur at any given place only once every 360 to 410 years, on average. Totality currently can never last more than seven minutes and 32 seconds. This value changes over the millennia and is currently decreasing.

Eclipses in ancient history

The earliest record of a solar eclipse that occurred was more than four millennia ago. In China, it was believed that the gradual blotting out of the Sun was caused by a dragon who was trying to consume the Sun, and it was the duty of the court astronomers to shoot arrows, beat drums and raise whatever discord they could to scare the dragon away.

In the ancient Chinese classic Shujing (or Book of Documents) is the account of Hsi and Ho, two court astronomers who were caught completely unaware by a solar eclipse, having gotten drunk just before the event began. In the aftermath, Zhong Kang, the fourth emperor of the Xia dynasty, ordered that Hsi and Ho be punished by having their heads chopped off. The eclipse in question was that of 22nd October, in the year 2134 BCE.

Danger of looking at the Sun

Looking directly at the photosphere of the Sun can cause permanent damage

to the retina of the eye even if we look at it just for a few seconds, because of the intense visible and invisible radiation that the photosphere emits. Viewing the Sun during partial and annular eclipses as well as during total eclipses outside the brief period of totality requires special eye protection, or indirect viewing methods, if eye damage is to be avoided. The Sun's disc can be viewed using appropriate filtration to block the harmful part of the Sun's radiation.

Phases observed during a total eclipse

First contact:	Second contact:	Totality:	Third contact:	Fourth contact:
When the moon's limb (edge) is exactly tangential to that of the Sun's.	Starting with Bailey's Beads and the diamond ring effect, almost the entire disc is covered.	The moon obscures the entire disc of the Sun and only the solar corona is visible.	When the first bright light becomes visible and the moon's shadow is moving away from the observer. Again, a diamond ring may be observed.	When the trailing edge of the moon ceases to overlap with the solar disc and the eclipse ends.

The moon covering the Sun in a partial eclipse. This happens when the moon passes in front of the Sun and hides it from being viewed by Earth.

FUN FACT

In the past, the moon was too close to Earth and during eclipses it completely blotted out the Sun's disc. The moon's orbit will continue to widen and in perhaps 600 million years, total solar eclipses will no longer occur.

The Sun as a Deity

Like other natural phenomena, the Sun has been an object of veneration in many cultures throughout history. Humanity's most fundamental understanding of the Sun is as the luminous disc in the sky, whose presence above the horizon creates day and whose absence causes night. In many prehistoric and ancient cultures, the Sun was thought to be a solar deity or other supernatural phenomenon.

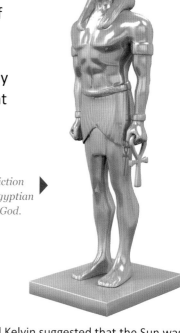

▶ *Depiction of Egyptian Sun God.*

Importance of the Sun

Worshipping the Sun was central to civilisations such as the ancient Egyptians, Incas of South America and Aztecs of Mexico. In religions such as Hinduism, the Sun is still considered as a deity. The Egyptians portrayed Ra (the Sun) as being carried across the sky in a solar barque, accompanied by lesser gods. To the Greeks, he was Helios, carried by a chariot drawn by fiery horses. From the reign of Elagabalus in the late Roman Empire, the Sun's birthday was a holiday celebrated as Sol Invictus, meaning "unconquered sun".

Development of scientific understanding

One of the first people to offer a scientific or philosophical explanation for the Sun was Greek Philosopher Anaxagoras, who reasoned that it was a giant flaming ball of metal and that the moon reflected the light of the Sun.

The Sun is the centre of our galaxy

During the third century BCE, Aristarchus of Samos, Ancient Greece, first proposed the theory that the Sun is the centre around which the planets move. During the early years of the modern scientific era, the source of the Sun's energy was a significant puzzle.

Lord Kelvin suggested that the Sun was a gradually cooling liquid body that was radiating an internal store of heat.

FUN FACT

According to Greek mythology, Helios, a solar deity, was a charioteer who drove his fiery vehicle through heaven by day. During the night, he floated back across the ocean in a golden bowl, to mount his chariot again the next morning.

▶ *Solar system with the Sun, planets and stars.*

PLANETS

▲ *A captivating view of the Sun and the planets that form the solar system.*

Our solar system consists of eight planets. Mercury, the closest planet to the Sun, is only a bit larger than Earth's moon. Venus, the second planet from the Sun, is terribly hot. Earth is the third planet from the Sun; two-thirds of this planet is covered with water and it is the only planet known to harbour life. Mars, the fourth planet, is a reddish planet that is cold and dusty.

Jupiter, the fifth planet, is the largest planet in the solar system. Saturn, the sixth planet, is known for its rings. The seventh planet, Uranus, is the only giant planet that orbits on its side. Neptune, the eighth planet, is known for strong winds. Until 2006, Pluto was considered to be a planet but was later demoted to a dwarf planet.

Mercury

Mercury is the smallest and closest planet to the Sun of the eight planets in the solar system.

Mercury

Mass: 330,104,000,000,000 billion kg (0.055 x Earth)

Equatorial diameter: 4879

Equatorial circumference: 15,329 km

Notable moons: None

Orbit period: 87.97 Earth days

Surface temperature: -173 °C to 427 °C

Mercury is named after the Roman deity Mercury, the messenger of the gods.

Internal structure

Mercury consists of approximately 70 per cent metallic and 30 per cent silicate material. Mercury's density is the second highest in the solar system at 5.427 g/cm^3. Geologists estimate that its core occupies about 42 per cent of its volume. In addition, its crust is believed to be 100 – 300 km thick.

Surface geology

Mercury possesses a "dorsa" or "wrinkle-ridges", moon-like highlands, montes (mountains), planitiae (plains), rupes (escarpments) and valles (valleys). There are craters on Mercury, which range in diameter from small bowl-shaped cavities to multi-ringed impact basins, 100 km wide. The largest known crater is "Caloris Basin", with a diameter of 1,550 km. The impact that created the Caloris basin was so powerful that it caused lava eruptions and left a concentric ring of over 2 km tall surrounding the impact at the crater.

▲

An image of the planet Mercury as captured by a space probe of NASA. It appears red because it is covered in red soil.

The surface of the planet Mercury is very similar to that of the moon in the sense that it is rough and full of craters and rocks. It is also dry and dusty seeing that it is the closest planet to the Sun.

▼

Atmosphere

The surface temperature of Mercury ranges from 100 K to 700 K at the most extreme places. The subsolar point reaches about 700 K during perihelion (when Earth is closest to the Sun), but only 550 K at aphelion (when Earth is farthest from the Sun). On the dark side of the planet, the temperatures average at about 110 K.

Magnetic field and magnetosphere

Despite its small size and slow 59-day-long rotation, Mercury has a significant magnetic field. Like that of Earth, Mercury's magnetic field is bipolar (magnetic poles of equal magnitude and opposite signs). Space probes have indicated that the strength and shape of the magnetic field are stable.

FUN FACT

Mercury is only the second hottest planet in the solar system despite being the closest to the Sun, with the hottest planet being Venus.

Location and Movement

Mercury has the most eccentric orbit among all the planets. It takes 87.969 Earth days to complete an orbit. Its higher velocity when it is near perihelion is clear from the greater distance it covers at each five-day interval.

Mercury's orbit and axis

Mercury's orbit is inclined by seven degrees to the plane of Earth's orbit. Its axial tilt is almost zero. At certain points on Mercury's surface, an observer would be able to see the Sun rise about halfway, then reverse and set before rising again, all within the same Mercurian day. To a hypothetical observer on Mercury, the Sun appears to move in a backward direction.

Longitude convention

The longitude convention for Mercury puts the zero of its longitude at one of the two hottest points on the surface. The two hottest places on the equator are at longitudes 0° W and 180° W, and the coolest points on the equator are at longitudes 90° W and 270° W.

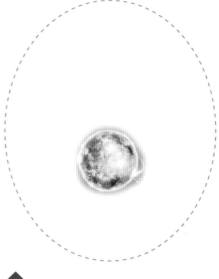

▲
The planet has a 3:2 spin-orbit resonance, rotating thrice for every two revolutions around the Sun.

Spin-orbit resonance

For many years, it was believed that this planet was tidally locked with the Sun at the same time, rotating once for each orbit and always keeping the same face directed towards the Sun, similar to the way that the same side of the moon always faces Earth. However, this is not true. It rotates thrice for every two revolutions around the Sun.

Observation

Observating Mercury is complicated due to its proximity to the Sun, as it is difficult to distinguish it in the Sun's glare. It can be observed for only a brief period either in the morning or evening twilight. Additionally, it can be seen during a total solar eclipse. Like the moon and Venus, it exhibits phases as seen from Earth.

▲
Unlike the moon whose one side faces Earth at all times, Mercury rotates twice for every revolution around the Sun.

FUN FACT

Just like humans, Mercury too has wrinkles. As the iron core of the planet cooled and contracted, the surface of the planet became wrinkled. Scientists have named these wrinkles "lobate scarps". These scarps can be up to 1.6 km high and hundreds of km long.

Venus

Venus is the second planet from the Sun and the second brightest object in the night sky, after the moon. It never appears to venture far from the Sun. It can also be seen during daytime from Earth. It is almost the same size as Earth and is also referred to as Earth's twin. This planet is named after the Roman goddess of love and beauty because of its brightness.

Venus

Mass: 4,867,320,000,000,000 billion kg (0.815 × Earth)

Equatorial circumference: 38,025 km

Known moons: None

Orbit's distance: 108,209,475 km (0.73 AU), having an orbit period of 224.70 Earth days

Surface temperature: 462 °C

Named after the Roman goddess of love and beauty, Venus is the second largest terrestrial planet.

FUN FACT

At one point, it was thought that Venus may be a tropical paradise, as the dense clouds of sulphuric acid around it make it impossible to view its surface from outside its atmosphere. It was only later that scientists observed and measured the extreme temperatures and hostile environment.

Appearance

Venus is sometimes called Earth's "sister planet" because of their similar size, mass, proximity to the Sun and bulk composition. However, it has also been shown to be radically different from Earth in other respects. It has the densest atmosphere of the four terrestrial planets, consisting of more than 96 per cent carbon dioxide. With a surface temperature of 462 °C (735 K), it is by far the hottest planet in the solar system, despite Mercury being the closest one to the Sun. Venus has no carbon cycle that converts carbon into rock, nor does it appear to have any organic life to absorb carbon into biomass.

Early studies

Ancient civilisations knew Venus as the "morning star" and "evening star", based on the assumption that these were two separate objects. The Greeks, too, thought of them as two separate stars, "Phosphorus" and "Hesperus". The Romans named the morning Venus "Lucifer", or Light-Bringer, and the evening one "Vesper". The Babylonians understood that the two were a single object. They referred to it as the "bright queen of the sky" in their tablet.

Atmospheric pressure on Venus is 92 times greater than Earth's.

The planet is bright enough to be seen in a mid-day clear sky and it can be easily seen when the Sun is low on the horizon.

Location and Movement

Venus orbits the Sun at an average distance of about 0.72 AU and completes an orbit every 224.65 days. Although all planetary orbits are elliptical, Venus' orbit is more circular. All the planets of the solar system orbit the Sun in an anti-clockwise direction as viewed from Earth's North Pole, but Venus rotates clockwise, called "retrograde" rotation, once every 243 Earth days. A Venusian day lasts longer than a Venusian year. The equator of Venus rotates at 6.5 km per hour.

Observation

Venus has no natural satellites, though the asteroid 2002 VE68 presently maintains a quasi-orbital relationship with it. Studies show that Venus is likely to have had at least one moon created by a huge-impact event billions of years ago. About 10 million years later, according to the study, another impact reversed the planet's spin direction and caused the Venusian moon to gradually spiral inward until it collided and merged with Venus.

Venusian phases

As it moves around its orbit, Venus displays phases like those of the moon in a telescopic view. The planet presents a small "full" phase when it is on the opposite side of the Sun. It shows a larger "quarter phase" when it is at its maximum elongations from the Sun and at its brightest in the night sky. It presents a much larger "thin crescent" in telescopic views as it comes around to the nearer side, between Earth and the Sun.

Due to retrograde rotation on Venus, the Sun rises in the West.

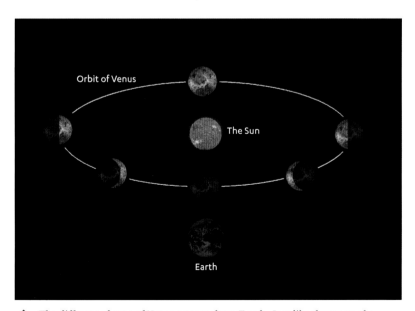

The different phases of Venus as seen from Earth. Just like the moon, the Sun illuminates parts of Venus as it orbits around it.

Surface of Venus

Venus has very high atmospheric pressure, low winds and very high temperatures. This is the reason why the surface of Venus can be called rocky. From a distance, the planet looks like any other planet. However, owing to the Soviet Union's Venera 13 lander, we were able to take a closer look at the surface of Venus. Although covered by clouds, there is a good amount of sunlight that shines through and lights up the surface. To be precise, the surface of Venus is flat and slabby. This is not unlike the sedimentary rocks present on Earth that are naturally layered. However, what has caused the land of Venus to become that way is yet to be discovered.

Transit of Venus

 A transit of Venus across the Sun occurs when the planet Venus passes directly between the Sun and Earth (or another planet), becoming visible against the solar disc. During a transit, Venus can be seen from Earth as a small black disc moving across the face of the Sun. The duration of such transits is usually measured in hours. It is similar to a solar eclipse by the moon. Venus appears smaller and travels more slowly across the face of the Sun, because it is much farther away from Earth.

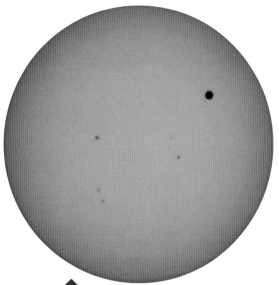

Transits of Venus are among the rarest of predictable astronomical phenomena. We see the shadow of Venus falling on the Sun.

Scientific importance

Venus transits are historically of great scientific importance as they were used to gain the first realistic estimates of the size of the solar system. Observations of the 1639 transit, combined with the principle of parallax, provided an estimate of the distance between the Sun and Earth that was more accurate than any other, up to that time.
The 2012 transit provided scientists with several research opportunities, especially to refine the techniques that are used to explore exoplanets (planets that are outside our solar system).

Ancient history

Ancient Indian, Greek, Egyptian, Babylonian and Chinese observers knew of Venus and recorded the planet's motions. The early Greek astronomers called Venus by two names, Hesperus, the evening star and Phosphorus, the morning star. Pythagoras is credited with realising that they were the same planet. There is no evidence that any of these cultures knew of the transits.

The eight-year itch

Currently, transits occur only in June or December and the occurrence of these

People watching Venus Transit at the David Dunlap Observatory on 5th June, 2012, in Richmond Hill, Ontario, Canada.

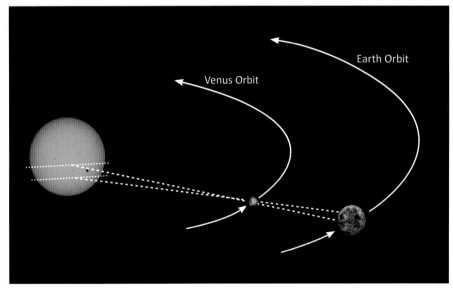

Diagram of Venus transits.

events slowly drifts, becoming later in the year by about two days every 243-year cycle. Transits usually occur in pairs, on nearly the same date eight years apart. This is because the length of eight Earth years is almost the same as 13 years on Venus, so every eight years, the planets are in roughly the same relative positions.

Earth

Earth is the third planet from the Sun. It is the largest of the terrestrial planets of the inner solar system, bigger than Mercury, Venus and Mars.

Earth's dimensions

The mean distance of Earth from the Sun is 1.49504 km. Earth's mean radius is 36,371 km. However, Earth is not quite round in shape. The planet's rotation causes it to bulge at the equator. Its equatorial diameter is 12,756 km, whereas from pole to pole, the diameter is 12,720 km; a difference of only 64 km.

Earth's circumference and density

Earth's circumference at the equator is about 40,075 km, but from pole-to-pole, it is only 40,008 km around. This shape, caused by the flattening at the poles, is called an "oblate spheroid". Earth's density is 5.52 grams/cm^3 and is the densest planet in the solar system because of its metallic core and rocky mantle. Jupiter, which is 318 times bigger than Earth, is less dense because it is made of gases, such as hydrogen.

Earth's mass and volume

Earth's mass is 5.9722 × 1024 kg and its volume is 1.08321 × 1012 km.

▼ *The Sun's light takes 8 minutes and 20 seconds to travel to Earth.*

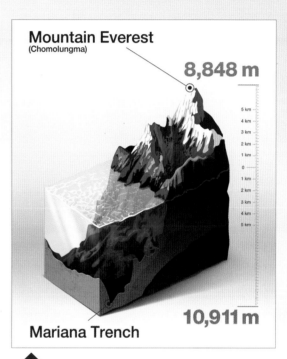

Mountain Everest
(Chomolungma)

8,848 m

5 km
4 km
3 km
2 km
1 km
0
1 km
2 km
3 km
4 km
5 km

10,911 m
Mariana Trench

▲
Vector form of the highest and deepest places on Earth.

Surface area

The total surface area of Earth is about 509 million km^2. About 71 per cent, i.e., 361,000,000 km^2, is covered by water and 29 per cent, i.e., 149,000,000 km^2, by land.

Zenith and Nadir

Mount Everest is the highest place on Earth that is above sea level, at 29,028 feet (8,848 m), but it is not the highest point on Earth. That title belongs to Mount Chimaborazo in the Andes Mountains in Ecuador.

The lowest point on Earth is the Mariana Trench in the western Pacific Ocean. It reaches down about 36,200 feet (11,034 m) below sea level.

Location and Movement

Earth rotates about an imaginary line that passes through the North and South poles of the planet, which is called the axis of rotation. Earth rotates about this axis once each day, approximately 24 hours. Rotation results in daytime when an area is facing the Sun and night time when an area is facing away from it. As we are on Earth, we do not sense its rotation, but we experience it by observing the Sun's motion.

North celestial pole
Axial tilt
Rotating axis
Celestial equator
Ecliptic
South celestial pole

The orbital and axial planes are not precisely aligned: Earth's axis is tilted approximately 23.4^{0} perpendicular to Earth-Sun plane.

Apparent diurnal motion

For an observer at a fixed position on Earth, its rotation makes it appear as if the sky is revolving around Earth. In other words, if one is standing for long enough in a field at night, it looks like the sky is moving, not you.

Earth's orbit

Earth orbits the Sun at a distance of about 150 million km every 365.2564 mean solar days or one sidereal year. Due to this motion, on an average, it takes 24 hours for Earth to complete a full rotation about its axis. When viewed from a vantage point above the north poles of both the Sun and Earth, Earth orbits in a counter-clockwise direction around the Sun.

Axial tilt and seasons

Due to Earth's axial tilt, the amount of sunlight reaching any given point on the surface varies over the year. This causes a seasonal change in the climate, with summer in the northern hemisphere occurring when the North Pole is pointing towards the Sun and winter occurring when the pole is pointed away. During summer, the days last longer and the Sun climbs higher in the sky. In winter, the days are shorter.

Above the Arctic Circle, an extreme point is reached where there is no daylight at all for a part of the year. It is dark for up to six months at the North Pole itself and is called a polar night. In the southern hemisphere, the situation is exactly reversed where the direction of the South Pole is oriented opposite to the North Pole.

Seasonal variation.

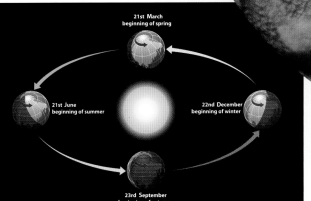

21st March
beginning of spring

21st June
beginning of summer

22nd December
beginning of winter

23rd September
beginning of autumn

FUN FACT

Without the axial tilt, there would be an eclipse every two weeks, alternating between lunar and solar eclipses.

Earth's Structure

The shape of Earth approximates an oblate spheroid; a sphere which is flattened along the axis from pole to pole such that there is a bulge around the equator. This bulge results from the rotation of Earth, and causes the diameter at the equator to be 43 km larger than the pole-to-pole diameter.

Inner core

It extends another 1,448 km towards the centre of Earth. It is believed that this inner core is a solid ball of mostly iron and nickel.

Outer core

It extends to a depth of around 4,828 km beneath the surface. It is believed that this outer core is made up of super-heated molten lava.

Earth's crust

The first layer consists of about 16 km of rock and loose materials that scientists call the crust. Beneath the continents, the crust is almost three times as thick as it is beneath the oceans.

The mantle

It extends to a depth of approximately 2,897 km and is made of a thick, solid, rocky substance that represents about 85 per cent of the total weight and mass of Earth. The first 80 km of the mantle is believed to consist of very hard and rigid rock. The next 241 km is believed to be super-heated solid rock that, due to the heat energy, is very weak.

What Earth is made up of

Earth is made of four distinct layers. These layers are the crust, mantle, outer and inner cores.

Chemical composition

Earth's mass is approximately 5.97×10^{24} kg. It is composed mostly of iron (32.1%), oxygen (30.1%), silicon (15.1%), magnesium (13.9%), sulphur (2.9%), nickel (1.8%), calcium (1.5%) and aluminium (1.4%), and the remaining 1.2% consists of trace amounts of other elements. Due to mass segregation, the core region is believed to be primarily composed of iron (88.8%), with smaller amounts of nickel (5.8%), sulphur (4.5%) and less than one per cent trace elements.

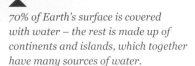

70% of Earth's surface is covered with water – the rest is made up of continents and islands, which together have many sources of water.

How Earth was Formed?

Earth was formed approximately 4.54 billion years ago and is the only known planet to support life. Although scientists estimate that over 99 per cent of all species that ever lived on the planet are extinct, currently 10 – 14 million species of life call Earth their home, including over 7.2 billion humans, who depend upon its biosphere and minerals.

FUN FACT

Earth is the only planet not named after a Roman god or goddess.

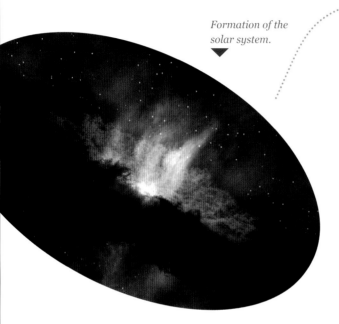

Formation of the solar system.

Geological history

Earth's atmosphere and oceans are formed by volcanic activity, and outgassing that included water vapour. The origin of the world's oceans occurred as condensation increased by water and ice that was delivered by asteroids, proto-planets, and comets. Around 3.5 billion years ago, Earth's magnetic field was established, which helped prevent the atmosphere from being stripped away by solar winds. A crust formed when the molten outer layer of Earth cooled to form a solid as the accumulated water vapour began to accumulate in the atmosphere.

Formation of continents

Continents were formed by plate tectonics, a process eventually driven by the continuous loss of heat from Earth's interior. In the last hundreds of millions of years, the supercontinents have formed and broken up thrice. Roughly 750 million years ago, one of the earliest known supercontinents, Rodinia, began to break apart. The continents later joined to form Pannotia, 540 – 600 million years ago, then finally Pangaea, which also broke apart 180 million years ago.

Formation

The formation and evolution of the solar system occurred along with the Sun. In theory, a solar nebula partitioned a volume out of a molecular cloud due to gravitational collapse, which began to spin and flatten into a circum-stellar disc, and then the planets grew out of that along with the star. A nebula contains gas, ice grains and dust. The assembly of the primordial Earth proceeded for 10 – 20 million years. The moon formed shortly thereafter, approximately 4.53 billion years ago.

Continents were formed by plate tectonics, The supercontinents have formed and broken up thrice.

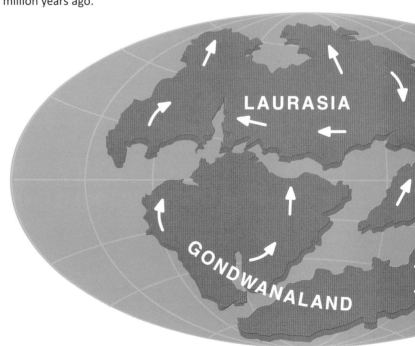

LAURASIA

GONDWANALAND

Earth's History

It seems impossible to imagine an Earth without any life on it. Millions of years ago, Earth was lifeless. And then, unicellular beings began to exist. They were formed in water. From single-celled to multi-celled to beings with complex cellular structures, Earth has come a long way and so have humans, along with it.

Beginning of life

The first life forms appeared between 3.5 and 3.8 billion years ago. Life remained mostly small and microscopic until about 580 million years ago, when complex multi-cellular life started appearing.

Geological change has been continually occurring on Earth since the time of its formation and biological change, since the first appearance of life. Species constantly evolve, taking on new forms, splitting into daughter species or going extinct in response to an ever-changing planet.

Hadean and Archean eons

The first eon during Earth's history, the Hadean, begins with Earth's formation and is followed by the Archean eon at 3.8 Ga. The oldest rocks found on Earth date to about 4.0 Ga, soon after the formation of Earth's crust and Earth itself. By the beginning of the Archean, Earth had significantly cooled. Most of the present life forms could not have survived in the Archean atmosphere, which lacked oxygen and also an ozone layer.

Formation of the moon

Earth's one and only natural satellite, the moon, is a larger relative of its planet than any other satellite in the solar system. Radiometric dating of rocks from the moon has shown that it was formed at least 30 million years after the solar system.

Origin of life

The first step in the appearance of life may have been chemical reactions that produced many of the simpler organic compounds, including amino acids, which are the building blocks of life.

The subsequent stage of complexity could have been reached from at least three possible starting points: self-replication, metabolism and external cell membranes, which allow food to enter and waste products to leave, but exclude unwanted substances.

Geochronological scale
millions of years ago

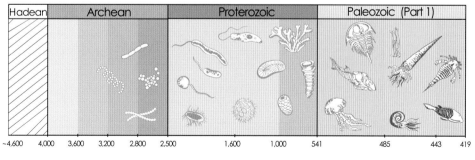

Hadean	Archean	Proterozoic	Paleozoic (Part 1)

~4,600 4,000 3,600 3,200 2,800 2,500 1,600 1,000 541 485 443 419

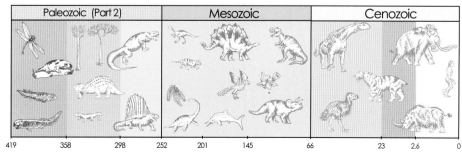

Paleozoic (Part 2)	Mesozoic	Cenozoic

419 358 298 252 201 145 66 23 2.6 0

Earth's Atmosphere

Earth's atmosphere is a thin layer of gases that surrounds it. It is composed of 78 per cent nitrogen, 21 per cent oxygen, 0.9 per cent argon, 0.03 per cent carbon dioxide and trace amounts of other gases. This thin layer insulates Earth from extreme temperatures; keeping heat within the atmosphere and also blocking it from the Sun's incoming ultraviolet radiation.

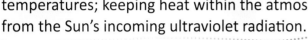

Earth's ability to support life depends on its atmosphere.

1 Exosphere

The exosphere is the outermost layer of Earth's atmosphere. The exosphere being from about 640–1,280 km above Earth.

2 Thermosphere

The thermosphere is a thermal classification of the atmosphere. In the thermosphere, the temperature increases with the altitude.

3 Mesosphere

The mesosphere is characterised by temperatures that quickly decrease as the height increases. The mesosphere extends from 17 to 80 km above Earth's surface.

4 Ionosphere

The ionosphere starts at about 70 – 80 km above Earth and continues for hundreds of kilometres (640 km). It contains many ions and free electrons (plasma). The ions are created when sunlight hits the atoms and strips off some of its electrons.

5 Stratosphere

The stratosphere is characterised by a slight temperature increase with height and the absence of clouds. The stratosphere extends from 17 – 50 km above Earth's surface. The ozone layer is located in the stratosphere. This layer absorbs a lot of ultraviolet solar energy.

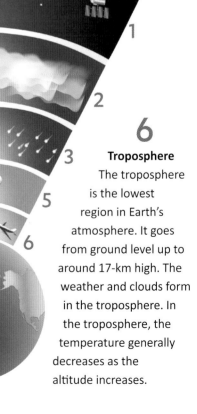

6 Troposphere

The troposphere is the lowest region in Earth's atmosphere. It goes from ground level up to around 17-km high. The weather and clouds form in the troposphere. In the troposphere, the temperature generally decreases as the altitude increases.

Formation of the atmosphere

Earth's atmosphere was formed by planetary degassing, a process in which gases like carbon dioxide, water vapour, sulphur dioxide and nitrogen were released from its interior from volcanoes and other processes. Life forms on Earth have modified the composition of the atmosphere since their evolution.

Northern lights (aurora borealis) in the night sky over a lake.

Life on Earth

A planet that can sustain life is termed "habitable", even if life did not originate there. Earth provides liquid water — an environment where complex organic molecules can assemble and interact, and there is sufficient energy to sustain metabolism. The distance of Earth from the Sun, as well as its orbital eccentricity, rate of rotation, axial tilt, geological history, sustaining atmosphere and protective magnetic field, all contribute to the current climatic conditions at the surface.

The biosphere

Life is everywhere on Earth; you can find living organisms from the poles to the equator, at the bottom of the sea to several miles in the air, from freezing waters to dry valleys to undersea thermal vents to groundwater thousands of feet below Earth's surface. Over the last 3.7 billion years or so, living organisms on Earth have diversified and adapted to almost every environment imaginable.

Human geography

It is estimated that one-eighth of Earth's surface is suitable for humans to live on. Three quarters of it is covered by oceans, leaving one quarter as land. Half of that land area is desert (14 per cent), high mountains (27 per cent) or other unsuitable terrain.

Natural resources and land use

Large deposits of fossil fuels are obtained from Earth's crust, consisting of coal, petroleum and natural gas. Earth's biosphere produces many biological products for humans, including food, wood, pharmaceuticals and oxygen.

 *Humans can use only about .003 per cent of the water on Earth.*

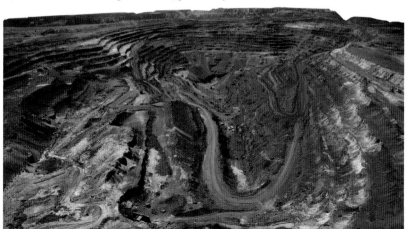

Natural and environmental hazards

Large areas of Earth's surface are subject to extreme weather such as tropical cyclones, hurricanes or typhoons. Many places are subject to earthquakes, landslides, tsunamis, volcanic eruptions, floods, droughts and other calamities. Many areas are subject to pollution, acid rain, loss of vegetation and erosion.

The most distant point from the centre of Earth is a volcano.

FUN FACT

In the past, Earth was believed to be flat. However, spherical Earth, a concept that has been credited to Pythagoras, displaced this.

Mars

In the night sky, you can sometimes see a very bright star that shines with a reddish twinkle. It is the planet of Mars. It is the fourth planet from the Sun and is at a distance of about 228 million km. It is the second smallest planet in the solar system, after Mercury. It is named after the Roman god of war. Interestingly, some parts of this planet look similar to the moon.

Mars

Mass: 641,693,000,000,000 billion kg (0.107 × Earth)

Equatorial diameter: 6,805

Equatorial circumference: 21,297 km

Notable moons: Phobos and Deimos

Orbit period: 686.98 Earth days (1.88 Earth years)

Surface temperature: -87 to -5 °C

It is described as the "Red Planet", because the iron oxide prevalent on its surface gives it a reddish appearance.

Internal structure

A silicate mantle that formed many tectonic and volcanic features on the planet surrounds the core, but it now appears to be dormant. Besides silicon and oxygen, the other abundant elements in the Martian crust are iron, magnesium, aluminium, calcium and potassium. The average thickness of the planet's crust is about 50 km, with a maximum thickness of 125 km as compared to the 40-km crust of Earth.

Etymology

The planet of Mars gets its name from the Roman god of war. In various cultures, Mars represents masculinity and youth. Its symbol, which is a circle with an arrow pointing out to the upper right, is also used as a symbol to denote the male gender.

Physical characteristics

Mars has approximately half the diameter of Earth. Its surface area is only slightly less than Earth's dry land. Even though Mars is larger and has more mass than Mercury, Mercury has a higher density. This evens them out and makes the two planets have an almost similar gravitational pull at the surface.

The reddish appearance of the Martian surface is caused by iron oxide, more commonly known as hematite, or rust. It sometimes also looks butterscotch, or golden, brown, tan and greenish, depending on the minerals.

Location and Movement

The planet orbits the Sun in 687 days and travels 9.55 AU in doing so, making the average orbital speed 24 km per second. As Earth completes its 24-hour-per-day spin, it results in the Coriolis "force". Earth is 40,000 km around at its widest part, the equator. Because it spins on its axis once in 24 hours, a point on its equator is moving about 1700 km per hour in relation to its axis.

Mars is visible from Earth

Mars reaches an opposition when there is a 180-degree difference between its geocentric longitudes and that of the Sun. Every opposition has some significance because Mars becomes visible from Earth, all night, high and fully lit, but the ones of special interest occur when Mars is near the perihelion, because this is when it is also the closest to Earth.

Laws of planetary motion

German astronomer Johannes Kepler formulated three laws of planetary motion. A key discovery was that the motion of Mars followed an elliptical path. This happened because his model with a circular orbit did not match the observations of Mars.

Surface geology

Mars is one of the terrestrial planets and consists of minerals containing silicon and oxygen, metals and other elements that rocks are ideally made of. The surface of Mars is primarily composed of tholeiitic basalt. Parts of the southern moorland include noticeable amounts of high-calcium pyroxenes. Localised concentrations of hematite and olivine have also been found. Quite a lot of the surface is deeply covered by fine iron oxide dust.

Martian soil has a basic pH of 7.7 and contains 0.6 per cent of salt perchlorate.
▼

▲
Mars in its orbit, fourth planet from the Sun.

Martian soil

Martian soil is slightly alkaline and contains elements such as magnesium, sodium, potassium and chlorine. These nutrients, necessary for plant growth, are found in the gardens on Earth.

Streaks across Mars are common and new ones frequently appear on steep slopes of craters, troughs and valleys. The streaks are dark at first and get lighter as they age. They have also been seen to follow the edges of boulders and other obstacles in their path.

Hydrology

Liquid water cannot exist on Mars due to its low atmospheric pressure, which is about 100 times thinner than Earth's, although, the polar ice caps seem to be made mainly of water.

FUN FACT

The amount of water ice in the south polar ice cap of Mars, if melted, would be sufficient to cover the entire surface up to a depth of 11 m.

Geology and Atmosphere

During the solar system's formation, Mars was created as a result of run-away accretion out of the proto-planetary disc that orbited the Sun. Mars has typical chemical features due to its position in the solar system. Elements with relatively low boiling points, such as chlorine, phosphorus and sulphur, are much more common on Mars than Earth.

Polar caps

Mars has two permanent polar ice caps. During winter at the pole, it is in continuous darkness, chilling the surface and converting the atmosphere into dry ice. When the poles are exposed to sunlight, the frozen CO_2 evaporates, creating enormous winds that sweep off the poles as fast as 400 km per hour.

These seasonal actions move huge amounts of dust and water vapour, giving rise to frost and large cirrus clouds, like on Earth.

Martian atmosphere

The solar wind interacts directly with the Martian ionosphere, lowering the atmospheric density by stripping away atoms from the outer layer. The atmospheric pressure on the surface ranges from 0.030 kPa on Olympus Mons to over 1.155 kPa in Hellas Planitia.

Atmospheric make up

The atmosphere of Mars comprises about 96 per cent carbon dioxide, 1.93 per cent argon and 1.89 per cent nitrogen with traces of oxygen and water. The atmosphere is rather dusty, containing particulates about 1.5 μm in diameter that gives the Martian sky an orange colour when observed from the surface of Earth.

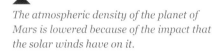

The atmospheric density of the planet of Mars is lowered because of the impact that the solar winds have on it.

Seasons of Mars

The seasons of Mars are similar to Earth's. The lengths of the seasons are about twice those of Earth's because Mars is farther from the Sun causing the Martian year to be around two Earth years long. Martian surface temperatures vary from about −143 to 35 °C. Mars also has the largest dust storms in the solar system. These vary from a storm over a small area, to massive storms covering the planet entirely. They tend to occur when Mars is the closest to the Sun and lead to increased global temperature.

▼ *Dust storm on Mars.*

FUN FACT

The shield volcano Olympus Mons is an extinct volcano in the vast upland region of Tharsis. Mount Olympus is approximately three times the height of Mount Everest.

Transit of Earth from Mars

A transit of Earth across the Sun as seen from Mars occurs when the planet Earth passes directly between the Sun and Mars, obscuring a small part of the Sun's disc for an observer on Mars. During a transit, Earth would be visible from Mars as a small black disc moving across the face of the Sun.

View from Mars

No one has ever seen a transit of Earth from Mars, but the next transit will take place on 10th November, 2084. The last transit of this type took place on 11th May, 1984. If viewed from Mars, during the event, it is possible for even the moon to be visible. However, the distance between Earth and its moon is such that they end up finishing their transits at different points in time.

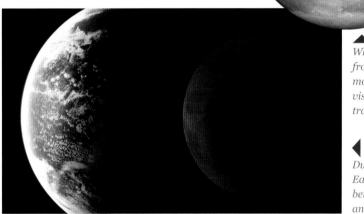

When viewed from Mars, the moon becomes visible during transit.

During the transit, Earth passes between the Sun and Mars.

View from Earth

A transit of Earth from Mars corresponds to Mars being perfectly and uniformly illuminated opposite Earth. More recently, using a radar from Earth has made better measurements of the oblateness of Mars possible. Also, better measurements have been made using artificial satellites that have been put into the orbit around Mars, including Mariner 9, Viking 1, Viking 2 and Soviet orbiters. These are the more recent orbiters that have been sent from Earth to Mars.

Grazing and simultaneous transits

Sometimes, Earth only grazes the Sun during a transit. In this case, it is possible that in some areas of Mars a full transit can be seen, while in other regions there is only a partial transit (no second or third contact). It is also possible that a transit of Earth can be seen from some parts of Mars as a partial transit, while in others, Earth misses the Sun.

Position of the Sun, moon and Mars during the transit.

> **FUN FACT**
>
> The simultaneous occurrence of a transit of Venus and Earth is extremely rare, and will next occur in the year 571,471.

Jupiter

Jupiter is the fifth planet from the Sun and the largest planet in the solar system. It is one of the gas giants with one-thousandth the mass of the Sun, but is two and a half times the total mass of all other planets in the solar system combined. When viewed from Earth, Jupiter can reach an apparent that is sufficiently bright to cast shadows.

Jupiter

Mass: 1,898,130,000,000,000,000 billion kg (317.83 x Earth)

Equatorial circumference: 439,264 km

Known moons: 67

Notable moons: Io, Europa, Ganymede and Callisto

Known rings: 4

Orbit period: 4,332.82 Earth days (11.86 Earth years)

The Romans named the planet after the roman God Jupiter.

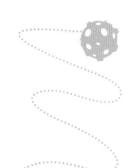

Jupiter takes 12 years to orbit the Sun.

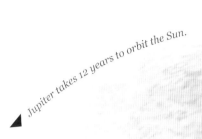

The illumination of Jupiter

Because the orbit of Jupiter is outside that of Earth's, the planet always appears nearly fully illuminated when viewed through Earth-based telescopes. It was only during spacecraft missions to Jupiter that crescent views of the planet were obtained. A small telescope will usually show Jupiter's four Galilean moons and the prominent cloud belts across Jupiter's atmosphere. A large telescope can show Jupiter's Great Red Spot when it faces Earth.

Etymology

The Romans named the planet after the Roman god Jupiter. To the Greeks, it represented Zeus, the god of thunder. For the Mesopotamians, Jupiter was the god Marduk and a patron of the city of Babylon. Germanic tribes saw this planet as Thor.

Earth overtakes Jupiter every 398.9 days as it orbits the Sun. This duration is called the synodic period. As it does so, Jupiter appears to undergo retrograde motion with respect to the background stars, i.e., for a period, Jupiter seems to move backward in the night sky, performing a loop in its motion.

Zodiac relation

Jupiter's 12-year orbital period corresponds to the dozen astrological signs of the zodiac, and may have been the historical origin of the signs, i.e., each time Jupiter reaches opposition, it has advanced eastward by about 30°, the width of a zodiac sign.

▼ *Jupiter as compared to Earth.*

EARTH

JUPITER

FUN FACT

Jupiter has the shortest day when compared with the seven planets. It orbits the Sun once every 11.8 Earth years.

Location and Movement

Jupiter is the only planet that has a centre of mass with the Sun that lies outside its volume, though by only seven per cent of the Sun's radius. The average distance between Jupiter and the Sun is 778 million km. The elliptical orbit of Jupiter is inclined 1.31 degrees compared to Earth. This planet does not experience significant seasonal changes, in contrast to Earth and Mars, as its axial tilt is relatively small.

It is the third brightest object in the night sky after the moon and Venus.

Fastest rotation

Jupiter's rotation is the fastest amongst all the planets in our solar system. It completes a rotation on its axis in a little less than 10 hours, creating an equatorial bulge easily seen through an amateur telescope. The planet is shaped as an oblate spheroid; this means that the diameter across its equator is longer than that between its poles. Since Jupiter is not a solid body, the rotation of Jupiter's polar atmosphere is about five minutes longer than its equatorial atmosphere.

Magnetosphere

Jupiter's magnetic field is 14 times as strong as Earth's, ranging from 0.42 metric tonne at the equator to 1.0 – 1.4 metric tonne at the poles, making it the strongest in the solar system. This field is believed to be generated by eddy currents (swirling movements of conducting materials) within the liquid metallic hydrogen core.

Formation of a magneto-disc

The gas ionised in the magnetosphere produces sulphur and oxygen ions, together with hydrogen ions. This forms a plasma sheet in Jupiter's equatorial plane. The plasma in the sheet rotates along with the planet, deforming the dipole magnetic field into that of a magneto-disc.

The four largest moons of Jupiter orbit within this magnetosphere, which protects them from the solar wind.

▼ *The dipole magnetic field of Jupiter.*

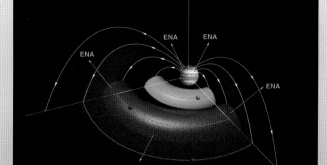

Atmosphere and Surface

Jupiter is composed chiefly of gaseous and liquid matter. It is the biggest of four gas giants and also the largest planet in the solar system. The density of Jupiter, 1.326 g per sq cm, is lower than any of the four terrestrial planets.

Composition

Jupiter's upper atmosphere is composed of about 88 – 92 per cent hydrogen and 8 – 12 per cent helium by per cent volume of gas molecules.

The atmosphere is about 75 per cent hydrogen and 24 per cent helium by mass; the remaining one per cent of the mass consists of other elements. The interior contains denser materials so that the distribution is roughly 71 per cent hydrogen, 24 per cent helium and five per cent other elements by mass. The atmosphere contains trace amounts of methane, water vapour, ammonia and silicon-based compounds. There are also traces of carbon, ethane, hydrogen sulphide, neon, oxygen, phosphine and sulphur. The outermost layer of the atmosphere contains crystals of frozen ammonia.

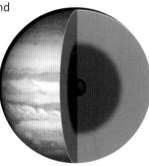

Jupiter's layers.

Rocky core

Jupiter is thought to consist of a dense core with a mixture of elements, a surrounding layer of liquid metallic hydrogen with some helium and an outer layer predominantly of molecular hydrogen. The core is often described as rocky, but its detailed composition is unknown.

Planetary rings

Jupiter has a faint planetary ring system of three main segments: an inner "torus" of particles known as the halo, a relatively bright main ring and an outer gossamer ring. These rings appear to be made of dust, rather than ice as with Saturn's rings. The main ring is probably made of material ejected from the satellites Adrastea and Metis. Material that would normally fall back to the moon is pulled into Jupiter because of its strong gravitational influence.

Great Red Spot

Latest evidence by the Hubble Space Telescope shows that there are three "red spots" adjacent to the Great Red Spot. Mathematical models suggest that the storm is stable and may be a permanent feature of the planet. The storm is large enough to be visible through Earth-based telescopes.

FUN FACT

The Great Red Spot is a huge storm on Jupiter that has raged for at least 350 years. It is so huge that three Earths could fit within it.

The planetary rings of Jupiter: The Inner halo, the bright main ring and the outer gossamer ring.

Saturn

Saturn is the sixth planet from the Sun and the second largest planet in the solar system, after Jupiter. It is named after the Roman god of agriculture; its astronomical symbol represents the god's sickle. Saturn is a gas giant with an average radius around nine times that of Earth. One-eighth the average density of Earth, Saturn is just over 95 times bigger.

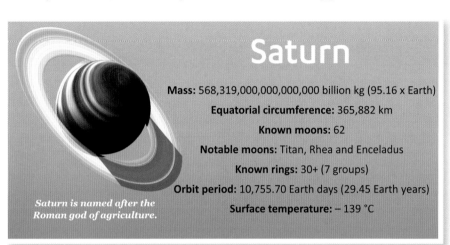

Saturn

Mass: 568,319,000,000,000,000 billion kg (95.16 x Earth)

Equatorial circumference: 365,882 km

Known moons: 62

Notable moons: Titan, Rhea and Enceladus

Known rings: 30+ (7 groups)

Orbit period: 10,755.70 Earth days (29.45 Earth years)

Surface temperature: – 139 °C

Saturn is named after the Roman god of agriculture.

One of the giant

Saturn is one of the giant planets in our solar system. It is oblate in shape, meaning that it is wider around the equator. It spins very fast, completing its rotation every 10.7 hours. Material is flung in an outward direction as it spins, which gives it a bulging equator. It is the least dense planet. Interestingly, if Saturn was to be placed in a huge ocean of water, it would float!

Saturn's rings

Saturn has a prominent ring system that consists of nine continuous main rings and three discontinuous arcs, composed chiefly of ice particles and some rocky debris and dust. The planet is orbited by 62 moons; out of which 53 are officially named. This does not include the multiple "moonlets" comprising the rings. Titan, Saturn's largest moon and the solar system's second largest moon is bigger than

Mercury, and is the only moon in the solar system to hold its own atmosphere.

Virtual image of Saturn and its rings. ▼

Occultation by the moon

Saturn is the farthest of the five planets that are easily visible to the naked eye.

The other four are Mercury, Venus, Mars and Jupiter. Saturn appears to the naked eye in the night sky as a bright, yellowish point of light. Twice every Saturnian year (approximately every 15 Earth years), the rings temporarily disappear from view, due to their angle and thinness. Periodically, the moon occults Saturn, i.e., the moon completely covers Saturn in the sky.

◀ *Comparison between Saturn and Earth.*

Location and Movement

The average distance between Saturn and the Sun is over 1.4 billion km (9 AU). It takes Saturn 10,759 Earth days (or about 29 and a half years), to finish one revolution around the Sun. The visible features on Saturn rotate at different rates depending on latitude. Multiple rotation periods have been assigned to various regions.

Saturn's rotational pattern

The latest estimate of Saturn's rotation (as an indicated rotation rate for the whole of Saturn), based on a compilation of various measurements, is 10 hours, 32 minutes and 35 seconds.

The gaseous giant

Saturn is termed as a gaseous giant because the exterior is chiefly composed of gas and it lacks a definite surface, although it may have a solid core. The rotation of the planet makes it take the shape of an oblate spheroid. Its equatorial and polar radii differ by almost 10 per cent. Saturn is the only planet in the solar system that is less dense than water (about 30 per cent less). Although Saturn's core is significantly denser than water, the average specific density of the planet is less due to the gaseous atmosphere.

Magnetosphere

Saturn has an intrinsic magnetic field that is a magnetic dipole. Its strength at the equator is approximately 1/20th of the field around Jupiter and slightly weaker than Earth's magnetic field. As a result, Saturn's magnetosphere is much smaller than Jupiter's. The magnetosphere is efficient at deflecting the solar wind particles from the Sun. The moon, Titan, that orbits it is in the outer part of Saturn's magnetosphere and contributes plasma from the ionised particles in Titan's outer atmosphere. Saturn's magnetosphere produces auroras, just like Earth.

Saturn is also known as the gaseous giant as it is majorly made of gases.

FUN FACT

Saturn orbits the Sun once every 29.4 Earth years. Due to its slow movement against the backdrop of stars, it got the nickname of "Lubadsagush" from the ancient Assyrians, which means "oldest of the old".

Atmosphere and Surface

Saturn is termed as a gas giant, but it is not completely gaseous. The temperature, pressure and density inside the planet rise steadily towards the core, which cause hydrogen to convert into a metal in the deeper layers of the planet.

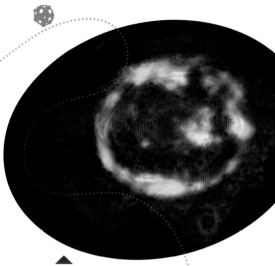

The planet chiefly consists of hydrogen.

Internal structure

The interior of Saturn is similar to that of Jupiter, having a small rocky core surrounded by hydrogen and helium with small amounts of various volatile substances. This core is also similar in composition to Earth, but denser. The core is about 9 – 22 times the mass of Earth. A thicker liquid layer of metallic hydrogen, followed by a liquid layer of helium-saturated molecular hydrogen that gradually transitions into gas with increasing altitude, surrounds this. The outermost layer spans 1,000 km and consists of a gaseous atmosphere.

Atmosphere

The outer atmosphere of Saturn contains 96.3 per cent molecular hydrogen and 3.25 per cent helium by volume. The proportion of helium is significantly deficient compared to the abundance of this element present in the Sun. The quantity of elements heavier than helium is not precisely known, but the proportions are assumed to match the primordial abundances from the formation of the solar system. The total mass of these heavier elements is estimated to be 19 – 31 times the mass of Earth, with a significant fraction located in Saturn's core region.

Shepherd moons

Saturn is best known for the system of planetary rings that makes it visually unique. The rings extend from 6,630 km to 120,700 km above its equator and are approximately 20 m thick. They are composed of 93 per cent water ice with traces of tholin impurities and 7 per cent amorphous carbon. Beyond the main rings, at a distance of 12 million km from the planet, is the thin Phoebe ring that orbits in retrograde fashion. Some of Saturn's moons, along with Pandora and Prometheus, act as shepherd moons to confine the rings and prevent them from spreading out.

A few moons on the outer edge of Saturn's rings keep the rings from expanding and are known as shepherd moons.

◀ *The other gas giants also have ring systems, but Saturn's is the largest and most visible.*

FUN FACT

Saturn has a hot interior, reaching 11,700° C at the core, and the planet radiates 2.5 times more energy into space than it receives from the Sun.

Uranus

Uranus is the seventh planet from the Sun. It has the third-largest planetary radius and fourth-largest planetary mass in the solar system. Its atmosphere, although similar to Jupiter's and Saturn's in its primary composition of hydrogen and helium, contains more "ices", such as water, ammonia and methane. It is the coldest planetary atmosphere in the solar system, with a minimum temperature of 49 K and has a complex, layered cloud structure. The interior of Uranus is mainly composed of ices and rock.

Uranus

The Greek god of the sky, Uranus, was the inspiration behind naming this planet.

Mass: 86,810,300,000,000,000 billion kg (14.536 × Earth)

Equatorial circumference: 159,354 km

Known moons: 27

Notable moons: Oberon, Titania, Miranda, Ariel and Umbriel

Known rings: 13

Orbit distance: 2,870,658,186 km (19.22 AU)

Surface temperature: -197 °C

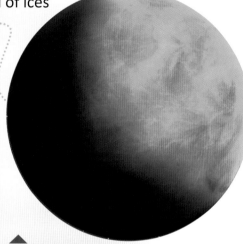

A rendering of the gas planet Uranus in a clear night sky.

All about Uranus

It is four times the size of Earth. Similar to other giant planets, it does not have a solid surface. Its surface is visible due to the layers of methane ice clouds present in its hydrogen-rich atmosphere. The methane gas present in the atmosphere absorbs the red wavelengths in sunlight, which makes the planet appear blue. Like other giant planets, Uranus has a ring system, a magnetosphere and numerous moons. The Uranian system has a distinctive configuration among other planets because its axis of rotation is tilted sideways. Its north and south poles, therefore, lie where most other planets have their equators.

Etymology

Uranus is named after the ancient Greek deity of the sky Ouranus, the father of Cronus (Saturn) and grandfather of Zeus (Jupiter). It is the only planet whose name is derived from a figure of Greek mythology and not Roman mythology.

Smallest giant planet

Uranus' mass is around 14.5 times that of Earth, making it the smallest of the giant planets. It is the second least dense planet, after Saturn. This indicates that it is mainly made of various ices, such as water, ammonia and methane. Hydrogen and helium constitute only a small part of the total (0.5 – 1.5 Earth masses).

Sir William Herschel discovered Uranus on 13th March, 1781.

FUN FACT

Uranus rotates in a retrograde direction, opposite to the way Earth and most other planets rotate.

Location and Movement

The average distance of Uranus from the Sun is around three billion km (about 20 AU). The variation of that distance is greater than that of any other planet, at 1.8 AU. The intensity of sunlight reduces quadratically with distance, and therefore, the intensity of light on Uranus is about 1/400th the intensity of light on Earth.

Rotation

The rotational period of the interior of Uranus is 17 hours, 14 minutes, clockwise (retrograde). Its upper atmosphere experiences strong winds in the direction of rotation. At some latitudes visible features of the atmosphere move much faster, making a full rotation in as less as 14 hours.

Axial tilt

Uranus has an axial tilt of 98 degrees, so its axis of rotation is approximately parallel with the plane of the solar system. This causes seasonal changes completely unlike those of the other major planets. Other planets can be thought to rotate like a tilted spinning top on the plane of the solar system, but Uranus rotates more like a tilted rolling ball. Each pole gets around 42 years of continuous sunlight, followed by 42 years of darkness. Uranus is hotter at its equator than at its poles.

Axial tilt of Uranus

-59°

Visibility

At opposition, Uranus is visible to the naked eye in dark skies and becomes an easy target even in urban conditions with binoculars. In larger amateur telescopes, Uranus appears as a pale cyan disc with distinct limb darkening. With a large telescope, cloud patterns as well as some of the larger satellites, such as Titania and Oberon, may become visible.

Uranus appears blue to us when observed from Earth. ▼

Unlike other planets, Uranus orbits the Sun on its side.

FUN FACT

Uranus makes one trip around the Sun every 84 Earth years.

Atmosphere and Surface

Uranus is a ball of ice and gas. If you tried to land a spacecraft on Uranus, it would just sink through the upper atmosphere of hydrogen and helium into its liquid icy centre. The peculiar orientation of the planet, which orbits the Sun tipped on its side, divulges that its inner core has a stronger influence on its weather patterns than the distant star. When we observe Uranus, we see the blue-green colour that comes from its surface. This colour is light from the Sun that is reflected off its surface.

Upper Atmosphere
(cloud tops)

Mantle
(water, Ammonia,
Methane ices)

Core
(rock, ices)

Atmosphere
(Hydrogen, Helium,
Methane gas)

The internal structure of Uranus.

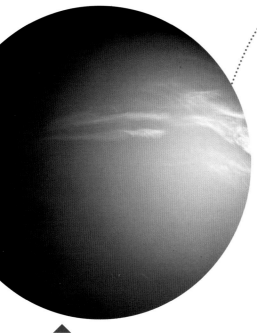

▲ *While Uranus appears blue, it has stripes similar to Jupiter and Saturn.*

Cloud patterns on Uranus

Although the planet appears blue, it contains stripes like Jupiter and Saturn. However, these bands are faint and are only visible in enhanced images. With respect to other gas giants, the zones are formed as the gases rise in the warm region, while in the belts, the gases fall to the planet as they cool. In the belts, the winds blow east, while they travel west within the zones. In 1986, Voyager 2 flew by the planet only observing 10 cloud patterns on the planet. With improvement in technology, higher resolution images taken from Earth revealed the existence of fainter clouds. The clouds in the troposphere, are carried by winds blowing up to 900 km per hour.

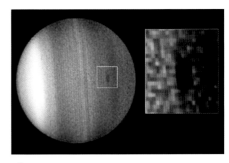

▲ *The stripes on Uranus are not visible because of the methane gas clouds that absorb the red light from the sunlight and reflect only the blue spectrum.*

Atmosphere

Uranus' atmosphere includes hydrogen and helium, and most importantly, it has large amounts of methane. This methane absorbs colour in the red end of the spectrum of light, while photons at the blue end of the spectrum are able to reflect off the clouds and go back into space. So, the full spectrum of the Sun's light goes in, the red and orange end of the spectrum is absorbed and the blue green end of the spectrum reflects back out. This is why the surface of Uranus has its colour.

FUN FACT

Did you know that Uranus's moons are named after characters created by William Shakespeare and Alexander Pope?

Neptune

Neptune is the eighth and farthest planet from the Sun in the solar system. It is the fourth-largest planet by diameter and the third largest by mass. Among the gaseous planets in the solar system, it is the densest. It is 17 times the mass of Earth and orbits the Sun at an average distance of 30.1 AU.

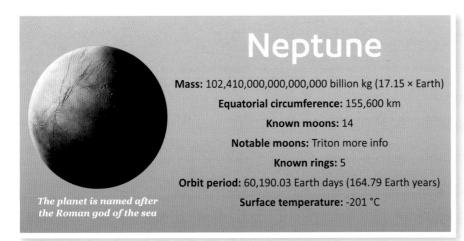

Neptune

Mass: 102,410,000,000,000,000 billion kg (17.15 × Earth)

Equatorial circumference: 155,600 km

Known moons: 14

Notable moons: Triton more info

Known rings: 5

Orbit period: 60,190.03 Earth days (164.79 Earth years)

Surface temperature: -201 °C

The planet is named after the Roman god of the sea

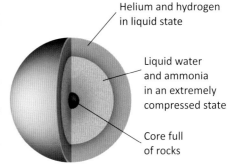

Helium and hydrogen in liquid state

Liquid water and ammonia in an extremely compressed state

Core full of rocks

Ice giant

Neptune's atmosphere is composed primarily of hydrogen and helium, along with traces of hydrocarbons and possibly nitrogen. It contains a higher proportion of "ices" such as water, ammonia and methane. Astronomers sometimes categorise Uranus and Neptune as "ice giants".

The interior of Neptune, like Uranus, is primarily composed of ices and rock. Perhaps the core has a solid surface, but the temperature would be thousands of degrees and the atmospheric pressure would be crushing. The planet's blue appearance is due to traces of methane in the outermost regions. In contrast to the hazy, relatively undistinguished atmosphere of Uranus, its atmosphere has active and visible weather patterns.

Neptune is similar in composition to Uranus, and their compositions differ from those of the larger gas giants, Jupiter and Saturn. ▶

Composition

The mass of this planet is midway between Earth and the larger gas giants; it is 17 times that of Earth, but just 1/19th that of Jupiter. Only Jupiter surpasses its surface gravity. Neptune's equatorial radius is nearly four times

that of Earth. It has been used as a metonym in search for extrasolar bodies: discovered bodies of similar mass are often referred to as "Neptunes", quite like astronomers refer to various extra-solar bodies as "Jupiters".

Location and Movement

The average distance between Neptune and the Sun is 4.50 billion km (about 30.1 AU). It completes an orbit, on an average, every 164.79 Earth years. The elliptical orbit of Neptune is inclined by 1.77° compared to that of Earth.

Axial tilt

The axial tilt of Neptune is 28.32 degrees, which is similar to the tilts of Earth (23°) and Mars (25°). Therefore, this planet experiences similar seasonal changes. The long orbital period of Neptune means that the seasons last for 40 Earth years.

Orbital resonances

Neptune's orbit has a massive impact on the region that is directly beyond it, known as the Kuiper belt. The Kuiper belt is a ring of small icy worlds similar to the asteroid belt, but far larger. Neptune's gravity influences the Kuiper belt. Over the age of the solar system, certain regions of the Kuiper belt became destabilised by Neptune's gravity, creating gaps in the Kuiper belt's structure.

The most heavily populated resonance in the Kuiper belt, having over 200 known objects, is the 2:3 resonances. Objects in this resonance complete two orbits for every three of Neptune and are known as "plutinos", because the largest of the known Kuiper belt objects, Pluto, is among them. Although Pluto crosses Neptune's orbit frequently, the 2:3 resonance ensures that they can never collide. The 3:4, 3:5, 4:7 and 2:5 resonances are less populated.

Trojan objects

A smaller celestial object that shares its orbit with a larger celestial object is called a Trojan object. Neptune possesses a number of Trojan objects occupying the Sun. Neptune Trojans stay in a 1:1 resonance with Neptune. Some Neptune Trojans are particularly stable in their orbits and are more likely to have formed with Neptune rather than being captured. Neptune also has a temporary quasi-satellite. The object has been a quasi-satellite of Neptune for about 12,500 years and will remain so for another 12,500 years, and is likely a captured object.

The blue planet, Neptune takes 165 years to orbit the Sun.

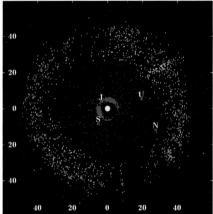

FUN FACT

Neptune has a very thin collection of rings, which are likely made up of ice particles mixed with dust grains and possibly coated with a carbon-based substance.

Atmosphere and Surface

 Neptune's internal structure resembles that of Uranus. Its atmosphere forms about 5 to 10 per cent of its mass and extends perhaps 10 to 20 per cent of the way towards the core, where it reaches pressures of about 100,000 times that of Earth's atmosphere. Increasing amounts of methane, ammonia and water are found in the lower regions of the atmosphere. The core of Neptune is composed of iron, nickel and silicates.

Atmosphere

At high altitudes, Neptune's atmosphere is 80 per cent hydrogen and 19 per cent helium along with a trace amount of methane. Prominent absorption bands of methane occur at wavelengths above 600 nanometre (nm), in the red and infrared portion of the spectrum. Since Neptune's atmospheric methane content is similar to that of Uranus, some unknown atmospheric constituent is thought to contribute to Neptune's colour.

Atmospheric division

Its atmosphere is divided into two regions: the lower troposphere, where the temperature decreases with altitude, and the stratosphere, where the temperature increases with altitude.
The stratosphere gives way to the thermosphere that gradually transitions to the exosphere.

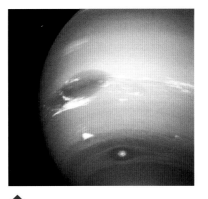

Bands of high-altitude clouds cast shadows on Neptune's lower cloud deck.
▼

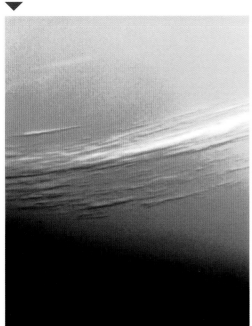

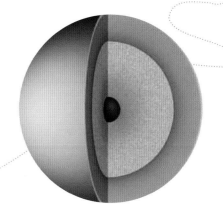

▲ *The internal structure of Neptune:*
1. Upper atmosphere, top clouds.
2. Atmosphere consisting of hydrogen, helium and methane gas.
3. Mantle consisting of water, ammonia and methane ices.
4. Core consisting of rock (silicates and nickel-iron).

Magnetosphere

Neptune resembles Uranus in its magnetosphere, with a strongly tilted magnetic field. Its magnetic field has an intricate geometry that includes relatively large contributions from non-dipolar components, including a strong quadrupole moment that might exceed the dipole moment in strength; whereas, Earth, Jupiter and Saturn have only relatively small quadrupole moments.

▲ *Neptune has very extreme weather changes that take place on its surface. It has storms, dark spots and cirrus-like clouds that are bright enough to be visible through satellite imaging. Although Neptune receives a thousand times less sunlight than Earth, it has a dynamic weather.*

FUN FACT

Neptune has a very active climate. Large storms whirl through its upper atmosphere and high-speed winds track around the planet at up to 600 m per second. One of the largest storms ever seen was called the "Great Dark Spot".

Volcanoes in Space

A volcano is a mountain that faces downward to a pool of molten rock below Earth's surface. When pressure builds up, eruptions occur. Gases and rocks shoot up through the opening and spill over or fill the air with lava debris. Eruptions cause lateral blasts, lava flows, hot ash flows, mudslides, avalanches, falling ash and floods. Volcanic eruptions have been known to destroy entire forests.

Mauna Loa

1. Mauna Loa

Mauna Loa is the world's largest volcano, which is located on the south-central part of the island of Hawaii. Frequently snow-capped during winter, it is a shield volcano that has erupted around three dozen times since its first well-documented eruption in 1843. It is a chain of active and inactive volcanic islands created, where the Pacific plate moves over a hot spot in Earth's mantle.

2. Vesuvius

When Earth's continental plates are forced one below another, frictional heating occurs, thereby resulting in volcanism. Mount Vesuvius near Naples, Italy, was created in this manner.

It did not erupt frequently, but when it did, it had a disastrous effect. Ash is blown up in the air and tsunamis are generated in the nearby sea.

3. Olympus Mons

Olympus Mons consists of a central structure that is 22 km high and 700 km wide. It is a global landmark on Mars. It is thrice as high as Mount Everest, making it the tallest mountain in the solar system. Its significant size has been attributed to the stability of the Martian crust as well as long accumulation time, which could be more than a billion years.

▲ *Without magma, Olympus Mons stopped increasing in length and size.*

▲ *An inactive Vesuvius.*

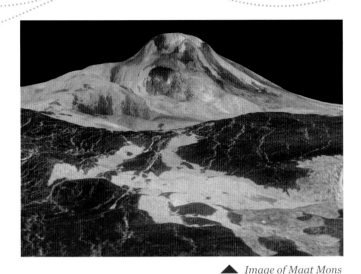

4. Volcanic Io

Io is the most active volcano in the solar system. Volcanic eruptions were first observed in 1979 by the Voyager spacecraft. They have also been witnessed in every flyby of the spacecraft Galileo, which is currently exploring the Jovian system. Volcanic activity on Io is so harsh that there are no signs of impact craters on its surface as they are rapidly filled with volcanic material the moment that they appear. Given the volcanic nature of Io, it is not surprising that its moons are named after various mythological characters associated with fire and volcanoes.

5. Maat Mons

Image of Maat Mons on Venus created by NASA using data from the Magellan spacecraft's radar.

Venus's surface is a volcanic plain, where the lava flow hardened more than 80 million years ago. This is true for more than three-fourths of its surface. There are several hundreds of volcanoes around the planet. Maat Mons is the highest, having its peak 5 km above the surface. If Maat Mons is active, this could explain the presence of sulphur dioxide and methane in its atmosphere.

This image acquired during Galileo's ninth orbit (C9) around Jupiter, shows two volcanic plumes on Io.

6. Triton

When the Voyager 2 spacecraft flew past Triton, Neptune's moon, it discovered plumes similar to geysers that were ejecting from its surface. These occurred as the result of a process called "cryovolcanism". The activity is triggered in regions where the Sun's light pierces the nitrogen ice that is frozen, which covers its surface. The subsurface icy material is heated and vaporised, thereby creating a greenhouse effect.

Triton, as seen from Voyager 2.

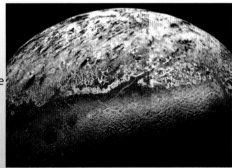

FUN FACT

Olympus Mons rises three times higher than Earth's highest mountain, Mount Everest, whose peak is 8.85 km above sea level.

Impact Factor

 When asteroids hit the surface of a planet, impact craters are formed. These are geologic structures that form when a large meteoroid, asteroid or comet crashes into a planet or satellite. The surfaces of the moon, Mars and Mercury record this rather evidently. However, on Earth, which has been even more heavily impacted than the moon, craters are continually eroded and re-deposited as well as erased by volcanic resurfacing and tectonic activity. As a result, only about 120 terrestrial impact craters have been recognised, the majority in geologically stable cratons of North America, Europe and Australia.

When asteroids strike

When an asteroid strikes the solid surface of a planet, a shock wave is created. This wave spreads outwards from the site of the impact. This shock wave breaks the rock, resulting in a large cavity that is much larger than the asteroid. The impact sprays material — ejecta — outwards in all directions. It gets shattered into small pieces and may melt or vaporise. At times, the force of the impact is so strong that it melts some of the local rock. If an asteroid is sufficiently large, some of the material pushed towards the edges of the crater fall back towards the centre. Then, the rock beneath the crater pushes back up, creating a central peak in the crater. The edges of these larger craters may also drop, creating terraces that step down into the crater.

Parts of a crater

Floor – It is the bottom of a crater that is either bowl-shaped or flat. It is usually below the level of the adjoining ground.

Central peaks – These form in the central area on the floor of a large crater. For larger craters, those that are a few tens of km in diameter, the

excavated crater becomes so great that it collapses on itself. This material that falls back into the crater pushes it up the mound, forming the central peak. Simultaneously, the rock beneath the crater bounces back up to add to the peak.

Walls – These are the interior sides of a crater that are generally steep. They may have huge stair-like terraces that are created when the walls fall due to gravity.

Rim – It is the edge of the crater. It is elevated above the nearby terrain as it is composed of material that is pushed up at the edge when it is excavated.

Ejecta – It refers to the rock material that is thrown out of the crater in the event of an impact. It is distributed outwards from the crater's rim onto the planet's surface as debris. It can be loose material or a blanket of debris that surrounds the crater, which thins out at the outermost region.

Rays – These are bright streaks that extend away from the crater. At times, these extend for great distances and are composed of ejecta debris and material.

 *An artist's representation showing the collision of Andromeda and Milky Way.*

Types of craters

1. Simple craters: These are small bowl-shaped, smooth-walled craters. Their maximum size depends on the planet they are formed on.

2. Complex craters: These are large craters with complicated features. Larger craters can have terraces, central peaks and numerous rings.

3. Impact basins: These are very large impact structures that are more than 300 km in diameter. The largest impact basin on the moon is 2500 km in diameter and more than 12 km deep. These are also found on other planets, including Mars and Mercury.

 A simple crater with smooth walls.

• Endurance crater

Mars is one such planet that has thousands of craters. One example is the endurance crater. It is 130 m wide. A space rover "Opportunity" examined the crater in 2004. It is circular to an extent and is surrounded by a ring of rough cliffs that slope down to the crater's floor. Sand and other materials envelop the crate's floor. This has led it to become shallow since it was formed.

• Lunar crater

The Daedalus crater is one that is found on the moon. It is 93 km wide and has mountainous peaks at its centre. This crater formed because the land that was struck by the asteroid sprung back after its initial impact. Simultaneously, the crater's edge was pushed outwards, forming a ring of mountains.

• Vredefort crater

The Vredefort crater impacted Earth around two billion years ago. This crater is located in Free State, South Africa. This crater has a radius of 190 km. It is the world's largest known impact structure. It was declared as a UNESCO World Heritage Site in 2005.

• Manicouagan crater

There are about 170 craters on Earth. Manicouagan is the fifth largest crater in Canada. It is 100 km across. It has undergone significant change since its existence approximately 214 million years ago. This crater has been eroded and water has also filled the lower ground, forming the Manicouagan reservoir.

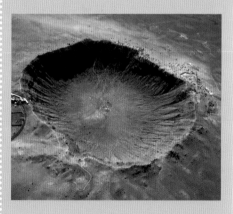

Large Magellanic Cloud

There are huge rings of material that encircle the four largest planets in our solar system, which extend beyond each planet's equatorial region. Interestingly, only Saturn's rings are visible from Earth. However, with progressive technology, spacecrafts have captured close-up images of all the four planet's rings. They seem solid, but are made of different materials that follow their own orbit around their respective planets. Saturn's ring is the most enormous ring system and was the first to be discovered.

Rings of Uranus.

Jupiter's rings

Jupiter has three rings circling it. Unlike Saturn's rings, which are clearly visible from Earth using small telescopes, Jupiter's rings are not clearly visible. Difficult to spot, they were discovered just a few years ago. They were first found by the Voyager 1 spacecraft in 1979. These rings have three parts: The innermost, cloud-like ring is called the halo ring. The next one is the main ring, which is quite narrow and thin. Beyond the main ring are the two nearly transparent gossamer rings. Its rings are made of tiny rock fragments and dust. Like Saturn's rings, they do not contain ice. They are continuously losing material and being re-supplied with new dust from micro-meteors that hit Jupiter's four inner moons.

Uranus's rings

The rings of Uranus were the first to be found around a planet besides Saturn. American astronomer James L. Elliot and his colleagues discovered the ring system from Earth in 1977, nine years before the Voyager 2 encounter. This happened during a stellar occultation by Uranus, i.e., when the planet passed between a star and Earth, temporarily blocking the star's light. They observed that the light from the star dimmed briefly for about five times at a considerable distance above Uranus's atmosphere both before and after the planet occulted the star. The decrease in brightness indicated that the planet was encircled by five narrow rings. Later, Earth-based observations revealed four additional rings. Voyager 2 detected a 10th ring and found indications of more. From the outer side of Uranus, the 10 are named 6, 5, 4, Alpha, Beta, Eta, Gamma, Delta, Lambda and Epsilon.

▼ *A satellite photographing Saturn*

▲ *Giovanni Domenico Cassini, an Italian astronomer, astrologer, mathematician and engineer, discovered the four moons of Saturn and explained its ring structure.*

Saturn's rings

Saturn, the sixth planet from the sun, is one of the most easily identified targets for astronomers, due to its large and distinct ring system. The rings of Saturn have fascinated stargazers for centuries, ever since telescopes were first pointed toward the sky. When Galileo Galilei first observed Saturn in 1610, he thought that the rings were enormous moons, one positioned on each side of the planet. Over several years of observations, he noted that the rings changed shape and even disappeared, as they changed their inclination with respect to Earth.

Ring particles

Saturn's rings are made up of billions of particles ranging from grains of sand to mountain-sized chunks. Composed predominantly of water ice, the rings also draw in rocky meteoroids as they travel through space. Though Saturn

▲ *Saturn has the largest rings in our solar system spanning up to 175,000 miles.*

appears to be surrounded by a single, solid ring when viewed by an amateur astronomer, numerous divisions exist. The rings are named alphabetically in the order of discovery. Thus, the main rings are, lying farthest from the planet to closest, A, B and C. A 4700 km wide gap, known as the Cassini Division, separates the A and B rings.

An artist's representation of the rings of ▼ *Saturn showing the division of the rings as explained by Cassini.*

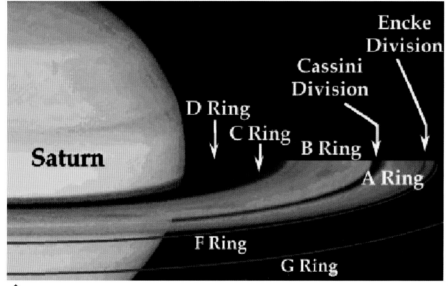

▲ *The B ring is the largest, brightest ring and has the most mass among Saturn's many rings.*

Cassini Division

Named alphabetically, in the order that they were discovered, the rings are relatively close to each other with the exception of the Cassini Division, a gap measuring 4700 km. The main rings are, working outward from the planet, known as C, B and A. The Cassini Division is the largest gap in the rings and separates rings B and A. In addition, a number of fainter rings have been discovered more recently. The D ring is exceedingly faint and closest to the planet. The F ring is a narrow feature just outside the A ring. Beyond that, are two far fainter rings named G and E. The rings show a tremendous amount of structure on all scales; some of this structure is related to gravitational perturbations by Saturn's many moons, but much of it remains unexplained.

FUN FACT

The planetary rings must constantly be refilled with new dust from the planet's moons to exist.

Space Storms

There are storms that occur on the giant planets, namely Saturn, Jupiter, Neptune and Uranus. Their upper atmospheres propel around in bands that are parallel to their equators. As gas is channelled at high speeds around the planets, it creates clouds and storms. The storms on Jupiter are easily visible as white and dark spots, which stand out against the planet's upper atmosphere.

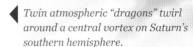

Jupiter's Great Red Spot is shrinking.

◀ *Twin atmospheric "dragons" twirl around a central vortex on Saturn's southern hemisphere.*

Great Red Spot

The Great Red Spot is a huge, long-lasting storm in Jupiter's atmosphere, on its southern hemisphere. It is a high pressure storm, similar to a hurricane. Its colour ranges from pink to orange. Interestingly, this whirlwind varies in size and colour every year. It is about 28,000 km long and 14,000 km wide. It is the biggest storm in our solar system. It is so big that three Earths would fit within it with room to spare. Jupiter's Great Red Spot was discovered in 1664 by English scientist Robert Hooke. The reason it has lasted so long in comparison to Earth's storms is because there is no landfall. On Earth, hurricanes lose most of their energy and die when they move over land.

Dragon Storm

The Dragon Storm was a powerful source of radio emissions, which occurred during mid-September 2004. The radio waves from the storm resemble the short bursts of static generated by lightning on Earth. Cassini detected the bursts only when the storm was rising over the horizon on the night side of the planet as seen from the spacecraft; the bursts stopped when the storm moved into sunlight. This on/off pattern repeated for many rotations over a period of several weeks and it was the clockwork-like repeatability which indicated that the storm and the radio bursts were related. Scientists have concluded that it is a giant thunderstorm whose precipitation generates electricity as with thunderstorms on Earth. The storm may be deriving its energy from Saturn's deep atmosphere.

In examining the images taken of Saturn's atmosphere over many months, imaging scientists found that the Dragon Storm arose in the same part of Saturn's atmosphere that had earlier produced large, bright convective storms. In other words, this storm appears to be a long-lived storm deep in the atmosphere that periodically flares up to produce dramatic, bright, white plumes that subside over time. One earlier sighting in July 2004 was also associated with strong radio bursts.

The spots are the shape of an ellipse with dimensions of 13,000 × 6,600 km, roughly the same size as Earth.

Great Dark Spot

The Great Dark Spot was a huge spinning storm in the southern atmosphere of Neptune, which was about the size of Earth. Winds were measured at speeds of up to 2414.02 km per hour. These were the strongest winds ever recorded on any planet in the solar system! It was first discovered when the Voyager 2 spacecraft flew by Neptune in 1989. When the Hubble Space Telescope looked at Neptune in 1994, the Great Dark Spot was gone and a new spot had appeared in the northern atmosphere of the planet.

Dynamic weather system

The Great Dark Spot was a very dynamic weather system, generating massive white clouds similar to high-altitude cirrus clouds on Earth. Unlike Earth's cirrus clouds, however, which are composed of crystals of water ice, Neptune's cirrus clouds are made up of crystals of frozen methane. Neptune's clouds are driven by winds of 1200 m per hour, the fastest winds of any planet in the solar system. How such high-velocity winds come to be on a planet so far from the Sun continues to remain a mystery.

Saturn's auroral storms are a result of the pressure of solar wind.

Saturn's aurora

Scientists first observed Saturn's auroras in 1979. Decades later, these shimmering ribbons of light continue to fascinate astrologers. They are magnificently tall, rising hundreds of km above the planet's poles. And unlike the bright displays on Earth that fizzle after only a few hours, the auroras on Saturn can shine for days. Auroras are produced when speeding particles accelerated by the Sun's energy collide with gases in a planet's atmosphere. The gases fluoresce, emitting flashes of light at different wavelengths. The process that triggers these auroras is similar to the phenomenon that causes fluorescent lamps to glow.

There are bright shapes that form on Saturn that are actually auroras, which can last for days.

Water and Space

Extraterrestrial liquid water is water in its liquid form that is found beyond Earth. It is a subject of wide interest because it is commonly thought to be one of the key prerequisites for the existence of extraterrestrial life. With oceanic water covering 71 per cent of its surface, Earth is the only planet known to have stable bodies of liquid water, which is essential to all known lifeforms.

Scientists using the Hubble telescope have discovered that Jupiter's largest natural satellite, Ganymede, has an ocean buried beneath its icy surface.

▲ *Reservoirs of ice still hidden below Mars' surface*

Icy Mars

Water on Mars exists today almost entirely as ice, with a small amount present in the atmosphere as vapour. Some liquid water may occur transiently on the Martian surface today but only under certain conditions. No large standing bodies of liquid water exist because the atmospheric pressure at the surface averages at just 600 pascals — about 0.6 per cent of Earth's mean sea level pressure — and because the global average temperature is far too low (210 K or –63 °C), it leads to either rapid evaporation or freezing.

Enceladus

Enceladus, a moon of Saturn, has shown geysers of water, confirmed by the Cassini spacecraft in 2005 and analysed more deeply in 2008. Gravimetric data in 2010-11 confirmed a subsurface ocean. In addition to water, these geysers form vents near the South Pole containing small amounts of salt, nitrogen, carbon dioxide and volatile hydrocarbons. The melting of the ocean water and the geysers appear to be driven by tidal flux from Saturn.

Ganymede

A subsurface saline ocean is theorised to exist on Ganymede, a moon of Jupiter, following observation by the Hubble Space Telescope in 2015. Patterns in auroral belts and the rocking of the magnetic field suggest the presence of an ocean. It is estimated to be 100 km deep with the surface lying below a crust of 150 km of ice.

Europa

Scientists' consensus is that a layer of liquid water exists beneath Europa's surface, and that heat from tidal flexing allows the subsurface ocean to remain liquid. It is predicted that the outer crust of solid ice is approximately 10 – 30 km thick, including a ductile "warm ice" layer, which could mean that the liquid ocean underneath may be about 100 km deep. This puts the volume of Europa's oceans at 3×10^{18} m³, slightly more than twice the volume of Earth's oceans.

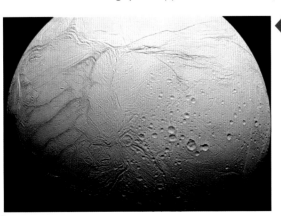

◀ *The blue-green "tiger stripes" are thought to be the source of Enceladus's water jets.*

The icy surface of Europa ▶ *is strewn with cracks, ridges and chaotic terrain, where the surface has been disrupted and ice blocks have moved around.*

DWARF PLANETS

▲ *Our solar system has six dwarf planets, namely, Ceres, Pluto, Haumea, Makemake, Eris and the unnamed V774104.*

Dwarf planets are similar to the solar system's eight planets, but are smaller. Like planets, they are large, roundish objects that orbit the Sun.

The category "dwarf planet" was created as a result of extreme debate as to whether Pluto should be called a planet. Pluto had been considered the solar system's ninth planet for 50 years. However, in 2006, the International Astronomical Union (IAU) defined "planet" in a manner that only eight bodies in the solar system qualified to be classified under the category. Simultaneously, it established a new, separate class of objects called dwarf planets.

Pluto

Pluto is the only dwarf planet to once have been considered as a major planet. It is now seen as one of the largest known members of the Kuiper belt. It was once thought of as the ninth planet and the one most distant from the Sun, a shadowy disc-like zone beyond the orbit of Neptune populated by many comets. It is the second most massive dwarf planet after Eris.

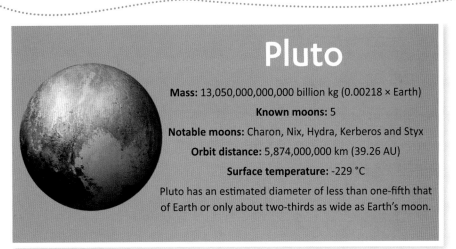

Pluto

Mass: 13,050,000,000,000 billion kg (0.00218 × Earth)

Known moons: 5

Notable moons: Charon, Nix, Hydra, Kerberos and Styx

Orbit distance: 5,874,000,000 km (39.26 AU)

Surface temperature: -229 °C

Pluto has an estimated diameter of less than one-fifth that of Earth or only about two-thirds as wide as Earth's moon.

Internal structure

Since the decay of the radioactive components would ultimately heat the ice enough for it to separate from the rock, scientists believe that Pluto's internal structure is differentiated, with the rough material having sunk into a dense core encompassed by a mantle of water ice. It is possible that such heating continues even today, making a subsurface sea layer of fluid water at the core-mantle boundary.

Theoretical structure of Pluto.

Temporary atmosphere

Pluto's orbit is exceedingly eccentric, or a long way from elliptical, which implies that its distance from the Sun can change significantly. Now and again, Pluto's orbit enters the path of Neptune's orbit. At the point when Pluto is closer to the Sun, its surface ice defrosts and temporarily forms a thin environment. For the most part, it consists of nitrogen, with some methane. Pluto's low gravity causes its atmosphere to extend farther beyond Earth's. As Pluto moves far from the Sun and gets colder, gasses noticeable all around settle onto the surface again. When Pluto is farthest from the Sun, its atmosphere may become negligible.

Pluto's surface

Pluto's surface is one of the coldest places in the solar system at roughly -225 °C. For a long time, astronomers did not know much about its surface, but the Hubble Space Telescope shows a reddish, yellowish, grey planet with a curious bright spot at the equator that may be rich in carbon monoxide.

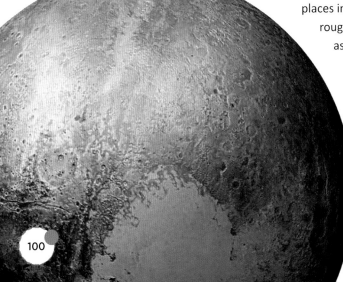

FUN FACT

Pluto was named by an 11-year-old girl, Venetia, after the Roman god of the underworld. Her grandfather then suggested it to Herbert Hall Turner, Professor of Astronomy at the University of Oxford.

Pluto's moons

Pluto has a very large moon nearly half its size, called Charon, named after the mythological demon who ferried souls to the underworld in Greek mythology. Pluto and Charon are 19,640 km apart, less than the distance between London and Sydney by flight. Charon's orbit around Pluto takes 6.4 Earth days and one Pluto rotation, i.e., a Pluto day. This is because Charon hovers over the same spot on Pluto's surface and the same side of Charon always faces Pluto, a phenomenon known as tidal locking.

While Pluto appears reddish, Charon seems greyish. Scientists suggest that Pluto is covered with nitrogen and methane, while Charon is covered with ordinary water ice. Compared with most of the solar system's planets and moons, the Pluto-Charon system is tipped on its side in relation to the Sun. Also, Pluto's rotation is retrograde compared to the other orbiting celestial bodies—it spins from east to west.

Pluto's other moons

Hydra and Nix (discovered in 2005); Kerberos, originally P4, (discovered in 2011); and Styx, originally P5, (discovered in 2012) are Pluto's other moons.

Pluto's formation and origin

The main hypothesis behind the development of Pluto and Charon is that a rising Pluto was hit by another Pluto-sized object. While most of the combined matter became Pluto, the rest spun off to become Charon.

▲ *The Sun and dwarf planet Pluto in a row.*

▲ *Charon is the largest of the five known moons of the dwarf planet Pluto.*

◀ *Pluto and its moon Charon.*

Ceres

Currently, Ceres is the smallest classified dwarf planet. It is the largest object in the asteroid belt, which lies between the orbits of Mars and Jupiter. It is composed of rock and ice. It is 950 km in diameter and contains a third of the mass of the asteroid belt.

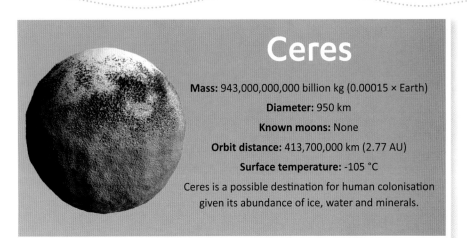

Ceres

Mass: 943,000,000,000 billion kg (0.00015 × Earth)

Diameter: 950 km

Known moons: None

Orbit distance: 413,700,000 km (2.77 AU)

Surface temperature: -105 °C

Ceres is a possible destination for human colonisation given its abundance of ice, water and minerals.

FUN FACT

Ceres' close proximity to Earth and low mass have led some scientists to suggest that it could serve as a potential site for manned landings and a launching point for manned deep space missions.

It is the largest asteroid and the only dwarf planet in the inner solar system. ▼

Ceres' features

Ceres has a density of 2.09 g per cubic centimetre, leading scientists to conclude that approximately a quarter of its weight is water. This would give the dwarf planet more fresh water than Earth. With temperature lows of -38 °C, water at the surface of Ceres would convert, potentially creating a thin atmosphere.

History and discovery

Sicilian astronomer Giuseppe Piazzi discovered what was then considered a planet, naming it Ceres after the Roman goddess of corn and harvests. Within a decade, four new objects were discovered in the same region, all considered as planets. Nearly 50 years passed before Ceres was demoted to the status of an asteroid. In 2006, Ceres was promoted to the status of a dwarf planet. It did not attain full planetary status because it failed to gravitationally clear its orbit of any debris.

What is Ceres made of?

The thin, dusty crust is thought to be composed of rock, while a rocky inner core lies at the centre. Observations of Ceres from Earth reveal that the surface contains iron-rich clays. Signs of carbonates have similarly been found, making Ceres one of the only bodies in the solar system known to contain these minerals, the other two being Earth and Mars. Carbonates are considered good potential indicators of habitability.

Close up of the dwarf planet Ceres. ▼

Comparison of the size of Ceres with Earth and moon. ▼

Haumea

Haumea is the third closest dwarf planet from the Sun. It has a unique elongated shape, making it the least spherical of all dwarf planets. It is one of the fastest rotating objects in our solar system. It completes a rotation on its axis every four hours. The rapid spinning has elongated the dwarf planet into the unique shape that astronomers discovered in 2003. It is almost the same size as Pluto. Like Pluto and Eris, Haumea orbits our Sun in the Kuiper belt. It was discovered in March 2003 at the Sierra Nevada Observatory in Spain. The official announcement of its discovery came in 2005, the same year that its moons were discovered.

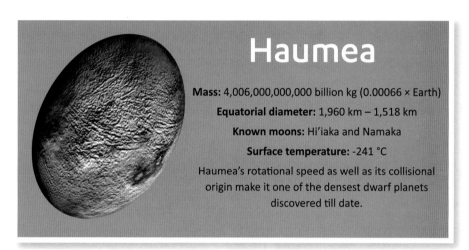

Haumea

Mass: 4,006,000,000,000 billion kg (0.00066 × Earth)

Equatorial diameter: 1,960 km – 1,518 km

Known moons: Hi'iaka and Namaka

Surface temperature: -241 °C

Haumea's rotational speed as well as its collisional origin make it one of the densest dwarf planets discovered till date.

Image of Haumea and its two moons, Hi'iaka (below) and Namaka (above).

Classification

Haumea is a "plutoid", a dwarf planet residing beyond Neptune's orbit. Haumea was classified as a Kuiper belt object until the IAU reclassified it as the fifth dwarf planet in the solar system, following Ceres, Pluto, Eris and Makemake. The plutoid was renamed after the Hawaiian goddess of childbirth and fertility. Its two moons were named after the goddess' two daughters, Hi'iaka and Namaka.

Special features

Size: Haumea is approximately 1/3rd the size of Pluto. It is the fastest spinning known large object in the solar system.

Orbit: Haumea takes 285 Earth years to orbit the Sun. At its closest, it only comes within 34 times of Earth–Sun distance, while at its farthest; it lies more than 51 times as far away.

Composition: The rapid spin of the dwarf planet permitted researchers to determine its density, in light of the fact that different materials would stretch out differently. Accordingly, researchers believe that it is almost completely made up of rock. Observations of the planet, on the other hand, uncover a brilliantly glimmering surface. Researchers have presumed that though most of the dwarf planet's interior is rough, it is secured by a thin icy shell.

The moons of Haumea

The two moons of Haumea are far smaller than the dwarf planet. The largest, Hi'iaka, is only about 0.5 per cent of Haumea, while the smaller, fainter Namaka is only 0.05 per cent of Haumea.

Hi'iaka was found on 26th January, 2005 by a group of space experts headed by Mike Brown of the California Institute of Technology. Namaka was discovered on 30th June, 2005, by the same group.

FUN FACT

Haumea also appears to have a dark red spot on its surface that may contain more minerals and organic compounds than the ice around it.

Pluto, Makemake and Haumea.

Makemake

Makemake is a dwarf planet in the outer solar system. It was the fourth body identified as a dwarf planet. When it was discovered, it was around the same time that Eris was a contender to be named as the 10th planet of the solar system. It was during this period that the IAU gave a clear definition of a planet. As a result, Makemake and Eris were classified as dwarf planets. Since Eris is bigger than Pluto, Pluto was downgraded to a dwarf planet.

The position of Makemake in the solar system.

Makemake as seen from the HST.

The Easter bunny

Makemake was first observed in March 2005 by a team of astronomers at the Palomar Observatory. Officially known as 2005 FY9, the tiny planetoid was nicknamed "Easter bunny" by the group. It is named after the god of fertility in Rapanui mythology. The Rapanui live on Easter Island in the south-eastern Pacific Ocean. Makemake was the chief god, the creator of humanity and god of fertility.

Characteristics

Makemake is one of the largest known objects in the outer solar system, just slightly smaller and dimmer than Pluto. Scientists think that it is about two-thirds the size of Pluto. It orbits beyond the range of Pluto, taking approximately 310 Earth-years to revolve around the Sun.

Surface: The dwarf planet is reddish-brown in colour, leading scientists to conclude that it contains a layer of methane on its surface. There are also signs of frozen ethane and frozen nitrogen.

Location: Similar to all the known dwarf planets except Ceres, Makemake travels through the Kuiper belt, the region of

Makemake is the second brightest object in the Kuiper belt, after Pluto.

The brightness of Makemake in space.

ice and rock at the outer edges of the solar system.

Rotation: Makemake spins on its axis once every 22.5 hours, with a day just shorter than Earth's.

Moons

Unlike Pluto and Haumea, Makemake has no moon, which makes it difficult to determine the dwarf planet's mass and density. Astronomers took advantage of the dwarf planet's passage in front of a star to determine that it lacks a significant atmosphere, a surprise given its similarities to Pluto, which has a thin one.

FUN FACT

Dwarf planets orbit on a different plain and not where the other eight planets are, going over and below them.

Eris

Eris is the Greek goddess of discord and strife, who inspired jealousy and envy among the goddesses, leading to the Trojan War. Eris is a Plutoid, i.e., it's a trans-Neptunian dwarf planet. Its orbital characteristics more specifically categorise it as a scattered-disc object (SDO). It is believed to have been "scattered" from the Kuiper belt into more distant and unusual orbits following gravitational interactions with Neptune as the solar system was forming.

Eris was only discovered in the year 2003.

Pluto

Characteristics

Orbit – Eris has an orbital period of 558 years.

Albedo – Studies show that the dwarf planet has a surface even more reflective than Earth's snow, suggesting it's covered in a thin layer of ice.

Surface – Infrared light from the object revealed the presence of methane ice, indicating that the surface may be similar to that of Pluto, which was the only TNO known to have surface methane at the time, and of Neptune's moon Triton, which also has methane on its surface.

Appearance – Eris appears almost grey. It is at a distance from the Sun that methane can condense onto its surface even in regions where the Albedo is low. The condensation of methane uniformly over the surface reduces any Albedo contrasts and would cover up any deposits of red tholins.

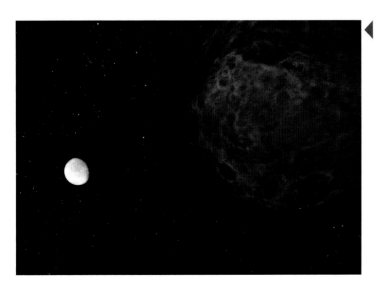

Artist's impression of Eris and Dysnomia. Eris is the main object, Dysnomia is the small grey sphere just above it. The flaring object on the top left is the Sun.

Eris's moon

When Eris received its official name from the IAU, the moon received the name Dysnomia, after the Greek goddess of lawlessness, who was Eris' daughter. It is a small moon that takes two weeks to orbit its dwarf planet. It is about eight times smaller than Eris. Astronomers are presently studying the relationship between Dysnomia and Eris. A better understanding of how they interact will allow them to gauge the mass of both the dwarf planet and its moon.

FUN FACT

All the objects in the asteroid belt could fit inside Eris. It is still smaller than Earth's moon, having about two-thirds of the moon's diameter and one-third of its volume.

Trans-Neptunian Objects

The outer edge of our solar system is not empty. There are many huge spheres of rock and ice out near Pluto's orbit and beyond. Astronomers have a name for everything further out than Neptune. These icy celestial bodies are called Trans-Neptunian Objects (TNOs). A trans-Neptunian object is any minor planet in the solar system that orbits the Sun at a greater distance on average than Neptune. The Kuiper belt, scattered disc and Oort cloud are three divisions of this volume of space.

Distribution and classification

As indicated by their distance from the Sun and their orbits, TNOs are classified under two major groups:

a) Kuiper belt objects, which are further arranged into the following two groups:

Resonant objects: These are locked in an orbital resonance with Neptune.

Classical Kuiper belt objects: These have no such resonance, moving on almost circular orbits, undisturbed by Neptune.

b) The scattered disc, which contains objects more distant from the Sun as a rule with extremely irregular orbits, for instance, Eris.

Appearance

Density: Small TNOs are thought to be low-density mixtures of rock and ice with some organic surface material such as tholin. On the other hand, the high density of Haumea suggests very high non-ice content.

Colours: TNOs display a wide range of colours from blue-grey (neutral) to very red. The distribution appears to be uniform. Classical objects seem to be composed of two different colour populations: the so-called cold (inclination <5°) population, displaying only red colours and the so-called hot (higher inclination) population,

Largest known trans-Neptunian objects along with their respective moons.

displaying the whole range of colours from blue to very red.

Size determination: It is hard to determine the diameter of TNOs. For massive objects, with extremely well-known orbital elements (like Pluto), diameters can be accurately measured by occultation of stars. For other big TNOs, diameters can be assessed by thermal measurements.

◀ *Size comparison between Earth's moon, Neptune's moon Triton and several large TNOs.*

FUN FACT

Scientists are believed to have found one TNO bigger than Pluto. This is officially known as 2003 UB313, nicknamed "Xena".

SATELLITES

▲ *It has been found that about 168 natural satellites orbit around the planets of the solar system.*

A satellite can be a moon, planet or machine that orbits a planet or star. For example, Earth is a satellite because it orbits the Sun. Likewise, the moon is a satellite because it orbits Earth. Usually, the word "satellite" refers to a machine that is launched into space and moves around Earth or another body in space.

Several artificial or human-made satellites orbit Earth. Some take pictures of the planet that help meteorologists predict weather and track hurricanes, while others take pictures of other planets, the Sun, black holes, dark matter or faraway galaxies. These pictures help scientists to better understand the solar system and the universe.

Earth's Moon

The moon is Earth's only natural satellite. Although not the largest natural satellite in the solar system, it is the largest among the satellites of major planets that is relative to the size of the object it orbits. The moon is a cold, rocky body that is about 3,476 km in diameter. It does not have a light of its own, but shines by the sunlight reflected from its surface.

Earth came first

The moon is thought to have formed nearly 4.5 billion years ago, not long after Earth. Although there have been several hypotheses behind its origin in the past, the current most widely accepted explanation is that the moon formed from the debris that was left over after a giant impact between Earth and a Mars-sized body named Theia.

Internal structure

The moon has a distinct crust, mantle and core. It has a very small core that consists of only one to two per cent of the total mass and is roughly 680 km wide. It mostly consists of iron, but may also contain large amounts of sulphur and other elements. Its rocky mantle

Moon surface ▼

is about 1,330 km thick and made up of dense rocks that are rich in iron and magnesium. The crust on top is about 70 km deep. The outermost part of the crust is broken due to all the large impacts it has received, a shattered zone that gives way to intact material below a depth of about 9.6 km.

Moon's atmosphere

The moon has a very thin atmosphere, so a layer of dust can sit undisturbed for centuries. Heat is not held near the surface without much of an atmosphere, so temperatures vary heavily. Temperatures range from 134 °C to -153 °C.

Gravity

The moon has a much weaker gravity than Earth, due to its smaller mass, so one would weigh about one-sixth (16.5%) of their weight on Earth.

Phases of the moon

One moon rotation lasts for the same amount of time that it takes to orbit Earth and therefore the same side faces us. While it is orbiting, its appearance keeps changing as sunlight falls on

different areas on its surface. While in orbit, the side where sunlight falls reduces and then grows. When it faces the Sun, it is fully lit up. We refer to this event as the full moon. These changes in appearance are referred to as phases. It takes 29 and a half days to complete an entire cycle of these phases.

Phases of Earth's moon.

Moon's soil

The moon's surface is covered by a mud-like layer that is several metres thick. On the moon's surface, this mud-like substance is fine. As you go deeper, the size of the particles starts getting much bigger. Solid rock lies at a depth of about 16.4 feet down on the moon and the soil is 32.8 feet deep in the mountainous regions. Asteroids hitting the moon's surface resulted in soil getting formed at a rate of 20 km per second. As a result, the rock got squashed and craters were produced.

Moon's surface

The moon's surface took form a few years after it came into existence. A few billion years of continuous asteroid showers were followed by volcanic welling up from the moon's interior and filling low-lying regions. The spots that we see on the moon from Earth are the craters that are formed by asteroid collisions.

The blue moon

According to modern folklore, a blue moon is the second full moon in a calendar month. In a month there is only one full moon. However, a second one could also occur. Full moons occur after a 29 days cycle, whereas most months consist of 30 or 31 days. Therefore, two full moons can appear in a single month. This phenomenon occurs every two and a half years, on average.

Is the moon really blue?

The date of a full moon does not affect the moon's colour. The moon on 31st July is usually pearly-grey. Interestingly there was a time, not long ago, when people saw blue moons almost every night. Full moons, half moons and crescent moons were all blue. On some nights, they would be green.

Why does it turn blue?

In 1883, an Indonesian volcano named Krakatoa exploded. Scientists equate the blast to a 100-megaton nuclear bomb. Plumes of ash rose to the very top of Earth's atmosphere, making the moon turn blue. Krakatoa's ash is the reason for the blue moon. White moonbeams shining through the clouds emerged blue and occasionally green. Blue moons lasted for years after the eruption. Other less potent volcanoes have turned the moon blue as well. Blue moons were also observed in 1983 after the eruption of the El Chichon volcano in Mexico. There are reports of blue moons caused by Mt St. Helens in 1980 and Mt Pinatubo in 1991 as well.

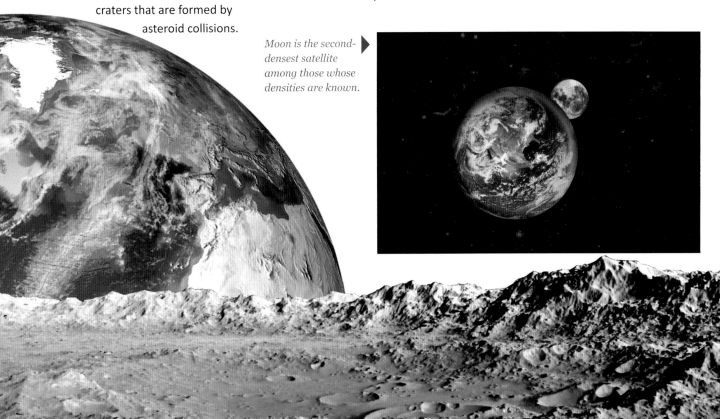

Moon is the second-densest satellite among those whose densities are known.

Lunar Eclipse

A lunar eclipse occurs when the moon passes directly behind Earth into its umbra (shadow). This can occur only when the Sun, Earth and the moon are aligned exactly with Earth in the middle. Hence, a lunar eclipse can only occur on the night of a full moon.

Types of lunar eclipse

A penumbral eclipse occurs when the moon passes through Earth's penumbra. The penumbra causes a subtle darkening of the moon's surface. A special type of penumbral eclipse is a total penumbral eclipse, during which the moon lies exclusively within Earth's penumbra. Total penumbral eclipses are rare and when these occur, that portion of the moon that is closest to the umbra can appear somewhat darker than the rest of the moon. A partial lunar eclipse occurs when only a portion of the moon enters the umbra.

When the moon travels completely into Earth's umbra, one observes a total lunar eclipse and it may last up to nearly 107 minutes.

However, the total time between the moon's first and last contact with the shadow is much longer and could last up to four hours.

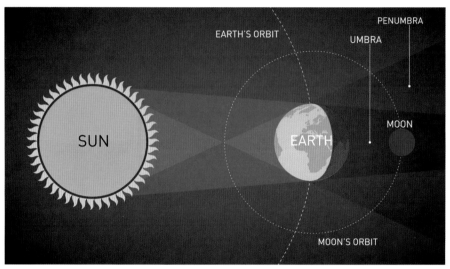

▲ *Lunar eclipse.*

Horizontal eclipse

A selenelion or selenehelion occurs when both the Sun and eclipsed moon can be simultaneously observed. This can only happen either before sunset or after sunrise. Both these bodies will appear just above the horizon at nearly opposite points in the sky. This arrangement has led to the phenomenon being referred to as a horizontal eclipse. Although the moon is in Earth's umbra, the Sun and eclipsed moon can both be seen at the same time because the refraction of light through Earth's atmosphere causes each of them to appear higher in the sky than their true geometric position.

Unlike a solar eclipse, lunar eclipses are safe to view without any special precautions, as they are dimmer than the full moon.

FUN FACT

Unlike a solar eclipse, which can only be viewed from a certain relatively small area of the world, a lunar eclipse may be viewed from anywhere on the night side of Earth. A lunar eclipse lasts for a few hours, whereas a total solar eclipse lasts for only a few minutes at any given place due to the smaller size of the moon's shadow.

Timing

The timing of a total lunar eclipse is determined by its contacts:

First contact: Beginning of the penumbral eclipse. Earth's penumbra touches the moon's outer limb.

Second contact: Beginning of the partial eclipse. Earth's umbra touches the moon's outer limb.

Third contact: Beginning of the total eclipse. The moon's surface is entirely within Earth's umbra.

The different phases of a lunar eclipse

Greatest eclipse: The peak stage of the total eclipse. The moon is at its closest to the centre of Earth's umbra.

Fourth contact: End of the total eclipse. The moon's outer limb exits Earth's umbra.

Fifth contact: End of the partial eclipse. Earth's umbra leaves the moon's surface.

Sixth contact: End of the penumbral eclipse. Earth's penumbra no longer makes contact with the moon.

Numerous early civilisations utilised the Moon's monthly cycle to quantify the passage of time. In fact, some calendars are synchronised to the phases of the Moon. The Hebrew, Muslim and Chinese calendars are all lunar calendars.

Blood moon

Due to its reddish colour, a totally eclipsed moon is sometimes referred to as a "blood moon". The most recent blood moon occurred on 8th October, 2014, and was visible across much of the Americas and Asia.

Lunar versus solar eclipse

There is often confusion between a solar and lunar eclipse. While both involve interactions between the Sun, Earth and moon, they are very different in their interactions. The moon does not completely disappear as it passes through the umbra because of the refraction of sunlight by Earth's atmosphere into the shadow cone. If Earth had no atmosphere, the moon would be completely dark during an eclipse. The red colouring arises because the sunlight reaching the moon must pass through a long and dense layer of Earth's atmosphere, where it is scattered.

A solar eclipse occurs in the day time at new moon, when the moon is between Earth and the Sun, while a lunar eclipse occurs at night when Earth passes between the Sun and the moon.

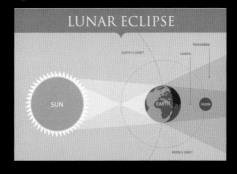

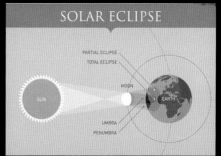

Lunar Tides

The moon's gravity pulls at Earth, causing predictable rises and falls in sea levels known as "tides". High tides are when water bulges upward and low tides are when water drops down. High tides result on the side of Earth that is nearest to the moon due to gravity. It also happens on the side farthest from the moon due to the inertia of water. Low tides occur between these two tidal humps.

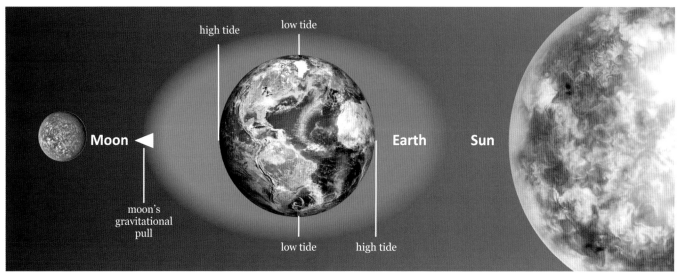

▲ *Illustration showing Earth, moon and tidal influence.*

The moon moves

The energy that Earth loses is picked up by the moon, increasing its distance from Earth, which means that the moon moves farther away by 3.8 cm annually.

Lunar eclipses

During eclipses, the moon, Earth and Sun are in a straight line, or nearly so. A lunar eclipse occurs when Earth gets directly or almost directly between the Sun and moon, and Earth's shadow falls on the moon.

A lunar eclipse can occur only during a full moon. A solar eclipse occurs when the moon gets directly or nearly directly between the Sun and Earth, and the moon's shadow falls on it. A solar eclipse can occur only during a new moon.

Effects of the Sun

The Sun also has an effect on the tidal timings of the oceans on Earth. The Sun has a gravitational force that keeps the entire solar system revolving around it. It is bound to exert a certain amount of gravitational pull on the water bodies on Earth. The Sun's gravity also causes tides. However, since the distance between the Sun and Earth is almost 400 times the distance between the moon and Earth, the force of gravity exerted on Earth's water is very less as compared to the force of the moon's gravity. For example, the tides that are formed in Tahiti are due to the Sun's gravity and are of lower amplitude.

An artist's representation of the moon affecting the tides. ▼

FUN FACT

The word "month" is derived from the moon's 29.5-day period of orbit around Earth. The phases of the moon are tracked on a lunar calendar and is different from the Georgian calendar.

Martian Moons

Mars has two moons, Phobos and Deimos, which are thought to be captured asteroids. Both satellites were discovered in 1877 by Asaph Hall. It is possible that Mars may have moons smaller than 50–100 m and a dust ring between Phobos and Deimos may be present, but none have been discovered yet.

Etymology

The names are based on the characters Phobos (fear) and Deimos (terror) who, in Greek mythology, accompanied their father Ares, god of war, into battle. Ares was known as Mars to the Romans. The motions of Phobos and Deimos would appear very different from that of our own moon. Speedy Phobos rises in the west, sets in the east and rises again in just 11 hours, while Deimos, being only just outside the synchronous orbit, rises as expected in the east, but very slowly.

Both moons are tidally locked, always presenting the same face towards Mars.

Captured asteroids

The origin of the Martian moons is still controversial. Based on their similarity, one hypothesis is that both moons may be captured main-belt asteroids. Both sets of findings support an origin of Phobos from material ejected by an impact on Mars that re-accreted in the Martian orbit, similar to the prevailing theory for the origin of Earth's moon.

However, both, Phobos and Deimos resemble asteroids more than moons.

Dimensions

Phobos is larger than Deimos and is 22 km in diameter. The smaller moon Deimos is only 13 km wide. This makes them both two of the smallest moons in the solar system.

FUN FACT

Phobos is so small that although it is closer to Mars as compared to any other moon and its planet, it only looks one-third the size of our moon when observed from Mars.

Phobos

Phobos (Mars I) is the larger and closer of the two natural satellites of Mars. Both moons were discovered in 1877. A small, irregularly shaped object with a mean radius of 11 km, it is seven times more massive than Mars's outer moon, Deimos. It is named after the Greek god Phobos, son of Ares (Mars) and Aphrodite (Venus), which was the personification of horror.

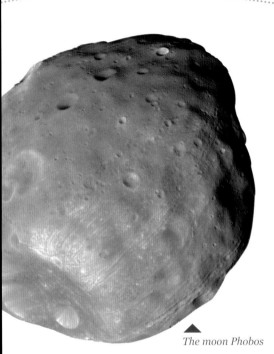

The moon Phobos

Appearance

Phobos is too small to be rounded under its own gravity. It does not have an atmosphere due to low mass and gravity. It is one of the least reflective bodies in the solar system. Its density is too low to be a solid rock and is known to have significant porosity.

Stickney crater

It is heavily cratered. The most prominent surface feature is the crater called Stickney, named after Asaph Hall's wife, Angeline Stickney Hall, Stickney being her maiden name. The impact that created Stickney must have nearly shattered Phobos. Many grooves and streaks also cover the oddly shaped surface. The grooves are typically less than 30 m deep, 100–200 m wide and up to 20 km long.

The unique Kaidun meteorite is thought to be a piece of Phobos but this has been difficult to verify since little is known about the detailed composition of the moon.

Predicted destruction

Tidal deceleration is gradually decreasing the orbital radius of Phobos.

Observations of Phobos's orbit leads to the conclusion that it will be destroyed in less than 30–50 million years. Given its irregular shape and assuming that it is a Mohr–Coulomb body, it will eventually break up when it reaches approximately 2.1 Mars radii.

Phobos and Deimos orbiting around Mars.

An artist's representation of the planet Mars along with one of its moons, Phobos, orbiting around it.

FUN FACT

It is speculated that Phobos is hollow due to its unusual orbital characteristics.

Deimos

Deimos (Mars II) is the smaller and further of the two natural satellites of Mars with a mean radius of 6.2 km, the other being Phobos. Deimos takes 30.3 hours to orbit Mars. In Greek mythology, Deimos is Phobos's twin brother. It means "terror".

They resemble asteroids more than the moons of the planet Mars.

orbits, which lie almost exactly in Mars's equatorial plane.

Solar transits

It regularly passes in front of the Sun. It is too small to cause a total eclipse, appearing only as a small black dot moving across the Sun. On 4th March, 2004, a transit of Deimos was photographed by Mars Rover Opportunity and on 13th March, 2004, a transit was photographed by Mars Rover Spirit.

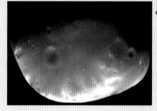

The Deimos looks like a smaller irregular moon.

The discovery

Based on the fact that Earth has a moon and Jupiter has four, Johannes Kepler suggested years ago that it was very possible for Mars to have atleast two moons. However, it wasn't till years later that Asaph Hall, after researching the area carefully and focus searching Mars' moons, discovered them on 12th August, 1877.

Appearance

Like most bodies of its size, it is highly non-spherical and half the size of Phobos. It is composed of rock that is rich in carbonaceous materials. It is cratered, but the surface is noticeably smoother than that of Phobos, caused by the partial filling of craters with regolith (a layer of loose, heterogeneous material covering solid rock). The regolith is highly porous. The two largest craters, Swift and Voltaire, each measure about 3 km across.

Orbits of Phobos and Deimos

Deimos' orbit is nearly circular and close to Mars' equatorial plane. Deimos, Mars' outer moon, is possibly an asteroid that was perturbed by Jupiter into an orbit that allowed it to be captured by Mars. Both Deimos and Phobos have very circular

▼ *Deimos, the smaller moon of Mars.*

Jovian moons

Jupiter has a total of 67 known moons, including four large moons known as the Galilean satellites. This almost qualifies it as another solar system. Its size plays a role in the number of moons orbiting it because there is a large area of gravitational stability around it to support many moons.

Orbital periods

The moons of Jupiter have orbital periods ranging from seven hours to almost three Earth years. Some of the orbits are nearly circular, while the moons farthest from Jupiter have more irregular orbits.

Galilean moons

Most of Jupiter's moons are small, which is less than 9.7 km in diameter. In January 1610, Italian astronomer Galileo Galilee discovered four of Jupiter's moons — now called Io, Europa, Ganymede and Callisto. He originally referred to the individual moons numerically as I, II, III and IV. Eight satellites—the four Galilean and four smaller moons—are closer to the planet and provide the dust that make up Jupiter's rings.

After alternatively using Roman names and numerals to address the moons of Jupiter that were discovered one after another, the IAU finally decided on a specific mean of nomenclature. In 1975, they decided to name the newly discovered moons after the lovers and favourites, and later according to the names of the daughters of Jupiter. Out of the 67 moons of Jupiter, moon number 66 has been named Megaclite and moon 67 still has to be named.

Jupiter was named after the mythological character Io, a priestess of Hera who became one of his lovers.

Jupiter and the four Galilean satellites.

The four Galilean moons orbiting around Jupiter.

FUN FACT

The Galilean moons are by far the largest and most massive objects in the orbit around Jupiter, with the remaining 63 moons and rings together comprising just 0.003 per cent of the total orbiting mass.

Io

Io is the innermost of the four Galilean moons of Jupiter. It is the fourth-largest moon. It has the highest density among all the moons and is the driest known object in the solar system.

Geologically active object

With over 400 active volcanoes, Io is the most geologically active object in the solar system. This extreme activity is because of tidal heating from friction that is generated within Io's interior as it is pulled between Jupiter and the other Galilean satellites—Europa, Ganymede and Callisto.

Several volcanoes produce plumes of sulphur and sulphur dioxide that climb as high as 500 km above the surface. Io's surface is also dotted with more than 100 mountains that have been uplifted by extensive compression at the base of Io's silicate crust. Some of these peaks are even taller than Mount Everest.

A representation of an artificial satellite capturing the image of Jupiter's moons.

Volcanoes

Io's volcanism is responsible for many of its unique features. Its volcanic plumes and flowing lava produce large surface changes. They paint the surface in various subtle shades of yellow, red, white, black and green, largely due to allotropes and compounds of sulphur.

Numerous extensive streams of lava, more than 500 km in length, also mark the surface. The materials produced by this volcanism make up Io's thin, patchy atmosphere and Jupiter's extensive magnetosphere. Io's volcanic ejecta (the particles ejected from a volcano) also produce a large plasma torus (the ring) around Jupiter.

FUN FACT

Besides Earth, Io is the only known body in the solar system to have observed active volcanoes.

Rotation and revolution

JUPITER

◀ Comparison between Jupiter and its moons.

Io orbits Jupiter at a distance of 421,700 km from Jupiter's centre and 350,000 km from its cloud tops. Its orbit lies between those of Thebe and Europa. Including Jupiter's inner satellites, Io is the fifth moon out from Jupiter.

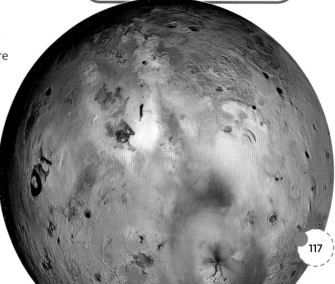

Europa

Europa (Jupiter II) is the sixth-closest moon of Jupiter and the smallest of its four Galilean satellites. But it is still the sixth-largest moon in the solar system. Like all the Galilean satellites, Europa is named after a lover of Zeus (the Greek counterpart of Jupiter), after the daughter of the king of Tyre.

Rotation and revolution

Europa takes almost four days to orbit Jupiter. Like its fellow Galilean satellites, it is tidally locked to Jupiter, with one hemisphere of Europa constantly facing Jupiter like Earth's moon.

Appearance

Europa is slightly smaller than the moon. At just over 3,100 km in diameter, it is the sixth-largest moon and 15th largest object in the solar system. However, by a wide margin, it is the least massive of the Galilean satellites. Nonetheless, it is comparatively larger than all the known moons in the solar system.

Internal structure

Europa has an outer layer of water around 100 km thick; some as frozen ice above the crust and some as liquid ocean beneath the ice.

Geological structures

Europa is one of the smoothest objects in the solar system. However, its equator has been thought to be covered in 10 m tall icy spikes called "penitents". These are formed by the effect of direct overhead sunlight on the equator and melting vertical cracks. Its most striking surface features are a series of dark streaks crisscrossing the entire globe, called "lineae". The edges of its crust on either side of the cracks have moved relatively to each other.

◄ *A series of dark lines known as lineae are seen across the surface of Europa.*

FUN FACT

The radiation level at the surface of Europa is sufficiently high, resulting in severe illness or even death in human beings, who are exposed to it even for a single day!

Subsurface ocean

Scientists believe that a layer of liquid water exists beneath Europa's surface. It is the heat from tidal flexing that allows the subsurface ocean to remain liquid.

▼ *The larger bands are more than 20 km across, often with dark, diffused outer edges, regular striations and a central band of lighter material.*

Ganymede

Ganymede (Jupiter III) is Jupiter's satellite. It is the largest moon in the solar system. It has a diameter of 5,268 km, eight per cent larger than Mercury, but has only 45 per cent of its mass. Its diameter is two per cent larger than Saturn's Titan, the second largest moon. It also has the highest mass of all planetary satellites, with 2.02 times the mass of Earth's moon. It is the seventh moon and third Galilean satellite on the outer side of Jupiter, orbiting at about 1.070 million km. It takes Ganymede about seven Earth days to orbit Jupiter.

Tidal lock

Ganymede orbits Jupiter at a distance of 1,070,400 km. It is third among the Galilean satellites and completes a revolution every seven days and three hours. Like most known moons, Ganymede is tidally locked, with one side always facing towards the planet.

Composition

Its average density suggests a composition of approximately equal parts rocky material and water, which is mainly ice. Some additional volatile ices such as ammonia may also be present.

Internal structure

It appears to be fully differentiated, consisting of an iron sulphide – iron core and silicate mantle. The precise thicknesses of the different layers in its interior depend on the assumed composition of silicates and a small amount of sulphur in the core.

Accretion of Ganymede

Ganymede was probably formed by an accretion in Jupiter's sub-nebula, a disc of gas and dust surrounding Jupiter after its formation. The accretion of Ganymede probably took about 10,000 years.

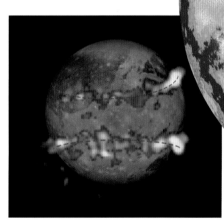

▲
Scientists have observed oceanic movements on the surface of Ganymede through the Hubble Telescope.

▲
Ganymede is the only Galilean moon of Jupiter named after a male figure, like Io, Europa and Callisto. He was a lover of Zeus.

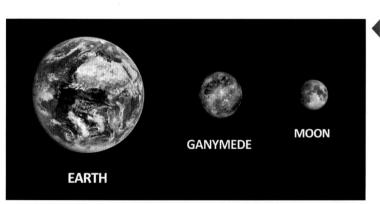

◀ *Ganymede compared with Earth and the moon.*

EARTH   GANYMEDE   MOON

FUN FACT

Larger than Mercury and Pluto, and only slightly smaller than Mars, Ganymede would easily be classified as a planet if it were orbiting the Sun rather than Jupiter.

Callisto

Callisto (Jupiter IV) is the most heavily cratered object in the solar system. It also has the oldest landscape. It is the outermost of the Galilean moons and has the lowest density compared to the four. It was named after the daughter of the King of Arcadia, Lycaon, who was a companion of Artemis, the hunting goddess.

Orbit

Like other moons, its rotation is locked in order to be synchronous with its orbit. The length of a Callistoan day and its orbital period is about 16.7 days. It also experiences less tidal influences than other Galilean moons because it orbits beyond Jupiter's main radiation belt.

Surface structure

Its surface is the oldest in the solar system. It does not show any signs that geological activity in general have ever occurred on it. It is thought to have evolved predominantly under the influence of impacts. Prominent surface features include multi-ring structures, variously shaped impact craters and chains of craters (catenae), and associated scarps, ridges and deposits. The absolute ages of the landforms are not known.

Callisto is roughly the same size as Mercury. It is the third largest moon in the entire solar system and the second largest in the Jovian system, after Ganymede. ▶

Darkest surface structure

While craters are its signature feature, its surface colouring is also the darkest of all the Galilean moons. Its composition consists of magnesium and iron-bearing hydrated silicates, carbon dioxide, sulphur dioxide and possibly ammonia and other organic compounds. It also consists of equal amounts of rocks and ices.

◀ *The crust and the interiors of the Galilean moon Callisto.*

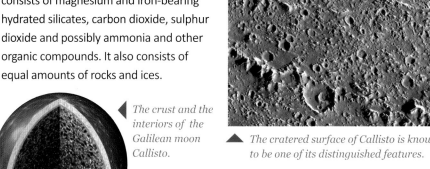

▲ *The cratered surface of Callisto is known to be one of its distinguished features.*

It is thought to be a long dead world, with hardly any geologic activity on its surface.

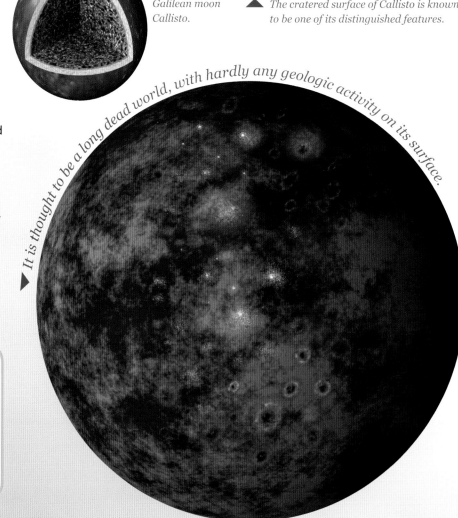

FUN FACT

The likely presence of an ocean within Callisto leaves a possibility that it could harbour life. Because of its low radiation levels, it has long been considered as the most suitable place for a human base for future exploration of the Jovian system.

Saturn's Moons

The moons of Saturn are several and diverse, ranging from tiny moonlets less than one km across to the gigantic Titan, which is larger than Mercury. Saturn has 62 moons with established orbits, 53 of which have names.

Discovery of the moons

Christiaan Huygens discovered the first known moon of Saturn in 1655 and it was Titan. Giovanni Domenico Cassini made the next four discoveries: Iapetus (1671), Rhea (1672), Dione (1684) and Tethys (1684). William Herschel discovered Mimas and Enceladus in 1789. The next two discoveries came at intervals of 50 or more years: Hyperion in 1848 and Phoebe in 1898.

Saturn's orbit

Saturn has 24 regular satellites; they have orbits not greatly inclined to Saturn's equatorial plane. They include the seven major satellites, four small moons that exist in a Trojan orbit with larger moons and two mutually co-orbital moons.

Irregular moon

The regular satellites are conventionally named after Titans and Titanesses associated with the mythological Saturn. The irregular satellites have been classified by their orbital characteristics into the Inuit, Norse and Gallic groups. Their names are chosen from the corresponding mythologies. The biggest

▲ *Saturn along with its satellites in space.*

irregular moon is Phoebe, the ninth moon of Saturn, which was discovered at the end of the nineteenth century. This moon belongs to the Norse group and like the rest of the moons in that group, its rotation is retrograde. The surface of Phoebe is scarred by approximately 130 craters, each one about 10 km wide. This moon is the source of the material required for the largest ring around Saturn.

The Saturnian moon system is very unbalanced. The other six ellipsoidal moons constitute roughly four per cent of the mass in orbit around the planet Saturn, while the remaining 55 small moons, with the rings, comprise only 0.04 per cent of it.

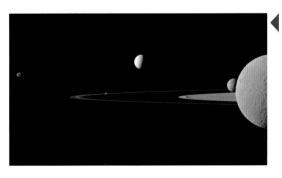

◀ *Titan comprises more than 96 per cent of the mass in orbit around the planet.*

▶

Phoebe contributes the material that is required to replenish the biggest ring around Saturn.

Titan

Titan (Saturn VI) is Saturn's largest moon. It is the only known moon to have a dense atmosphere. It is also the only object besides Earth, where clear evidence of stable bodies of surface liquid has been found. It is the sixth ellipsoidal moon from Saturn. It was the first known moon of Saturn and the fifth known satellite of another planet.

Titan has an atmosphere thicker than Earth's.

Atmosphere

Titan's atmospheric composition in the stratosphere is 98.4 per cent nitrogen and 1.6 per cent of methane and hydrogen. There are trace amounts of other hydrocarbons, such as ethane, diacetylene, methylacetylene and other gases.

Geological structures

The surface of Titan has been described as "complex, fluid-processed and geologically young". It has streaky features, some of them hundreds of kilometres in length, which seem to be caused by windblown rocky particles.

The surface is fairly smooth; the few objects that seem to be impact craters appear to have been filled in, perhaps by raining hydrocarbons or volcanoes.

Its surface is marked by broad regions of bright and dark terrain. The convoluted region is filled with hills and cut by valleys and chasms.

Large areas of Titan's surface are covered with sand dunes made of hydrocarbon. Dunes on Titan may resemble those of the Namibian desert in Africa.

Rotation and revolution

Titan orbits Saturn once every 15 days and 22 hours. Its rotational period is identical to its orbital period. Titan is, thus, tidally locked in synchronous rotation with its host and always shows one face to the planet.

A comparison between Earth, its moon and Saturn's moon Titan.

Saturn's system

It is believed that Saturn's system began with a group of moons similar to Jupiter's Galilean satellites, but they were disrupted by a series of giant impacts, which would go on to form Titan.

▼ *A representation of the surface of Titan.*

Porous icy crust

Alkanofer in porous icy crust

Expanding clathrate layer in porous icy crust

Non-porous icy crust

Iapetus

Iapetus is the third-largest moon of Saturn, and eleventh-largest in the solar system. It was discovered by Giovanni Cassini in 1672. He first spotted the moon on the west side of the planet, but when he tried to observe it days later on the eastern side, he could not spot it. This led him to surmise that the moon was tidally locked, with one face darker than the other.

Appearance

Unlike most of the moons, Iapetus has a bulging equator and compressed poles. It has low density and is known to be composed primarily of water, with fewer rocks.

A series of high mountains encircle the equator, going more than halfway around the moon. The ridge stretches more than 1,300 km around the moon's circumference. Some of the peaks reach heights of more than 20 km. They are among the highest mountains in the solar system. Iapetus is heavily cratered, and atleast five of these craters are over 350 km wide. The widest crater, Turgis, has a diameter of 580 km. Its rim is extremely steep and includes a scarp about 15 km high.

Two-faced moon

The most striking feature of Iapetus is its dual colouration. The leading hemisphere of the satellite is coal-black, while its rear is brighter. When the moon is facing Earth, its dark leading side keeps it hidden. The coal black region is called Cassini Regio, after the Italian astronomer. One theory suggests that eruptions of dark hydrocarbons from ice volcanoes could have caused the differentiation.

An image showing the bright trailing hemisphere, with part of the dark area appearing on the right. The large crater Engelier is near the bottom.

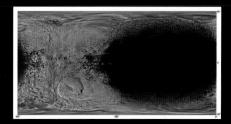

An image providing a closer look at the dark side of Iapetus, that helps it hide when observing from Earth.

An image showing the dark Cassini Region and its border with the bright Roncevaux Terra, Turgis, the largest crater, on the right, and the equatorial ridge.

FUN FACT

Temperature ranges from -143 °C on the warmer dark side to -173 °C on the bright side, which absorbs less heat and is cooler.

Rhea

Rhea is the second-largest moon of Saturn and the ninth-largest moon in the solar system. It is the smallest body in the solar system established in hydrostatic equilibrium. It is the second largest moon of Saturn, resembling a dirty snowball of rock and ice. It is the only moon that has oxygen in its atmosphere. Even though it is thin, it is one of the most heavily cratered satellites in the solar system.

◀ *Virtual image of Rhea, named after the Titan Rheaww of Greek mythology, "mother of the gods". It is also designated as Saturn V.*

Appearance

It has a density that is 1.233 times that of liquid water, which implies that it is three-quarters ice and one-quarter rock. Rhea has two huge impact basins on its hemisphere. They are between 400 and 500 km across. The northern of the two is called "Tirawa".

Rhea's surface

Its surface can be divided into two different areas based on crater density: the first area contains craters, which are larger than 40 km in diameter while the second area, in parts of the polar and equatorial regions, has craters less than 40 km. The leading hemisphere is heavily cratered and uniformly bright. As a result, Saturn's gravitational pull is less effective on the moon.

Atmosphere

A very faint oxygen atmosphere exists around it, the first direct evidence of an oxygen atmosphere on a body besides Earth. The main source of oxygen is radiolysis of water and ice at the surface by ions supplied by the magnetosphere of Saturn.

In addition to the oxygen, carbon dioxide has also been found in traces, which indicates that it is possible for life to exist on this heavenly body. It has been suggested that the air on Rhea might be breatheable for humans.

There is an impact crater that is prominent because of an extended system of bright rays, called "Inktomi", and is nicknamed "The Splat".

▼ *Earth, its moon and Saturn's moon Rhea.*

FUN FACT

The atmosphere around Rhea is so thin that oxygen is around five trillion times less dense than that found on Earth!

Dione

Dione, a moon of Saturn, was discovered by Italian astronomer Giovanni Domenico Cassini in 1684. It is named after the Titaness Dione of Greek mythology. It is also designated as Saturn IV. Its orbital period is one-tenth of the moon.

▲ *An artist's representation of Dione in comparison to the other moons of Saturn.*

▲ *Fractures dividing older craters on Dione. The ones running from upper right to lower left are the Carthage Fossae, while Pactolus Catena runs more horizontally on the lower right.*

Appearance

Dione is the 15th largest moon in the solar system. It is composed primarily of water ice, but since it is the third densest moon of Saturn, it has denser material like silicate rock in its interior. It has similar albedo features and terrain as Rhea. Both these have dissimilar leading and trailing hemispheres. Its leading hemisphere is cratered and homogeneously bright. Its trailing hemisphere contains a network of bright ice cliffs, which is a distinctive surface feature.

The ice cliffs

Photographs of Dione show wispy features covering its trailing hemisphere. The origin of these features is puzzling, as all that was known was that the material has a high albedo and is sufficiently thin so that it cannot hide the surface beneath. Studies revealed that the wisps were, in fact, not deposits but rather bright ice cliffs created by tectonic fractures.

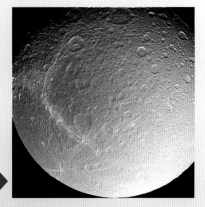

Dione as seen from Voyager 1; the craters on the upper and lower left are Dido and Aeneas. ▶

Craters

Dione's surface includes a heavily cratered terrain, fairly cratered plains, lightly cratered plains and areas of tectonic fractures. The heavily cratered terrain has several craters that are larger than 100 km in diameter. The plain areas have craters less than 30 km in diameter. The heavily cratered terrain is located on the trailing hemisphere, while the less cratered plains are present on the leading hemisphere.

FUN FACT

Dione has two Trojan moons, Helene and Polydeuces, which are located within its Lagrangian points L4 and L5, 60° ahead and behind Dione, respectively.

Tethys

Tethys or Saturn III is a mid-sized moon of Saturn about 1,060 km across. It was discovered by G. D. Cassini in 1684 and is named after the Titan Tethys of Greek mythology. Its surface is very bright, making it the second-brightest moon of Saturn after Enceladus and neutral in colour. It has two co-orbital moons, Telesto and Calypso.

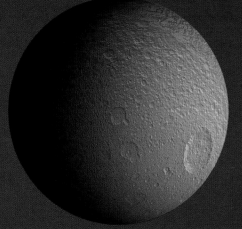

Tethys is the third closest of the major moons.

Frozen surface

Like many satellites around Saturn, Tethys is made up of water ice. The frigid surface is highly reflective, a characteristic increased by the shower of water ice particles from the plumes of the moon Enceladus.

Colour patterns

Its surface has many large-scale features distinguished by their colour and sometimes brightness. The trailing hemisphere gets increasingly red and dark as the anti-apex of motion is reached. The leading hemisphere, too, reddens lightly as the apex of the motion is approached, but does not darken.

Odysseus crater

Even though most impact craters are quite small, a giant one known as the Odysseus Crater covers almost two-fifth of the moon's diameter. At 400 km across, it is around the size of Saturn's smallest major moon, Mimas. The crater is quite shallow and its floor conforms to the shape of the moon.

Ithaca Chasma

A large trench runs from the moon's North Pole to its South Pole. It extends up to 2,000 km, spanning almost three-quarters of the planet's circumference. The Ithaca Chasma is 100 km wide and five km deep. The Chasma is believed to be created by the same impact that formed the Odysseus crater. The second cause could be that the surface froze before the core, leading it to expand and crack the crust.

Huge, shallow crater Odysseus, with its raised central complex, the Scheria Montes, is shown at the top of this image.

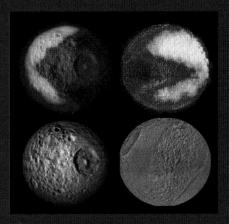

NASA's Cassini spacecraft found a Pac-Man-like shape on Tethys (left).

Tethys pictured along with its planet, Saturn.

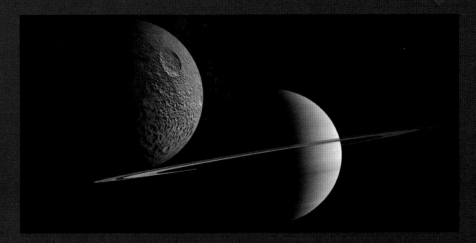

Uranian Moons

Uranus has 27 known moons, which are named after characters from the works of William Shakespeare and Alexander Pope. Uranian moons are divided into three groups: 13 inner moons, five major moons and nine irregular moons.

▼ Uranus and its five major moons.

Inner moons

Uranus is known to hold 13 inner moons. Their orbits lie inside Miranda's orbit. All inner moons are closely connected to the rings of Uranus. The two innermost moons (Cordelia and Ophelia) are known as shepherds, while the small moon (Mab) is a source of Uranus's outermost ring.

Irregular moons

Uranus has nine irregular moons, which orbit at a greater distance than Oberon, the farthest of the large moons. All the irregular moons are thought to be captured objects that were trapped by Uranus soon after its formation. Uranus' irregular moons range in size from 150 km (Sycorax) to 18 km (Trinculo).

Large moons

Uranus has five major moons – Miranda, Ariel, Umbriel, Titania and Oberon. They range in diameter from 472 km (Miranda) to 1,578 km (Titania). The major moons of Uranus are thought to have formed in the accretion disc. This existed around Uranus for some time after its formation or resulted from the large impact suffered by Uranus early on.

The skygazers

William Herschel, who discovered the planet of Uranus itself, was the one to discover two of its moons in 1787, Oberon and Titania. William Lassell, an English astronomer, was the one to spot Umbriel as well as Ariel in 1851. Before the space age began, the last moon was discovered by Gerard P. Kuiper in 1948; this was the frankenstein moon, Miranda.

A schematic image of the Uranian moon-ring system. ▶

FUN FACT

Caliban, one of Uranus' many moons, moves in an inclined orbit that is opposite to the rotation of Uranus. This shows that it was not formed from Uranus but was a body captured by Uranus' gravity.

Ariel

Ariel (Uranus I) is the fourth-largest of the 27 known moons of Uranus. It orbits and rotates in the equatorial plane of Uranus, which is almost perpendicular to Uranus's orbit and therefore has an extreme seasonal cycle.

Composition and structure

It is the fourth largest of the Uranian moons. It roughly consists of equal parts water ice and a dense non-ice component, which could be rock and carbonaceous material including heavy organic compounds known as tholins. Given its size and rock and/or ice composition, its interior is divided into a rocky core surrounded by an icy mantle.

Albedo and colour

It is the most reflective of Uranus's moons. Its surface is neutral in colour. The trailing hemisphere appears to be slightly redder than the leading hemisphere. Canyons have the same colour as the cratered terrain.

Geological structures

Its surface can be divided into three terrain types: cratered terrain, ridged terrain and plains. The main surface features are impact craters, canyons, fault scarps, ridges and troughs. The cratered terrain, a rolling surface covered by multiple impact craters, is the moon's oldest and most extensive unit. It is intersected by a network of scarps, canyons and narrow ridges. The longest canyon is Kachina Chasma, at over 620 km in length.

The second main terrain type, ridged terrain, consists of bands of ridges and troughs. Within each band, which can be up to 25 to 70 km wide, are individual ridges and troughs. The newest terrains observed on Ariel, the plains, are relatively low-lying smooth areas. The plains are seen on the floors of canyons and in a few irregular depressions in the heart of the cratered terrain.

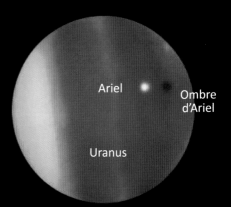

Canyons seen on upper left and the prominent noncircular crater below and left of centre is Yangoor.

Ariel   Ombre d'Ariel

Uranus

The shadow of Ariel falls on Uranus when it transits through.

Among Uranus's five major moons, Ariel is the second closest to the planet, orbiting at the distance of about 190,000 km.

FUN FACT

Ariel, along with the four major moons, has planetary mass and so would be considered as a dwarf planet if it directly orbited the Sun.

Miranda

Miranda or Uranus V is the smallest and innermost of Uranus's five round moons. Similar to the other Uranian moons, it orbits in Uranus's equatorial plane.

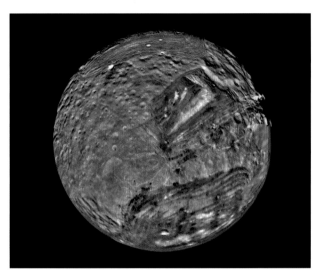

▲ *A close-up of Verona Rupes, the largest known cliff.*

Geological structures

Miranda's surface has mixed regions of broken terrain representing intense geological activity in the past and is criss-crossed by large canyons. It also hosts the largest known cliff in the solar system, Verona Rupes, which has a drop-off of over 5 km. Three giant racetrack-like grooved structures called "coronae" are each at least 200 km wide and up to 20 km deep, named Arden, Elsinore and Inverness. This was discovered on the moon's southern hemisphere. These may have formed via extensional processes at the tops of diapirs or upwelling of warm ice.

Miranda's past geological activity is supposed to have been a result of tidal heating when it was in orbital resonance with Umbriel.

Orbit

Miranda is the only satellite that orbits closest to it, at more or less 129,000 km from the surface. Its orbital period is 34 hours and, like the moon, is synchronous with its rotation period. This means that it always shows the same face to Uranus, a condition known as tidal lock. Its orbital inclination is abnormally high for a body this close to a planet and approximately 10 times that of the other Uranian satellites.

Appearance

Miranda is the least dense of Uranus' round satellites. This suggests a composition of more than 60 per cent water ice. Miranda's surface may be mostly water ice. With the low-density body, it probably contains silicate rock and organic compounds in its interior.

▲ *Uranus along with its five moons.*

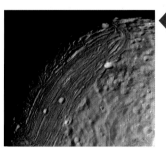

◄ *Most of the geological structures on Miranda remain unexplained and are said to be the result of the moon breaking apart and reassembling.*

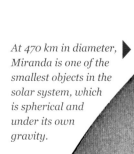

At 470 km in diameter, ▶ *Miranda is one of the smallest objects in the solar system, which is spherical and under its own gravity.*

Titania

Titania (Uranus III) is the largest of the moons of Uranus and the eighth largest moon in the solar system. Titania was discovered by William Herschel in 1787. It is named after the queen of fairies in Shakespeare's *A Midsummer Night's Dream*.

 Brightnesswise, Titania lies midway between the dark Oberon and Umbriel and the bright Ariel and Miranda.

◀ *Comparison of the sizes of Earth, its moon and Titania. Titania is about one-third the size of Earth's moon.*

Orbit

It is the second farthest from the planet among its five major moons. Its orbital period is about 8.7 days. It is synchronised with its rotational period, which means that it is a tidally locked satellite, with one face always pointing towards Uranus. Its orbit lies inside the Uranian magnetosphere; hence, its trailing hemisphere is struck by charged particles, which may have led to the darkening of the trailing hemispheres. This is observed for all Uranian moons except Oberon.

Composition

Titania's much higher density indicates that it consists of almost equal proportions of water ice and dense non-ice components. These could be made of rock and carbonaceous material including heavy organic compounds. Water ice absorption bands are slightly stronger on the leading hemisphere than on the trailing hemisphere. Besides water, the only other compound identified on Titania's surface is carbon dioxide, which is found mainly on the trailing hemisphere. It is divided into a rocky core surrounded by an icy mantle.

Geological structures

Its surface is generally slightly red. Three classes of geological features are seen on Titania: craters, canyons and scarps. Some craters, for instance, Ursula and Jessica, are surrounded by bright impact rays comprising fresh ice. All large craters on Titania have flat floors and central peaks, except Ursula, which has a pit in the centre.

Atmosphere

The presence of carbon dioxide on the surface suggests that it may have a weak seasonal atmosphere, similar to the Galilean-Jovian moon Callisto.

FUN FACT

There are fewer craters on Titania than on Oberon, which tells scientists that it is actually the younger moon.

Oberon

Oberon, also designated Uranus IV, is the outermost major moon of Uranus. It is the second largest and second biggest Uranian moon. It is also the ninth most massive moon in the solar system. It was discovered by William Herschel in 1787.

A virtual image of Oberon. The large crater with the dark floor (right) is Hamlet; the crater Othello is to its lower left, and the "canyon" Mommur Chasma is to the upper left.

Orbit

It is the farthest from the planet among Uranus' five major moons. Its orbital period is around 13.5 days, same as its rotational period. It is a synchronous satellite, tidally locked, showing only one face toward the planet. It spends a significant part of its orbit outside the Uranian magnetosphere. So, its surface is directly struck by the solar wind. Bombardment of magnetospheric particles in objects that orbit inside its magnetosphere leads to the darkening of the trailing hemispheres, which is observed in all of Uranus's moons except Oberon.

Composition and internal structure

Its density is higher than the typical density of Saturn's satellites, indicating that it consists of roughly equal proportions of water ice and a dense non-ice component. Water ice absorption bands are stronger on Oberon's trailing hemisphere rather than the leading one, in contrast to observations on other Uranian moons. It may be differentiated into a rocky core surrounded by an icy mantle.

Geological structures

It is the second-darkest large moon of Uranus after Umbriel. Two classes of geological features are observed on Oberon: craters and canyons. Its surface is the most heavily cratered compared to other Uranian moons. The high number of craters show that it has the most ancient surface among Uranus' moons. The crater diameters go up to 206 km for the largest known crater, Hamlet. Many large craters are surrounded by bright impact rays consisting of fresh ice. Oberon's surface is crossed by a system of canyons, which are less widespread than those found on Titania. The most prominent canyon in Oberon is Mommur Chasma.

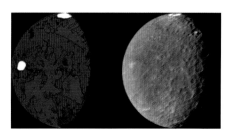

A view of Oberon.

Oberon in comparison with Titania.

Umbriel

Umbriel (Uranus II) was simultaneously discovered with Ariel. It was named after a character in Alexander Pope's poem *The Rape of the Lock*.

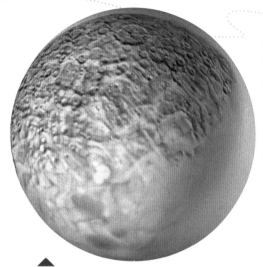

Umbriel's surface is the darkest of the Uranian moons.

Orbit

Umbriel is the third farthest moon from Uranus. Its orbit has a small eccentricity and is slightly inclined towards Uranus' equator. Its orbital period is around 4.1 Earth days; coinciding with its rotational period. Its orbit lies completely inside the Uranian magnetosphere; thus, its trailing hemisphere is struck by charged particles leading to the darkening of the trailing hemisphere. Umbriel also acts as a sink for the magnetospheric charged particles, which creates a pronounced dip in the energetic particle count near its orbit.

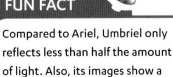

FUN FACT

Compared to Ariel, Umbriel only reflects less than half the amount of light. Also, its images show a mysterious bright ring about 140 km in diameter at one of its poles.

Composition and internal structure

Umbriel is the third largest and fourth most massive of Uranian moons. The moon's density indicates that it chiefly consists of water ice, with a dense non-ice component constituting around 40 per cent of its mass. The presence of water ice is supported by infrared spectroscopic observations, which have revealed crystalline water ice on the surface of the moon. Water ice absorption bands are stronger on Umbriel's leading hemisphere than on the trailing hemisphere.

Geological structures

Only one form of geological feature is found on Umbriel-craters. Its surface has several and bigger craters than Ariel and Titania. It shows the least geological activity. The crater diameters range from a few km to 210 km. All recognised craters on Umbriel have central peaks but not rays. The most prominent surface feature is the Wunda crater. It has a diameter of about 131 km and has a large ring of bright material on its floor, which appears to be an impact deposit. Nearby, seen along the terminator, are the craters Vuver and Skynd, which possess bright and tall central peaks.

View of Umbriel from Voyager 1.

Umbriel is a synchronous satellite, with one face perennially pointing towards Uranus.

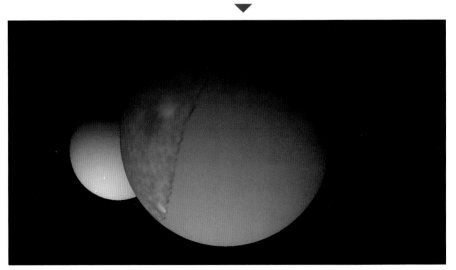

Moons of Neptune

Neptune has 14 known moons. All of these are named after minor water deities in Greek mythology, due to Neptune's position as the god of sea in Roman mythology.

History and background

Triton is the largest of Neptune's moons by far. William Lassell discovered Triton on 10th October, 1846. This is just 17 days after the discovery of Neptune itself. More than a century passed before the discovery of its second moon, Nereid. Neptune's "Nesois" is the moon that orbits the farthest from its planet in the solar system. It has an orbital period of about 26 years.

Characteristics and classification

The moons of Neptune can be divided into two groups, namely, regular and irregular moons. The first group of moons includes the seven inner moons. These moons follow circular prograde orbits. These orbits lie in the equatorial plane of Neptune. The irregular moon group consists of all other moons including Triton. They generally follow inclined, eccentric orbits. These are often retrograde orbits that are far from Neptune. Triton is the only exception to this. It orbits close to Neptune, following a circular orbit. This orbit is still retrograde and inclined.

Regular moons

The regular moons of Neptune are Naiad, Thalassa, Despina, Galatea, Larissa, S/2004 N 1 and Proteus. These are arranged according to increasing distance from the planet. Naiad is the closest regular moon as well as the second smallest among the inner moons. S/2004 N 1 is the smallest regular moon. Prior to its discovery,

Naiad was the smallest. Proteus is the largest regular moon as well as the second largest moon of Neptune. The regular moons were probably formed in a place around Neptune.

A picture of Neptune and its various moon in their orbits.

Irregular moons

The irregular moons of Neptune are Triton, Nereid, Halimede, Sao, Laomedeia, Neso and Psamathe. These are arranged in the order of their increasing distance. The five outer moons of Neptune are similar to the irregular moons of other giant planets like Uranus and Jupiter. They are believed to have been gravitationally captured by Neptune, as opposed to the regular moons.

A picture of Neptune with its moons.

133

Triton

 Triton is Neptune's largest moon. English astronomer William Lassell discovered it on 10th October, 1846. Triton is one of the very few moons in the solar system known and confirmed to be geologically active.

Discovery

Triton was discovered a mere 17 days after the discovery of Neptune. It is said that when John Herschel received news of Neptune's discovery, he wrote to Lassell suggesting that he search for possible moons of Neptune.

Naming

Triton is named after the Greek sea god Triton, the son of Poseidon. Poseidon is the Greek equivalent of the Roman Neptune. Camille Flammarion initially proposed the name Triton in his 1880 book called *Astronomie Populaire*. It was officially adopted many decades later. Triton was commonly known as "the satellite of Neptune" until the discovery of the second moon about 100 years later.

Orbit

▲ *Image showing the orbit of Triton*

Triton is unique among all large moons in the solar system. It has a retrograde orbit around its planet. It orbits in a direction opposite to Neptune's rotation. It is worth noting that most irregular moons of Jupiter and Saturn

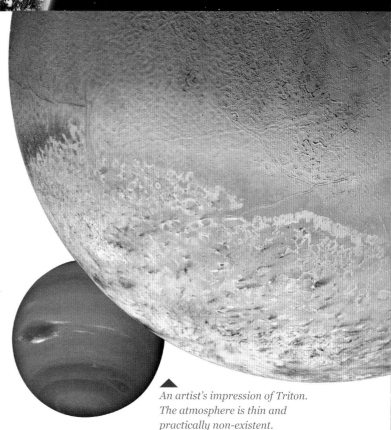

▲ *An artist's impression of Triton. The atmosphere is thin and practically non-existent.*

also have retrograde orbits as well as some outer moons of Uranus. However, these moons are all much farther from their planets. They are small compared to Triton. The largest of these moons, Phoebe, has only eight per cent of the diameter and only 0.03 per cent of the mass of Triton.

Capture and atmosphere

Triton was likely "captured" by Neptune. The process would have mostly destroyed the existing satellites into dust and rubble. It has a thin atmosphere of nitrogen and is less than 1000 times as dense as Earth.

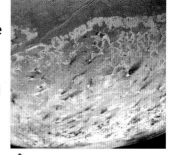

▲ *The photo of Triton as taken by Voyager 2.*

FUN FACT

Lassell claimed to have also discovered the rings of Neptune. Neptune was later confirmed to in fact have rings. However, they are so faint and dark that it is doubted that he actually saw these rings.

William Lassell discovered Triton after taking Herschel's advice. ▶

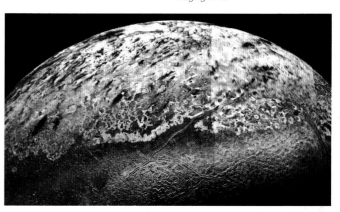

Proteus

Proteus is the second largest Neptunian moon and Neptune's largest inner satellite. It is also occasionally known as Neptune VIII. It is probably not an original body that formed with Neptune. It may have accreted later from the debris that was created when Triton was captured from the Kuiper belt.

Nomenclature and discovery

Proteus was discovered through the images taken by the Voyager 2 space probe two months before its flyby of Neptune in August 1989. It was temporarily designated as S/1989 N 1. Stephen P. Synnott and Bradford A. Smith announced the discovery on 7th July, 1989, with the words "17 frames taken over 21 days". This gives a probable discovery date of sometime around 16th June. On 16th September, 1991, S/1989 N 1 was named after Proteus. It was originally the shape-changing sea god of Greek mythology.

Orbit

Proteus orbits Neptune at a distance that is approximately around 4.75 times the equatorial radius of Neptune. Its orbit is slightly eccentric. It is inclined by about 0.5 degrees to the Neptune's equator. It is the largest of Neptune's regular satellites with a prograde orbit. It rotates synchronously with the orbital motion of Neptune. This means that only one face of Proteus always points to the planet.

Appearance

It is about 420 km in diameter. This makes it larger than Nereid, which was discovered second. Earth-based telescopes did not discover Proteus because it is very close to the planet. Nereid is usually lost in the glare of reflected sunlight from Neptune.

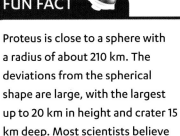

Proteus orbiting Neptune: a close-up as taken by the Voyager 2.

Shadow of Proteus on Neptune as seen from another planet.

Nereid

Nereid is Neptune's third largest moon. It has a highly eccentric orbit and is noted for the same. Gerard Kuiper discovered Nereid in 1949. It was, thus, that Neptune's second moon was discovered.

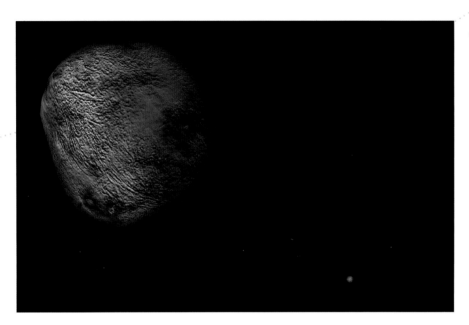

◀ *The image of Nereid as captured by Voyager 2 on its fly-by.*

Theories for eccentricity

The unusual eccentric orbit has three theories:

● it may be a captured asteroid

● it was a Kuiper belt object

● it was an inner moon in the past that was moved into an existing orbit during the capture of Triton.

The phenomena

Astronomers who have observed Nereid over a long period of time have seen a large variation in the brightness of the moon. This happens quite erratically. It is known to happen over a few days, a couple of months or even years! Explorers adhere this change to its extremely elliptical orbit. In fact, there are some astronomers who have not noticed these changes in brightness at all. This means that there is no known pattern to this change and the way it happens is quite chaotic. Astronomers still struggle to explain this phenomena.

Nomenclature and discovery

Nereid was discovered on 1st May, 1949, by Gerard P. Kuiper. He saw it on photographic plates that were taken with an 82-inch telescope by the McDonald Observatory. The name Nereid was mentioned in the report of his discovery. It is named after the Nereids. They were the sea-nymphs of Greek mythology and served as attendants of Neptune.

It was the second and last moon of Neptune to be discovered through Earth-based means. Only after the arrival of Voyager 2 did we make new discoveries.

Appearance

Nereid has an average radius of about 170 km. It is fairly large for an irregular satellite. The shape of Nereid is not known with any certainty. It appears neutral in colour. Astronomers have detected water ice on its surface.

Rotation and revolution

Nereid orbits Neptune in the prograde direction, i.e., in the same direction as Neptune's rotation, at an average distance of 5,513,400 km. However, its highly eccentric orbit takes it as close as 1,372,000 km at its closest point and moves as far as 9,655,000 km at the furthest point.

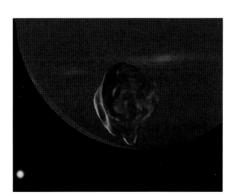

FUN FACT

The only spacecraft to visit Nereid has been Voyager 2. It passed Nereid at a distance of 4,700,000 km. This fly-by occurred between 20th April and 19th August, 1989.

OBJECTS IN SPACE

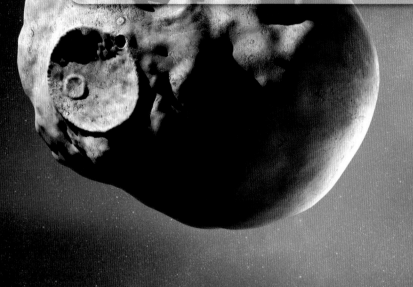

▲ *A view of an asteroid floating in space with Earth and its moon moving along their orbits in the background.*

We are learning about space all the time. However, there is still a lot more that we do not know. Most of the asteroids in our solar system are found in the asteroid belt between Mars and Jupiter. Some of these asteroids are so big that they have their own satellites. There are about 140 satellites orbiting the planets in our solar system.

Often, people think of asteroids and meteors hitting our planet as being a catastrophic event, but it is a common occurrence. At least one or two meteorites reach the surface of our planet every day. It is not a huge problem because the average size of a meteorite is that of a sugar cube.

Comets

A comet is a small, icy, solar system body. When passing close to the Sun, comets heat up and begin to outgas. This causes them to display a visible atmosphere or coma. Sometimes, they also exhibit a tail. Comet nuclei can range from a few hundred metres across to tens of kilometres across. They are composed of loose collections of ice, dust and small rocky particles.

Etymology

The word comet is derived from the Old English "cometa" and from the Latin words "comēta" or "comētēs". The word itself is a latinisation of the Greek phrase for "wearing long hair".

The Oxford English Dictionary notes that the term or phrase in Greek already meant "long-haired star", or comet, in ancient astronomy. It was derived from a Greek fashion slang that meant, "to wear the hair long". All these came about as the original term used to mean "the tail of a comet".

Nucleus of the comet

The nucleus is a solid, core structure of a comet. It is composed of an amalgamation of rock, dust, water ice and frozen gases. The gases are mainly carbon dioxide, carbon monoxide, methane and ammonia. Comets are popularly described as "dirty snowballs" due to Fred Whipple's model of comets. However, some comets may have higher dust content than the mean range. This leads to them being called "icy dirtballs".

The nucleus of Comet 103P/ Hartley as seen during a spacecraft flyby. This nucleus is about 2 km in length.

The astronomical symbol for comets also consists of "a small disc with three hair-like extensions", reflecting the etymology of the word.

FUN FACT

Comets had given rise to some very strong superstitions. Nero, a Roman emperor, took the sighting of a comet as an indication of danger to his life and killed all his surviving successors.

Coma or Tail

The force exerted on the comet by the Sun's radiation, pressure and solar wind causes streams of dust and gas to be released. These form a huge and extremely thin atmosphere called the "coma". As it approaches nearer, an enormous "tail" is formed. This tail points away from the Sun.

Exocomets

Exocomets are comets that have been detected beyond our solar system. They may be common in the Milky Way. The first exocomet system was detected in 1987. It was orbiting around Beta Pictoris, which is a very young type A V star. So far, a total of 11 such exocomet systems have been identified as of 2015. This has been done using the absorption spectrum caused by the large clouds of gas that are emitted by the comets when they pass close to their star.

Two tails?

When a comet moves in space, it forms two distinct tails; one each for the trail of dust and gas. An antitail is formed when a curved tail can be seen in the comet's orbit by the stream of dust that is pointing towards the Sun. While the dust tail points at the Sun, the gas tail points away from it and continues along the lines of the solar wind. This is because it is affected by the magnetic

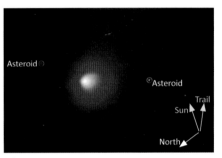

The nucleus of a comet with its two tails pointing in either directions as shown.

field of its plasma. This gas tail takes the shape of the magnetic field instead of the shape of its orbital path. When this phenomena is viewed from Earth, we could end up seeing a comet with two tails pointing in opposite directions because of Parallax.

◀ *A picture that shows the various parts of the comet.*

Dimensions of a coma

Usually, the main body of the comet, also known as the nucleus of the comet, is about 50 km in diameter. However, the tail or the coma following the nucleus could be greater than the size of the Sun itself! In some cases, it has been measured to be 3.8 AU long.

There is an unusual event recorded on 3rd February, 2007, when the Ulysses spacecraft had passed through a comet's tail!

FUN FACT

The meteor shower that we see from Earth is actually the dust trail of a comet. When Earth passes through the orbit of a comet, we see this sparkly meteor shower.

Halley's Comet

Halley's comet or Comet Halley is a short-period comet visible from Earth every 75 – 76 years. It is officially designated as 1P/Halley. Halley's Comet is the only short-period comet that is clearly visible to the naked eye from Earth.

Edmund Halley, the one who discovered Halley's comet.

▲ *Halley's Comet as seen in 1910.*

Pronunciation

Halley's Comet is commonly pronounced "hæli". This rhymes with valley. Another pronunciation is "heili", which rhymes with daily. Spellings of Edmond Halley's name during his lifetime included Hailey, Haley, Hayley, Halley, Hawley and Hawly. As a result, the contemporary pronunciation is uncertain.

Theory of comet orbit

Originally promoted by Aristotle, the philosophical consensus on the nature of comets held that they were disturbances in Earth's atmosphere. Tycho Brahe disproved this idea in 1577. He used parallax (displacement) measurements to show that comets must lie beyond the moon.

Periodic nature of comets

Edmond Halley used Newton's new laws to calculate the gravitational effects of Jupiter and Saturn on cometary orbits. He determined that the orbit of the comet that appeared in 1682 was very similar to the two comets that appeared in 1531. Thus, Halley's Comet became the first comet to be recognised as periodic.

Structure and composition

Planetary scientists got their first view of Halley's surface and structure from the Giotto and Vega missions. Halley's Comet has a nucleus that is relatively small. It is barely 15 km long, eight km wide and around eight km thick. The nucleus' shape

The Giotto Photo of Halley's Comet. ▲

vaguely resembles that of a peanut. The flyby images of Halley's Comet reveal an extremely varied topography. It has hills, mountains, ridges, depressions and at least one crater. Halley's Comet consists of water, carbon monoxide, carbon dioxide and other ices as well as coal.

Comet ISON

Comet ISON was a sun grazing comet discovered on 21st September, 2012, by Vitali Nevski of Vitebsk, Belarus, and Artyom Novichonok of Kondopoga, Russia. The comet was formally known as C/2012 S1. The discovery of this comet was made using the 0.4 m reflector of the International Scientific Optical Network (ISON) near Kislovodsk, Russia. Comet ISON derives its name from this.

Orbit

The ISON comet came to perihelion on 28th November, 2013. It passed at a distance of 0.0124 AU or 1,860,000 km from the centre point of the Sun. ISON's trajectory appeared to be hyperbolic. This suggested that it was a dynamically new comet that was freshly emerging from the Oort cloud.

Brightness and visibility

At the time of its discovery, Comet ISON's apparent magnitude was far too dim to be seen with the naked eye. However, it was bright enough to be viewed by amateurs with large telescopes.

Comet ISON as seen from the Mount Lemmon Sky Centre, 8th October, 2013. ▼

On 14th November, 2013, Comet ISON was reported to be visible to the naked eye. This was true only for experienced observers located at dark sites. On 17th–18th November it was brighter and much closer to the

morning twilight. Unfortunately, due to the full moon and the glow of twilight, it had not become bright enough to be seen without optical aid. By 28th November, it could have become extremely bright if it had remained entirely intact, but it disintegrated.

Media coverage

Some media sources called Comet ISON the "Comet of the Century". They speculated that it may outshine the full moon. Astronomer Karl Battams severely criticised the media's suggestion that Comet ISON would be "brighter than the full moon". The members of the Comet ISON Observing Campaign did not foresee ISON becoming that bright.

FUN FACT

Comet ISON has been compared to Comet Kohoutek, which was seen in 1973 – 74. Both these were highly anticipated Oort cloud comets that peaked early and eventually fizzled out.

Asteroids

Asteroids are minor planets. These are found especially in the inner solar system. The term has historically been applied to any astronomical object orbiting the Sun, but it did not show the disc of a planet and was not observed to have the characteristics of an active comet.

Definition

As minor planets in the outer solar system were discovered, their volatile-based surfaces were found to resemble comets more closely. These were often distinguished from traditional asteroids. Thus, the term asteroid has now come increasingly to refer specifically to "the small bodies of the inner solar system outside of the orbit of Jupiter".

Classification and grouping

Asteroids are grouped with the outer bodies as minor planets. These include centaurs, Neptune Trojans and trans-Neptunian objects. Minor planets is the term currently preferred in astronomical circles. Here, the term "asteroid" is used exclusively to refer to the minor planets of the inner solar system.

Origin

There are millions of asteroids. Many of these are thought to be the shattered remnants of planetesimals. Planetesimals were bodies within the Sun's solar nebula that didn't grow large enough to be classified as planets.

Location

A large majority of known asteroids orbit in the asteroid belt. The belt lies between the orbits of Mars and Jupiter. Some of these are co-orbital with Jupiter. They are referred to as the Jupiter Trojans. However, other orbital families of asteroids exist with significant populations. These include the near-Earth asteroids. Majority of the asteroids fall into three main groups: C-type, S-type and M-type. They are named for their compositions. They are generally identified by carbon-rich, stony and metallic compositions, with the same initials, respectively.

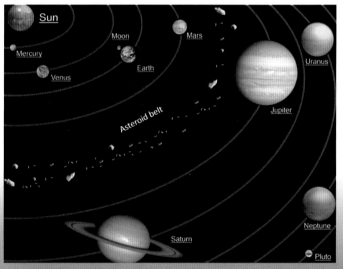

▲ *The asteroid belt that lies between the orbits of Mars and Jupiter.*

FUN FACT

The larger asteroids have also been called planetoids.

◄ *An artist's conception of a planetoid in space. Most asteroids are classified as planetoids.*

Extinction Events due to Asteroids

An extinction event is a widespread and rapid decrease in the amount of life on Earth. It is also known as mass extinction or biotic crisis. The most recent extinction occurred approximately 66 million years ago. This was the Cretaceous – Paleogene extinction event, which was mostly caused by asteroid impact.

FUN FACT

The chemical signature of each asteroid family is significantly different. Their chemical signatures can easily distinguish asteroids families.

An artist's rendition of an impact event: Dinosaurs were killed by the Cretaceous-Paleogene extinction event.

Mechanism on land

The impact of a sufficiently large asteroid or comet could cause food chains to collapse both on land and at sea. It could produce dust and particulate aerosols. These could block sunlight and reduce photosynthesis. Any impacts on sulphur-rich rocks could emit sulphur oxides. These could travel into the atmosphere and precipitate as poisonous acid rain. Large impacts may also cause mega-tsunamis and/or global forest fires.

Sea impacts

Carbon dioxide (CO_2) is present in very large quantities in seawater. However, it is soluble in seawater only below 50 °C. Sea surface temperatures are normally well below 50 °C. However, they will easily exceed that temperature when an asteroid strikes the ocean due to

the induction of a large thermal shock. This would cause very large quantities of CO_2 to erupt from the ocean. As a heavy gas, the CO_2 would quickly spread around the world. It would become present in concentrations sufficient to suffocate air-breathing fauna. Due to its weight, this would occur selectively at low altitudes.

Cretaceous – Paleogene extinction

The Cretaceous – Paleogene or K – Pg or Chicxulub impact is the most widely accepted candidate for the mentioned mass extinction event. A 2007 hypothesis argued that the impact actually belonged to the Baptistina family of asteroids. In 2010, another hypothesis implicated the newly discovered asteroid P/2010 A2, a member of the Flora family of asteroids, to be a remnant of the Chicxulub cohort.

A representation of the impact that will cause the mass extinction of life on Earth.

Kuiper Belt

The Kuiper belt is a region of the solar system beyond the planets. It extends from the orbit of Neptune to approximately 50 AU from the Sun. It is sometimes called the "Edgeworth – Kuiper belt".

Composition

The Kuiper belt mainly consists of small bodies that are remnants from the solar system's formation. Unlike most asteroids that are composed primarily of rock and metal, most Kuiper belt objects are composed largely of frozen volatiles. These are termed as "ices", such as those of methane, ammonia and water.

Dwarf planets

The Kuiper belt is home to at least three dwarf planets, namely Pluto, Haumea and Makemake. Neptune's moon Triton and Saturn's moon Phoebe are some of the solar system's moons that have originated in the region.

How it got its name

The Kuiper belt was named after Dutch-American astronomer Gerard Kuiper. Since its discovery in 1992, the number of known Kuiper belt objects, or KBOs, has increased to over a thousand. More than 100,000 KBOs over a 100 km in diameter exist.

An artist's conception of the view from the Kuiper belt.

An academic vector illustration showing the Kuiper belt's location.

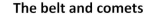

The belt and comets

The Kuiper belt was thought to be the main repository for periodic comets, whose orbits lasted less than 200 years. Studies since mid-1990s show that it is dynamically stable. The comets' place of origin is the disc, which is a dynamically active zone. The outward motion of Neptune 4.5 billion years ago created the disc.

FUN FACT

The Kuiper belt is similar to the asteroid belt. However, it is far larger, being 20 times as wide and 20 to 200 times as massive.

Meteorites

Meteorites are fragments of rock and/or metal that fall from space to Earth. Meteorites break away from large extraterrestrial bodies. They can measure anything from a fraction of a millimetre to the size of a football pitch and bigger. Captured by Earth's gravitational force, they are accelerated to speeds of over 11.2 km per second. As they enter Earth's thick atmosphere, they rapidly slow down due to the friction and glow, moving across the sky like a flash of light, before finally crashing to the ground.

View of the planet Earth from space during a meteorite impact.

Where are meteorites found?

There are many meteorites that are seen hitting the ground. Most of them fall into the sea. However, thousands of new meteorites are found each year. Meteorites can be found all over the world, but are easiest to spot in dry places, such as deserts, where they do not erode quickly and are less likely to be hidden by vegetation.

Where do they come from?

Most meteorites are fragments that have broken away as two asteroids collide. Asteroids are irregular-shaped rocks that orbit the Sun. There are thousands of asteroids in our solar system, most in an orbit between Mars and Jupiter, known as the asteroid belt. A small proportion of meteorites come from the moon and the planet Mars. These meteorites are much younger than those from asteroids, some as young as 2,500 million and 180 million years old, respectively.

Space rocks on Earth

At 60 tonnes, the Hoba meteorite found at Namibia is the heaviest meteorite rock to have been found by humans. It is estimated that it had fallen to Earth as recent as 800,000 years ago. Since it is flat, it is said that when it did fall to Earth, it skipped across the surface, much like a stone skipping across water.

Iron meteorite Gibeon from Namibia. ▼

Hoba meteorite - the largest meteorite ever found. ▼

Meteoroids and Meteors

A meteoroid is a small, rocky or metallic body travelling through space. They are significantly smaller than asteroids and range in size from small grains to one-metre wide objects.

A meteorite trail near Chelyabinsk, Russia.

Space dust

Objects that are smaller than 1 m are classified as micrometeoroids or space dust. Most meteoroids are fragments from comets or asteroids, while others are collision impact debris ejected from bodies such as the moon or Mars.

Shooting stars

A meteor or a "shooting star" is the passage of a meteoroid or micrometeoroid into Earth's atmosphere. Here, it becomes incandescent from air friction and starts shedding glowing material in its wake. This is sufficient to create a visible streak of light.

Location and etymology

Meteors typically occur in the mesosphere. This is at altitudes between 76 and 100 km from Earth's surface. The root word of meteor comes from the Greek "meteōros", which means "high in the air".

Mechanism

When an object enters Earth's atmosphere at a speed above 20 km per second, it rubs against the atmosphere. Aerodynamic heating produces a streak of light, both from the glowing object as well as the trail of glowing particles that it leaves in its wake.

Meteorite

Incoming objects that are larger than several metres, such as asteroids or comets, can explode in the air. If a meteoroid, comet, asteroid or any piece thereof withstands the wear from its atmospheric entry and impacts the ground, it is called a meteorite.

Frequency

Millions of meteors arrive in Earth's atmosphere daily. Most of them are about the size of a grain of sand. Meteors may occur in showers. These arise when Earth passes through a stream of debris left by a comet. They also arise as "random" or "sporadic" meteors. These are not associated with a specific stream of space debris.

▼ *A star trail image of meteors during meteor showers.*

FUN FACT

The observation of many amateur astronomers has allowed us to classify and distinguish between various meteor showers.

Meteor Shower

A meteor shower is "a celestial event in which a number of meteors are observed to radiate or originate from one point in the night sky". Streams of cosmic debris called meteoroids enter Earth's atmosphere at extremely high speeds, causing meteors. The IAU's Task Group on Meteor Shower Nomenclature as well as the IAU's Meteor Data Centre keeps track of meteor shower names.

Dust trail

A meteor shower is caused by an interaction between a planet such as Earth and streams of debris from a comet. Comets can produce debris by water vapour drag. Fred Whipple first demonstrated this in 1951. Each time a comet swings by the Sun in its orbit, some of its ice vaporises and a certain amount of meteoroids are shed. These meteoroids spread out along the entire orbit of the comet to form a meteoroid stream. This stream is also known as a "dust trail". This is distinguished from a comet's dust tail, which is caused by the very small particles that are quickly blown away by solar radiation pressure.

Etymology

Meteor showers are named after the nearest constellation or bright star. A Greek or Roman letter is assigned to the name of the constellation that is close to the radiant position at the peak of the shower. Then, the grammatical declension of the Latin possessive verb form is replaced by "id" or "ids". For example, meteors radiating from near the star delta Aquarii, whose declension is "-i", are called delta Aquariids.

Radiant drift

▲ *A four-hour time lapse photo of the leonids showing the shower from space.*

Meteor shower particles are all travelling in parallel paths at the same velocity. Thus, they all appear to an observer to radiate away from a single point in the sky. This "radiant point" is the effect of perspective.

This apparent "fixed point" slowly moves across the sky during the night. This is due to Earth turning on its axis. It is also the same reason that the stars appear to slowly march across the sky. The radiant also moves slightly from night to night against the background stars due to Earth revolving in its orbit around the Sun. This is termed as the radiant drift.

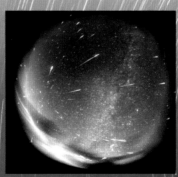

▲ *A meteor shower captured through a telescope.*

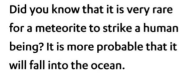

FUN FACT

Did you know that it is very rare for a meteorite to strike a human being? It is more probable that it will fall into the ocean.

Quadrantids

The Quadrantids, or QUA, are a January meteor shower. The Zenithal Hourly Rate (the number of meteors a single observer would see during an hour of peak activity) of this shower is often as high as that of two other reliably rich meteor showers — the Perseids in August and Geminids in December. However, these meteors are not seen as often as meteors in the other two showers. This is because the peak intensity is exceedingly sharp, it sometimes lasts only hours.

Intensity

The meteor rates exceed one-half of their highest value for about eight hours as compared to August Perseids, which do so for two days. Physically, this means that the stream of particles that produces this shower is narrow. Apparently, it has been deriving within the last 500 years from some other orbiting body.

Parent body

Peter Jenniskens tentatively identified the parent body of the Quadrantids in 2003 as the minor planet 2003 EH1. This minor planet may in turn be related to the comet C/1490 Y1. Chinese, Japanese and Korean astronomers observed this some 500 years ago, fitting the timeline.

A camera trick shot of a meteor shower.

Radiant point

The radiant point of the Quadrantids is an area inside the constellation Boötes, and not far from the Big Dipper. It lies "between the end of the handle of the Big Dipper and the quadrilateral of stars marking the head of the constellation Draco", as described by amateur skygazers and astronomers.

Etymology

The name Quadrantids comes from Quadrans Muralis, a former constellation created in 1795 by French astronomer Jérôme Lalande. It is now a part of Boötes. In January 1825, Antonio Brucalassi in Italy reported, "the atmosphere was traversed by a multitude of luminous bodies known by the name of falling stars".

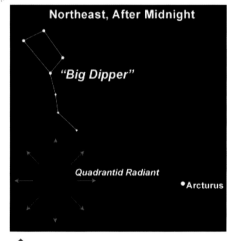

The radiant point of Quadrantid meteor shower, as seen next to the Big Dipper in this diagram.

These meteors appeared to radiate from Quadrans Muralis. In 1839, Adolphe Quetelet of Brussels Observatory, Belgium, and Edward C. Herrick of Connecticut, USA, independently suggested that the Quadrantids are an annual shower.

FUN FACT

When the IAU devised a list of 88 modern constellations in 1922, it did not include the constellation Quadrans Muralis. Therefore, the IAU officially adopted this list in 1930, but this meteor shower still retains the name Quadrantids, based on the original and now-obsolete constellation.

Leonids

The Leonids are a prolific meteor shower. They are associated with the comet Tempel-Tuttle. When this comet debris enters Earth's atmosphere and vaporises we see the Leonid meteor shower. They peak in the month of November. They occur when Earth passes through the debris left by the comet Tempel-Tuttle. The comet takes around 33 years to make one orbit around the Sun. People can view about 20 meteors an hour at the peak of the Leonids meteor shower.

A camera trick shot of the Leonid meteor shower.

Naming

The Leonids get their name from the location of their radiant, which lies in the constellation Leo. Meteors appear to radiate from that point in the sky. Their proper Greek name should be "Leontids". However, the word was initially constructed as a Greek or Latin hybrid based on its structure. It has been in use ever since.

Mechanism

Earth moves through the meteoroid stream of particles left from the passages of a comet during its revolution around the Sun. This stream comprises solid particles, known as meteoroids, ejected by the comet as its frozen gases evaporate under the heat of the Sun when it is sufficiently close enough, which means it is closer than Jupiter's orbit. The Leonids are a fast-moving stream. They encounter the path of Earth at an average of 72 km per second. Larger Leonids, namely those which are about 10 mm across, have a mass of half a gram. These are known for generating bright meteors.

Scientific background

The meteoroids left by the comet are organised in trails in orbits that are similar to that of the comet. The planets, in particular Jupiter, differentially disturb them. They are disturbed to a less extent by radiation pressure from the Sun. This is known as the Poynting – Robertson effect as well as the Yarkovsky effect.

Frequency

Old trails are spatially not dense and compose the meteor shower with a few meteors per minute. In case of the Leonids, density tends to peak around 18th November. However, some are spread through several days on either side of the peak and the specific peak changes every year.

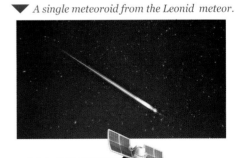

A single meteoroid from the Leonid meteor.

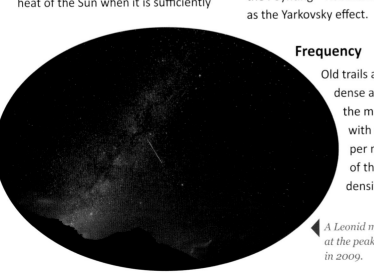

A Leonid meteor as seen at the peak of the shower in 2009.

FUN FACT

An annual Leonid shower may deposit over 12 or 13 tonnes of particles across the entire surface of the planet.

Lyrids

The April Lyrids, or LYR, are a meteor shower that lasts from 16th April to 26th April each year. It is designated as IAU shower number 6. The radiant of this meteor shower is located in the constellation Lyra. It is near the constellation's brightest star, Alpha Lyrae, that is also known as Vega. Their peak is typically around 22nd April each year.

Origin

The source of the shower is particles of dust shed by the long-period comet, C/1861 G1 Thatcher. April Lyrids are the strongest annual meteor shower from the debris of a long-period comet. This is mainly because compared to other intermediate long-period comets, they have a relatively short orbital period of about 415 years. The Lyrids have been observed for the past 2600 years.

Peak and observable meteorites

Meteor showers typically range from five to 20 meteors per hour. Some meteors can be fairly bright. These are known as "Lyrid fireballs". These fireballs cast shadows for a split second and leave behind smoky debris trails that can last for minutes.

Notable Lyrid observations

A strong storm of up to 700 meteors per hour occurred in 1803. This was observed by a journalist based in Richmond, Virginia:

"Shooting stars. This electrical [sic] phenomenon was observed on Wednesday morning last at Richmond and its vicinity, in a manner that alarmed many, and astonished every person that beheld it. From one until three in the morning, those starry meteors seemed to fall from every point in the heavens, in such numbers as to resemble a shower of sky rockets ..."

Another such outburst is the oldest known. The Lyrid shower on 23rd March in 687 BCE was recorded in ZuoZhuan. The shower is described as "On day xīn-mao of month 4 in the summer (of year 7 of King Zhuang of Lu), at night, fixed stars are invisible and at midnight, the stars dropped down like rain".

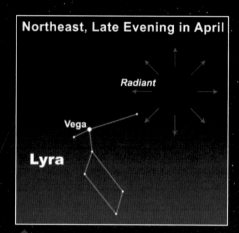

Northeast, Late Evening in April

Radiant

Vega

Lyra

The radiant point of the April Lyrid meteor shower, as seen next to Vega in this diagram.

The April Lyrid meteor shower.

FUN FACT

Skygazers have been blessed with the sight of as many as 100 Lyrid meteors per hour as happened in America, 1982.

Oort Cloud

The Oort cloud or Öpik – Oort cloud is a spherical cloud of predominantly, icy planetesimals that are believed to surround the Sun at a distance of up to 50,000 AU. It is named after Dutch astronomer Jan Oort and Estonian astronomer Ernst Öpik. It is thought to comprise mainly two regions: a spherical outer Oort cloud and a disc-shaped inner Oort cloud. The inner cloud is also called the Hills cloud.

Origin

The original proto-planetary disc, which came to be formed around the Sun approximately 4.6 billion years ago, could be the origin of the Oort cloud. It is widely accepted that the Oort cloud's objects initially assembled much closer to the Sun. The planets and asteroids were formed due to the same process. However, they were pulled into long elliptical or parabolic orbits due to the gravity of young gaseous giant planets like Jupiter.

Other theories

Recent research by NASA hypothesises that a large number of Oort cloud objects are the product of an exchange of materials between the Sun and its sibling stars. This exchange occurred as they formed and drifted apart. It is currently suggested that most Oort cloud objects were not formed in close proximity to the Sun. NASA simulations on the evolution of the Oort cloud, starting from the beginning of the solar system to the present, suggest that the cloud's mass peaked around 800 million years after its formation. At this point, the pace of accretion and collision slowed, and depletion began to overtake supply.

A schematic diagram of the structure of the Oort cloud.

Hypothesis and discovery

Estonian astronomer Ernst Öpik postulated in 1932 that long-period comets must have originated in an orbiting cloud at the outermost edge of the solar system. Oort independently revived this idea as a means to resolve a paradox about comets. Oort reasoned that a comet could not have formed while in its current orbit. Thus, it must have been held in an outer reservoir for most of its existence.

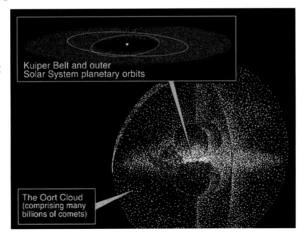

Kuiper Belt and outer Solar System planetary orbits

The Oort Cloud (comprising many billions of comets)

An artist's rendering of the Oort cloud and Kuiper belt. ▶

Oort's paradox

The orbits of comets are unstable over the course of the solar system's existence. Dynamics dictate that a comet must eventually either collide with the Sun, a planet or be ejected from the solar system by planetary perturbations. Moreover, a comet's volatile composition means that as they repeatedly approach the Sun, radiation gradually boils the volatiles off. This keeps occurring until the comet either splits or develops an insulating crust that prevents further outgassing. This was not possible in the solar system itself. Thus, comets existing solely in the solar system were paradoxical.

Space Debris

Space debris is the collection of defunct objects in orbit around Earth. It is also popularly known as orbital debris, space junk and space waste. Space debris include spent rocket stages, old satellites and fragments from disintegration, erosion and collisions. As their orbits overlap with new spacecrafts, debris may collide with operational spacecrafts and pose a significant hazard.

Magnitude of the problem

As of 2009, about 19,000 pieces of debris larger than 5 cm are being tracked. There are over 300,000 pieces larger than 1 cm that are estimated to exist below the 2000 km altitude. For a standard of comparison, the International Space Station orbits in the 300 – 400 km range. Both the 2009 collision and 2007 anti-satellite test events occurred at between 800 and 900 km.

Size and origin

Most space debris are smaller than 1 cm. They include the following:

● dust from solid rocket motors

● products of surface degradation, such as paint flakes

● frozen coolant droplets that are released from RORSAT nuclear-powered satellites

▲ *A comparatively big piece of space debris, measuring about 5 cm.*

Hazards posed

Impacts of debris particles cause erosive damage in a manner similar to sandblasting. Damage can be reduced by the addition of ballistic shielding to the spacecraft. An example is a "whipple shield", which is used to protect some parts of the International Space Station.

The number of objects in space influence the chance of collision. Thus, there is a critical density where the creation of new debris is theorised to occur faster than the various natural forces that remove them.

▲ *Space debris in Earth's orbit.*

Kessler syndrome

Beyond this critical density, a runaway chain reaction may occur, known as the "Kessler syndrome". This would rapidly increase the number of debris objects in orbit. It would, therefore, greatly increase the risk to operate satellites.

Repercussions

The Kessler syndrome would make it difficult to use the polar-orbiting bands. The cost of space missions would increase greatly. Hence, measurement, growth mitigation and removal of debris are activities that are taken seriously within the space industry today.

FUN FACT

Astronomers debate if the critical density has already been reached in certain orbital bands due to the sheer mass of debris present in them.

▶ *An artist's conception of an orbital band of garbage and junk circling Earth.*

STARS

▲ *An artist's representation of the stars and constellations in a clear sky at twilight.*

Stars are described as large, hot and flaming balls of gas. The star most familiar to us is the Sun. However, stars are not really made up of gas. They are massive, luminous spheres of plasma.

They are held together due to their own gravity, which gives them their characteristic spherical shape. The sphere minimises the area of the star's surface to a given mass.

Thus, it is the most efficient way for gravity to arrange the star's mass.

They originate with the gravitational collapse of a gaseous nebula. They are primarily composed of hydrogen, along with helium and trace amounts of heavier elements.

Life Cycle of a Star

Stars are born in a nebula. Huge clouds of dust and gas collapse under gravitational forces, forming proto-stars. These young stars undergo a further collapse, forming main sequence stars. They expand as they grow old. As the core exhausts its hydrogen and then helium, it contracts and the outer layers expand, cool and become less bright. This is a red giant or a red super giant, depending on the initial mass of the star. It will finally collapse and explode. Depending on the original mass of the star, it will either become a black dwarf, neutron star or black hole.

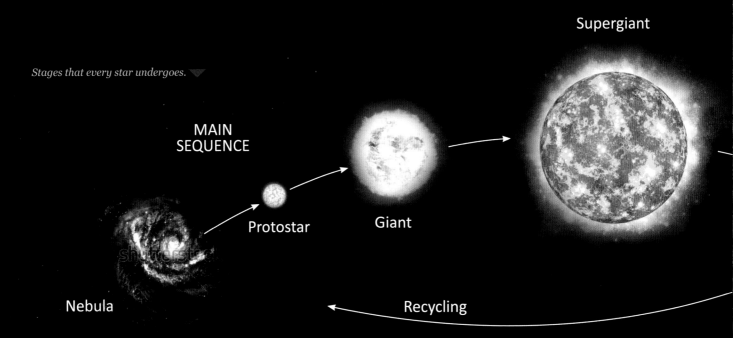

Stages that every star undergoes. ▼

Supergiant

MAIN SEQUENCE

Protostar

Giant

Nebula

Recycling

1. The Sun

It is a main sequence star. Hydrogen is converted into helium in the centre through nuclear fusion. Light and heat energy are produced during this process. The Sun has been doing this for more than 4.5 billion years. This process will continue for another five billion years or more. As it progresses and matures, it will move on from its current stage into a new one. This process will lead to a change in its appearance as it has been doing so all this while.

2. Main sequence stars

All stars pass through the main sequence stage. Most of them spend the majority of their lives as main sequence stars. These stars come in a variety of masses, sizes, colours and luminosity. Altair is a main sequence star and is about 1.6 times the diameter of the Sun.

3. Giants and supergiants

After a star leaves the main sequence, its core contracts and heats up. Burning hydrogen ignites in a shell around the centre, causing the envelope to expand, but as it does, it cools. The cooler, but bigger star becomes redder and more luminous. Eventually, the temperature at the core reaches 100 million degrees and burning helium ignites in the core. The star, at this point, has a surface temperature of about 3200 °C and a radius equal to Mercury's orbit. It has now transformed into a red giant.

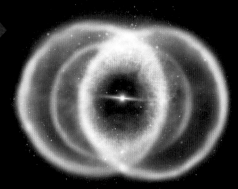

The cat's eye nebula is so called because the intersection of the two halos formed by the nebula looks like a cat's eye. Astronomers suspect that this is a twin star.

6. Cat's eye nebula

Three thousand light years away, the Cat's eye nebula is a dying star that throws off shells of glowing gas. Research reveals that this nebula is one of the most complex planetary nebulae known. In fact, the features seen here are so complex that it leads astronomers to suspect that the bright central object may in fact be a binary star system. The term planetary nebula is misleading. Although these objects may appear round and planet-like in small telescopes, high-resolution images reveal that they are stars surrounded by cocoons of gas blown off in the later stages of stellar evolution.

7. Red rectangle nebula

The Red Rectangle Nebula, also known as HD 44179, is so called because of its red colour and unique rectangular shape. It is a bipolar, proto-planetary nebula, which is located about 2,300 light years away towards the constellation Monoceros. Proto-planetary nebulas are formed by old stars, which are in the process of becoming planetary nebulae. In a few thousand years, once the expulsion of mass is complete, a very hot, white dwarf star will remain and its luminous ultraviolet radiation will cause the surrounding gas to glow. The star at the centre of this nebula known as MWC 922, was similar to our Sun, but is now ejecting its outer layers to create the nebula, giving it the distinctive shape. The shedding of the outer layers began about 14,000 years ago and is ejected from the star in opposite directions.

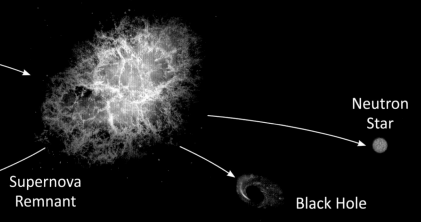

Type II Supernova

Neutron Star

Supernova Remnant

Black Hole

4. White dwarfs

These are the burned-out cores of collapsed stars that, like dying embers, slowly cool and fade away. They are the leftovers of low mass stars, among the dimmest objects observable in the universe. They are low to medium main sequence stars, which burned through their reservoirs of both hydrogen and helium. Then, they passed through the giant phase and were not sufficiently hot to ignite their carbon, puffing off their outer layers to form colourful planetary nebula. They finally collapsed

5. The ant nebula

Ant Nebula, also known as Menzel 3, or Mz 3, is a young bipolar planetary nebula about two light years in diameter, which is radially expanding at a rate of about 50 km per second. It is located some 8000 light years away in the constellation Norma. It gets its name because it resembles the head and thorax of an ant. The nebula has arguably the most complex bipolar morphology, consisting of a bright core, three nested pairs of bipolar lobes and an equatorial ellipse.

Star Quality

There are billions of stars, including the Sun, in the Milky Way. Quiet interestingly, there are billions of galaxies in the universe. So far, we have learned that hundreds of stars also have planets orbiting them. Since the beginning of civilisation, stars have played a significant role in religion and have proven to be crucial to navigation. Astronomy, the study of the heavens, may be the most ancient of the sciences.

1. Colour and temperature

A star's colour is determined by its temperature. Its colour keeps changing with changes in its temperature. An early schema from the 19th century ranked stars from A to P. After several transformations, the classification includes seven main types today: O, B, A, F, G, K and M. These are further classified based on colours. Blue stars 30,000 – 60,000 K, blue-white stars 30,000 – 54,000 K, white stars 11,000 – 19,800 K, yellow-white stars 7,500 – 13,500 K, yellow stars 6,000 – 10,800 K, orange stars 5,000 ¬ 9,000 K and red stars 4,000 – 7,200 K.

2. Gravity and pressure

A star's gravity pulls the star's gas towards its centre. Simultaneously, the pressure of the dense core pushes out the material. The two forces balance each other, maintaining the star's size. Most of the stars are almost spherical, though the rapid spinning makes them bulge around the equator. When two stars are in close proximity, their shapes are distorted due to gravity pulling one to the other.

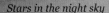

Stars in the night sky

3. Luminosity

Luminosity is the total amount of energy that is emitted by a star, galaxy or other astronomical object. It is related to the brightness of an object in a given spectral region. The most luminous stars emit more than six million times the Sun's light and the least luminous ones emit less than one ten-thousandth of it. It is an indication of a star's actual brightness as viewed from Earth. If the Sun was at a further distance, it would be dimmer, although it would still have the same luminosity.

Rigel, the star larger than our Sun.

4. Star size

Stars come in different sizes. The smallest stars, also called M-type stars or M stars are massive enough to initiate nuclear fusion in their core. If they were smaller, they would be brown dwarfs, yet many times bigger than the biggest planet in our solar system, Jupiter. The smallest stars out there are the tiny red dwarfs. These are stars with not more than 50 per cent of the mass of the Sun and they can have as little as 7.5 per cent its mass. This is the minimum mass required for a star to be able to support nuclear fusion in its core. An example of a star larger than our Sun is the blue supergiant Rigel in the constellation Orion. This is a star with 17 times the mass of the Sun, which puts out 66,000 times as much energy. Rigel is estimated to be 62 times as big as the Sun.

5. Rotation

Stars rotate around themselves at a high speed. The younger they are, the faster they spin. The B-class star Acherner spins as fast as 225 km per second. This is very close to 300 km per second when a star will disintegrate as its mass will get flung outwards in all directions. The Acherner gets its shape because of its high rotation. Its equator has been pushed outwards and is twice the size of its circumference around the poles. The Sun also rotates, however, at a stable rate of about 2 km per second.

Black Holes

We've seen that medium stars die off by fading into black dwarfs, and giants and supergiants explode into supernovas. But it is interesting to know that this explosion doesn't really dissipate all the matter of the star. In fact, while most of the mass of the star is blown away, the rest forms a core. Depending on the size of the core, it behaves differently.

Pre-conditions for black holes

Most giants form a neutron star that manifests as a pulsar or X-ray burster. The largest stars, however, can leave a core larger than four times the mass of the Sun. These form black holes. A black hole is mathematically defined as a region of space so dense that nothing can escape its gravitational field.

Origin of theory

The idea of black holes was proposed in the theory of relativity written by Einstein. This theory predicts that a sufficiently compact mass will distort space-time to form a black hole. However, the idea originated when John Michell first put the idea of a body so massive that even light could not escape, in a letter written to Henry Cavendish in 1783.

He quoted, "If the semi-diameter of a sphere of the same density as the Sun were to exceed that of the Sun in the proportion of 500 to one, a body falling from an infinite height towards it would have acquired at its surface greater velocity than that of light, and consequently supposing light to be attracted by the same force in proportion to its visinertiae, with other bodies, all light emitted from such a body would be made to return towards it by its own proper gravity".

An artist's impression of an accretion disc. An accretion disc is formed due to the heating of matter as it enters the black hole and would be a very bright phenomenon that would be visible through instruments, if not the naked eye.

Black holes and relativity

In 1916, Karl Schwarzschild found the first modern solution of general relativity that would characterise a black hole. However, until the 1960s, black holes were considered as a mathematical curiosity. They were something that mathematics predicted the existence of, but did not have any proof of its existence. The discovery of neutron stars generated interest in gravitationally collapsed compact objects as a possible reality in astrophysics.

Many spiral galaxies may have black holes at their centre.

The Milky Way has a massive

A black hole keeps sucking in light as well as everything that lies within its gravitational reach. ▶

black hole at the centre with a mass 4.6 million times that of the Sun.

Observing black holes

Due to the fact that nothing escapes the field of a black hole, including light, X-rays, radio waves and other forms of electromagnetic radiation, they are very hard to detect. Black holes must be detected by their interactions with the rest of the universe. Once stabilised, they have three basic independent properties: mass, charge and angular momentum. These are also the properties that can be used to detect them externally. The simplest static black holes have only mass, but neither electric charge nor angular momentum. They are commonly referred to as Schwarzschild black holes after Karl Schwarzschild.

Event horizon

The defining feature of a black hole is the appearance of an event horizon. The event horizon is a boundary in space-time through which matter and light can only pass inward towards the black hole. Nothing, not even light, can escape from within the event horizon. The boundary is named as an event horizon because no information about an event occurring inside this horizon will pass outside. Thus, all events within it have an information horizon.

Distorting space-time

An interesting thing about black holes is a by-product of their distortion of time and space. They tend to warp the space around them as well as cause time dilation, where time passes slower and slower as you get closer to the black hole. As a result, they may create wormholes that allow faster-than-light time travel.

A diagrammatic representation of the fabric of time with a wormhole that can allow time travel faster than the speed of light. ▶

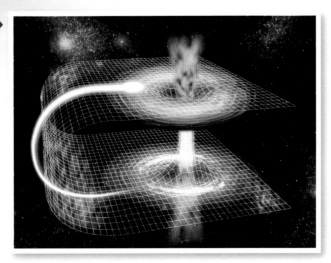

FUN FACT

Did you know that you cannot see a black hole directly?

Nova

A nova and supernova are both bright events in the sky that are generally visible during the night to the naked eye. Until very recently, they were used very interchangeably. However, recent discoveries have found that the two have completely different causes.

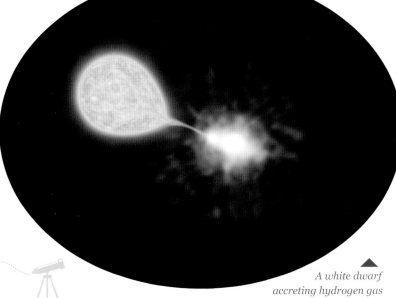

A white dwarf accreting hydrogen gas from a red giant star that has moved too close to its orbit.

Origin

Tycho Brahe coined the term "nova" after observing the supernova SN 1572 in the constellation Cassiopeia in the sixteenth century. He described it in his book *De Stella nova*, which is Latin for "concerning the new star". It was from here that the term nova was coined, though strictly speaking, the observed event was a supernova.

Cataclysmic nuclear explosion

A nova is a cataclysmic nuclear explosion on a white dwarf. A nova is caused by the accretion of hydrogen onto the surface of the star. Due to the closeness, hydrogen accumulates on the surface of a white dwarf in a binary system, after being bled off from the larger star. It then ignites and starts nuclear fusion in a raging manner.

Mechanism

The gases are compacted on the white dwarf's surface by its intense gravity, compressed and heated to very high temperatures as additional material is drawn in. As the white dwarf is dying and composed of degenerate matter, it does not absorb the material and inflate — as another star like the Sun would.

For most binary system parameters, the hydrogen burning is thermally unstable once it has reached the required fusion temperatures. As a result, it rapidly converts a large amount of the hydrogen into other heavier elements in a runaway reaction. This liberates an enormous amount of energy, blowing the remaining gases away from the white dwarf's surface and producing an extremely bright outburst of light.

Nova Eridani 2009 as seen on the night of a full moon.

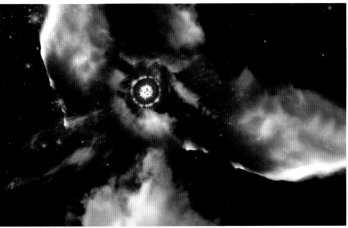

A nova as represented by an artist.

FUN FACT

Astronomers estimate that the Milky Way experiences roughly 30 to 60 novae per year. Few novae like the RS Ophiuchi recur every few decades and are relatively rare.

Supernova

A supernova is a stellar explosion that briefly outshines an entire galaxy. The amount of energy that is radiated is as much as the Sun or any ordinary star is expected to emit over its entire lifespan, but over a brief burst. The supernova fades from view over a period of weeks or months.

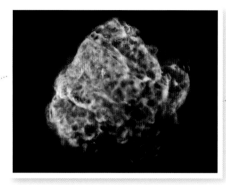

Remnants of a supernova continue to be bright for a while. Most gas clouds are formed by supernova events.

Earliest observation and discovery

The earliest recorded supernova was SN 185, which was viewed by Chinese astronomers in 185 AD. SN 1006 is the brightest recorded supernova in human history. Earlier, supernovae were considered as a brighter form of novae. Walter Baade and Fritz Zwicky at Mount Wilson Observatory did early work on what was originally believed to be simply a new category of novae. The term "super-novae" was first used during 1931 lectures held at Caltech by this pair. The hyphen had been lost and the modern name was in use by 1938.

Rare events

Supernovae are relatively rare events within a galaxy, occurring about thrice in a century in the Milky Way. Supernovae cannot be predicted with any meaningful accuracy and must be observed in progress. Thus, both amateurs and professionals conduct extensive supernova searching. Supernova searches fall mainly into two classes: those searches focussed on relatively nearby events and those looking for explosions farther away.

Format

Supernova discoveries are reported to the IAU's Central Bureau for Astronomical Telegrams. The name of a supernova is in the following format: SN followed by the year of discovery, suffixed with a one or two-letter designation.

Classification

Supernovae are classified as follows:

Type	Average peak absolute magnitude	Approximate energy (foe)	Days to peak luminosity	Days from peak to 10% luminosity
Ia	−19	1	approx. 19	around 60
Ib/c (faint)	around −15	0.1	15 − 25	unknown
Ib	around −17	1	15 − 25	40 − 100
Ic	around −16	1	15 − 25	40 − 100
Ic (bright)	to −22	above 5	roughly 25	roughly 100
II-b	around −17	1	around 20	around 100
II-L	around −17	1	around 13	around 50
II-P (faint)	around −14	0.1	roughly 15	unknown
II-P	around −16	1	around 15	Plateau then around 50
IInd	around −17	1	12 − 30 or more	50 − 150
IIn (bright)	to −22	above 5	above 50	above 100

Extreme Helium Star

Most stars consist of hydrogen as their primary component. However, there are certain stars that are extremely low or almost devoid of hydrogen. This category of stars is termed as "hydrogen-deficient stars".

Hydrogen deficient stars

Cool carbon stars like R Coronae Borealis, helium-rich spectral class O or B stars, population I Wolf-Rayet stars, AM CVn stars, white dwarfs of spectral type WC and transition stars like PG 1159 are all hydrogen deficient. An extreme helium star, often abbreviated as "EH", is a low-mass supergiant that is almost devoid of hydrogen.

Discovery

Daniel M. Popper discovered the first known extreme helium star at the McDonald Observatory in Austin, USA, in 1942. By 1996, 25 possible helium stars were identified. This was further narrowed to 21 by 2006. Extreme helium stars are characterised as those that displays no lines of hydrogen in their spectrum, but strong helium lines as well as the presence of carbon and oxygen.

Size and composition

The known extreme helium stars are "supergiants". Hydrogen is less abundant by a factor of 10,000 or more,

and surface temperatures range from 9,000 – 35,000 K. There are two popular theories as to how these stars are formed and why they have their unique composition.

The double-degenerate (DD) model:
This explains stars forming in a binary system. It has a small helium white dwarf and a more massive carbon – oxygen white dwarf. Gravity causes them to collide and form a dwarf that ignites into a supergiant.

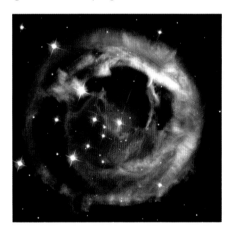

The final-flash (FF) model:
It says that helium ignites in a shell around the core, causing the dwarf to rapidly expand.

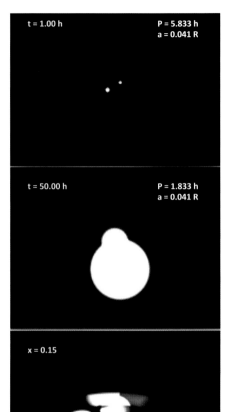

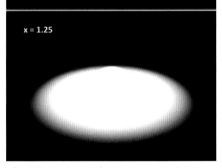

▲ *The various stages as postulated by the DD model – from the binary star to the EHe.*

An image of an extreme helium star *being formed in the galaxy.*

FUN FACT

It must be noted that the composition of examined EHes matches those predicted by the DD theory.

Red Giant

A red giant is a luminous giant star of low or intermediate mass. Its mass usually ranges between 0.3 to eight times that of our Sun. These stars are usually in a very late phase of stellar evolution. Red giants have radii tens to hundreds of times larger than that of the Sun. Their outer envelope is lower in temperature, about 5,000 K and below.

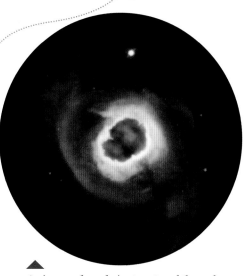

An image of a red giant captured through a thermal imaging telescope.

Formation

When a star initially forms from a collapsing molecular cloud in the interstellar medium, it primarily contains hydrogen and helium, with trace amounts of "metals", i.e., any element heavier than helium. When the star exhausts the hydrogen fuel in its core, nuclear reactions can no longer continue, and thus the core begins contracting due to its own gravity. This causes the remaining hydrogen to undergo fusion in a shell around the core at a faster rate. The outer layers of the star then expand greatly. This begins the red giant phase of a star's life.

Colour and naming

Since the expansion of the star greatly increases its surface area, red giants tend to be cooler and burn with an orange hue. Despite their name, they are closer to orange in reality. The M-type stars HD 208527, HD 220074 and K-giants including Pollux, Gamma Cephei and Iota Draconis are some examples of red giants with planets.

Life around red giants

It has traditionally been suggested that life could not evolve on planets orbiting them. However, current research suggests that there would be a habitable zone at twice the distance from Earth to Sun for a billion years. At a distance of nine AU, such a habitable zone would only exist for 100 million years. As of June 2014, 50 giant planets have been discovered around giant stars. These giants are much larger than those found around sun-sized stars.

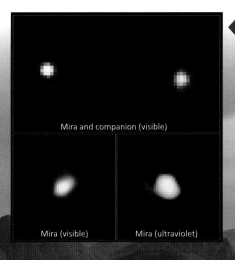

Mira and companion (visible)

Mira (visible)

Mira (ultraviolet)

The bright yellow dot in the top left corner is a star the size of the Sun. It serves as a comparison to show how big a red giant could be.

An artist's conception of a red giant at sunset on one of its orbiting worlds.

VY Canis Major

VY Canis Majoris or VY CMa is a red hypergiant star. It is located in the constellation Canis Major. It is one of the largest and brightest red hypergiants observed so far. It has a diameter of 1800 solar radii. This star emits energy very quickly and therefore, only exists for a few million years. It is estimated to be 4900 light years away from Earth. This star shows periodic light changes that last for approximately 2200 days.

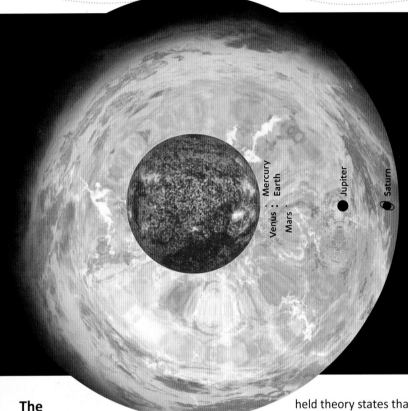

VY CANIS MAJORIS
RADIUS: 1.5 BILLION KM

Mercury
Earth
Venus
Mars
Jupiter
Saturn
Uranus
Neptune

A comparison of planets in our solar system to the VY Canis Majoris.

The crimson star

The first known recorded observation of VY Canis Majoris is in the star catalogue of Jérôme Lalande, who recorded it on 7th March, 1801. Since 1847, VY CMa has been known to be a crimson star. Originally, University of Minnesota Professor Roberta M. Humphreys approximated that the radius of VY CMa is 1800 – 2100 times that of the Sun. This would make it the largest known star based on its radius.

A big star

There have been conflicting opinions of the properties of VY CMa. A commonly held theory states that the star is a very large and luminous red hypergiant. However, various larger estimates of the size and luminosity fall outside the bounds of current stellar theory. In another theory, the star is a normal red supergiant, with a radius around 600 times that of our Sun.

Surface of VY CMa

This star also illustrates the conceptual problem of defining the "surface" of very large stars. This is very important for multiple reasons, including determining its radius and thus its size. It is a hundred thousand times less dense than the atmosphere of Earth (air) at sea level. Its average density is 0.000005 to 0.000010 kg per m³. Additionally, the star is constantly losing mass at an astounding rate. The boundary of such a star is usually defined by its "Rosseland Radius", which is based on its opaqueness to light.

The brightest point is VY Canis Majoris. This is an actual image taken by the Rutherford observatory on 7th September, 2014.

Sirius

Sirius is the brightest star system in Earth's night sky. The name "Sirius" is derived from the Ancient Greek "Seirios", which means "glowing" or "scorcher". What appears to be a single star to the naked eye is actually a binary system of a white star with a faint white dwarf. This system is formally known as Alpha Canis Majoris or alpha CMa.

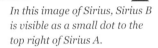

In this image of Sirius, Sirius B is visible as a small dot to the top right of Sirius A.

Sirius in ancient Egypt

Sirius is recorded in the earliest astronomical records. It was known in ancient Egypt as "Sopdet", which is written in Greek as "Sothis". The Egyptians based their calendar on the heliacal rising of Sirius. This heliacal rising marked the flooding of the Nile in ancient Egypt and the "dog days" of summer for the ancient Greeks.

Sirius to Polynesians

To the Polynesians in the southern hemisphere, it marked winter. The heliacal rising of Sirius refers to the day it becomes visible just before sunrise after moving far away from the glare of the Sun.

Dog star

Due to its prominent position in Canis Majoris (greater Dog) constellation, Sirius is often also referred to as the "Dog star".

Brightness

Sirius is the brightest star system in the night sky with almost twice the brightness of the second brightest star, Canopus. However, it is not as bright as the moon, Venus or Jupiter. In fact, even Mars and Mercury appear brighter than Sirius at times.

Types of Sirius

The two stars of the Sirius system are termed as Sirius A and Sirius B. Sirius A is a white main-sequence star with an estimated surface temperature of 9,940 K. It has an estimated mass which is twice that of the Sun. Sirius B is a star that has already evolved off the main sequence and transformed into a white dwarf. It has a mass almost equal to that of the Sun. It is one of the most massive white dwarfs known to us.

A Chandra X-ray observatory image of the Sirius star system.

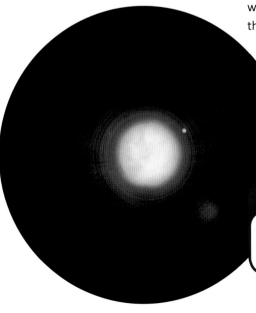

FUN FACT

The Sirius binary system is thought to be around 230 million years old.

Red, blue or white?

Greek astronomer Ptolemy had described the star of Sirius to be red in colour around 150 CE. However, poet Marcus Manilius described it as blue in his poems around 1 CE and ancient China has been describing it as white since 4 CE. Astronomers believe that this star keeps changing its colour. However, the reason is still being debated upon.

Arcturus

Arcturus is the brightest star in the northern celestial hemisphere. It lies in the constellation "Bootes" and is known as "Alpha Bootes". It is the fourth brightest star in the night sky, after Sirius, Canopus and Alpha Centauri. It lies barely 36.7 light years from Earth, making it very close by celestial standards.

FUN FACT

Arcturus became famous when its light was rumoured to be the mechanism used to open the 1933 Chicago World's Fair. The star was chosen as it was thought that light from Arcturus had started its journey at about the time of the previous Chicago World's Fair in 1893. The star is 36.7 light years from Earth and the light started its journey in 1896.

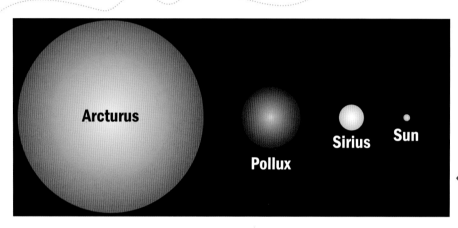

An image showing the sizes of various stars, relative to one another.

Early observations

Arcturus has been significant to observers since recorded antiquity. It was linked to the God Enlil and is also known as "Shudun", meaning yoke, in ancient Mesopotamia. Ptolemy of ancient Greece described Arcturus as "subrufa" or slightly red. Prehistoric Polynesian navigators knew Arcturus as "Hōkūleʻa", the star of joy. This civilisation used Arcturus as a navigational guide. The use of Arcturus is one of the methods by which Polynesians became such fabled sailors without any instruments.

Visibility

Arcturus can be observed during the day with a telescope. French mathematician and astronomer Jean-Baptiste Morin did this in 1635, making it the first star to be seen during the day. Arcturus is a type K0 III red giant star. Visibly, it is at least 110 times brighter than the Sun. However, most of the light given off by it is infrared and not visible to the naked eye. This is because the surface is cooler than the Sun.

Binary system

It is suggested that Arcturus is actually a part of a binary star system. The secondary star seems to be about 20 times dimmer than the primary one and orbits so close to Arcturus that it is not possible as of yet to distinguish it from the main star. There have been many focussed observations undertaken for this but the results remain inconclusive.

Arcturus as observed from a telescope.

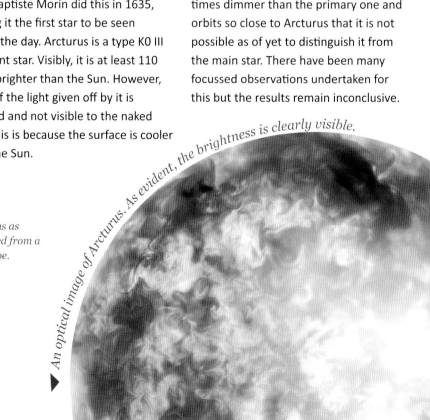

An optical image of Arcturus. As evident, the brightness is clearly visible.

Betelgeuse

Betelgeuse is the ninth brightest star in the night sky and second brightest in the constellation of Orion. It is also known by its official name or Bayer designation "alpha orionis". This is often shortened to alpha-orionis or alpha ori. The star's name is derived from the Arabic Yad al-Jauzā, which means "the hand of Orion". It refers to the star's position in the Orion constellation.

Classification

The star is classified as a red supergiant. It is one of the largest and most luminous observable stars. If Betelgeuse were in the solar system in place of the Sun, its surface would extend past the asteroid belt. It would possibly extend to the orbit of Jupiter and beyond. The resulting mass would be completely engulfing Mercury, Venus, Earth and Mars. Betelgeuse has a mass estimated to be around 30 times that of the Sun.

Variable brightness

It is one of the stars with greatly varying brightness. Sir John Herschel, in *Outlines of Astronomy*, first described the variation in Betelgeuse's brightness in 1836. This makes it easy to spot and identify with the naked eye. It also has a distinctive reddish-orange colour.

Eventual fate

Its fate depends on its mass. This is a critical factor that is not well understood. The most likely scenario is that the supergiant will continue to burn and fuse elements until its core is iron, at which point Betelgeuse will explode as a type II supernova. As of 2014, the most recent theory suggests

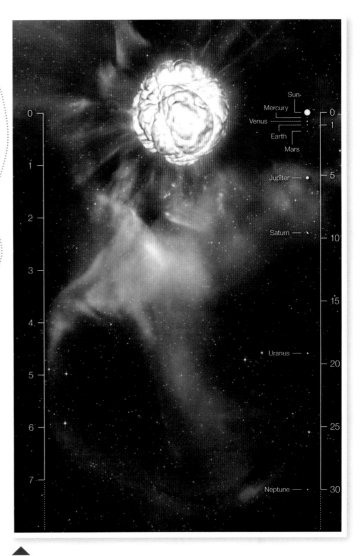

▲ *A computer generated image of Betelgeuse going supernova. The rest of the planets can be seen faintly.*

that it will explode as a supernova within 100,000 years. The event is expected to leave a neutron star 20 km in diameter.

Cultural significance

This star is popular in science fiction. The star's unusual name inspired the title of the 1988 film *Beetle juice*. It was reported that scriptwriter Michael McDowell was impressed by how many people made the connection between the film and the star. The red star Borgil in *Lord of the Rings* may also have been inspired by Betelgeuse.

◄ *A comparison between Aldebaran, Rigel, Antares and Betelgeuse.*

FUN FACT

Medieval translators misread the Arabic character for Y as B, which gave the star its current name.

Polaris

Polaris is the brightest star in the constellation Ursa Minor and the 45th brightest star in the night sky. It is very close to the north celestial pole and is commonly used for navigation. Thus, it is also commonly known as the pole star, lodestar or guiding star.

Star system of Polaris

It is actually a multiple star system. It consists of one main star, Alpha UrsaMinoris (UMi) Aa and two smaller companions, Alpha UMi B and Alpha UMi Ab. There are also two distant components, Alpha UMi C and Alpha UMi D.

Classification and characteristics

Alpha UMi Aa is a yellow supergiant with a mass 4.5 times that of the Sun. The two smaller companions are as follows:

● **Alpha UMi B** - is a main-sequence star orbiting at a distance of 2400 AU and a mass 1.39 times that of the Sun.

● **Alpha UMi Ab** - is a very close main sequence star at a distance of 18.8 AU and a mass 1.26 times that of the Sun.

Alpha UMi Aa is visible to the naked eye and even a modest telescope can see Alpha UMi B. The system is at an approximate distance of 434 light years from Earth.

Pole star

Because Alpha UMi nearly lies in a direct line with the axis of Earth's rotation "above" the North Pole, it stands almost motionless in the sky. As a result, all the stars of the Northern sky appear to rotate around Polaris. It makes an excellent fixed point to draw measurements for celestial navigation and astrometry.

An artist's rendering of the Polaris system, based on images captured through telescopes.

A photographer's trick shot recording the movement of stars due to the rotation of Earth.

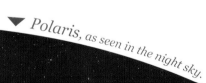

Polaris, as seen in the night sky.

FUN FACT

The celestial North Pole is not fixed. It moves due to Earth's motion. As a result, Polaris wasn't always a pole star and will not be one after a few centuries.

Alpha Centauri

Alpha Centauri is the brightest star in the southern constellation of Centaurus and the third brightest star in the night sky. It is actually a binary star system although it appears as a single object to the unaided eye. This system is located 1.34 parsecs or 4.37 light years from the Sun. This makes it the closest star system to our solar system.

Discovery

English explorer Robert Hues brought Alpha Centauri to the attention of European observers in his 1592 work *Tractatus de Globis*. He wrote, "Now, therefore, there are but three stars of the first magnitude that I could perceive in all those parts, which are never seen here in England. The first of these is that bright star in the sterne of Argo, which they call Canobus. The second is in the end of Eridanus. The third (referring to Alpha Centauri) is in the right foote of the Centaure". Argo and Canobus refer to Arcturus and Canopus, respectively. Jean Richaud first observed the binary nature of Alpha Centauri AB in December 1689. An astronomer and Jesuit priest, he made the finding incidentally while observing a passing comet from his station in Puducherry, India.

Alpha Centauri A

Alpha Centauri A is the primary member of the binary system. It is a sun-like main sequence star, but slightly larger and more luminous. It is about 1.1 times the Sun's mass with an orbit about 23 per cent greater. As an individual star, it is the fourth brightest, being slightly dimmer than Arcturus.

Alpha Centauri and Beta Centauri as seen through a camera; it is impossible to distinguish the two binary stars here. ▼

The Alpha Centauri appears as a bright star through a normal telescope.

Alpha Centauri B

Alpha Centauri B is the secondary member of the binary system. It is slightly smaller and less luminous than the Sun. It is mainly orange in colour, has 0.9 times the mass of the Sun and is 14 per cent smaller in radius. Without Alpha Centauri A, Alpha Centauri B would be a distant 21st brightest star in the night sky.

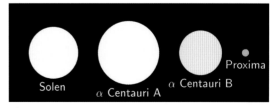

▲ *Comparision between the sizes of Solen, Alpha Centauri A, Alpha Centauri B and Proxima.*

Alpha Centauri C

Alpha Centauri C is the third star found in the proximity of Alpha Centauri A and B. It is also called Proxima. It is a much smaller star than the other two. This star could be called a part of a triple star system with the other two; however, its orbital period is too long.

Proxima Centauri

Proxima Centauri is a red dwarf that is about 4.24 light years from the Sun. It lies inside the G-cloud in the constellation of Centaurus. Scottish astronomer Robert Innes, the Director of the Union Observatory in South Africa, discovered it in 1915. It derives its name from the Latin word "proxima", meaning "close to" or "closest". This is because Proxima Centauri is the closest star to the Sun.

Star system

It is a very likely part of a triple star system with Alpha Centauri A and B. The gravitational pull of the two stars and their short distance makes this highly likely. However, its orbital period may be greater than 500,000 years. As a result, we are not sure of this fact.

Brightness

Proxima has a very low average luminosity. However, it is a flare star that undergoes random dramatic increases in brightness because of magnetic activity. When it was discovered, it was found to be the lowest-luminosity star known at the time.

Size

Being a red dwarf, it is a small star. Its radius is one-seventh and mass is only 12.3 per cent of the Sun. The star's relatively low energy-production rate suggests that it will be a main-sequence star for another four trillion years. This is nearly 300 times the current age of the universe. It is hypothesised that a life-sustaining planet could exist in orbit around it and other red dwarfs. Its habitable zone lies between 0.023 and 0.054 AU from the star. Such a planet would have an orbital period of 3.6 – 14 days.

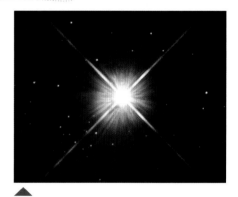

A Hubble telescope image of Proxima Centauri.

Travelling to Proxima

Astronomers consider that it is possible to travel to Proxima Centauri as it is bound to pass relatively close to Earth on its orbit before moving far away again. However, it could take about thousands of years for a spacecraft from Earth to land on a planet that is orbiting this red dwarf star.

An enlarged image of the red dwarf star of Proxima Centauri.

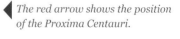

The red arrow shows the position of the Proxima Centauri.

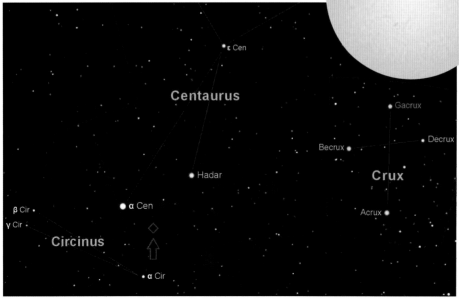

ε Cen

Centaurus

Gacrux

Decrux

Becrux

Hadar

Crux

β Cir
γ Cir

α Cen

Acrux

Circinus

α Cir

FUN FACT

If such a planet exists, Proxima Centauri moves little in the planet's sky and most of the surface experiences either day or night perpetually.

OGLE-TR-122/123

OGLE refers to the Optical Gravitational Lensing Experiment. It is a Polish astronomical project based at the University of Warsaw. While chiefly concerned with discovering dark matter through the use of the micro-lensing technique, it has discovered two notable and similar star systems.

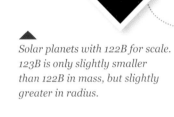

Star systems

OGLE-TR-122 and OGLE-TR-123 are binary stellar systems. Each contains one of the smallest main-sequence stars, whose radius has been measured. The orbital period for OGLE-TR-122 is approximately 7.3 days. The orbital period for OGLE-TR-123 is approximately 1.8 days.

Stars of 122

The primary star for OGLE-TR-122, which is also known as OGLE-TR-122A, is thought to resemble the Sun. The smaller star, OGLE-TR-122B, is estimated to have a radius around 0.12 times that of the Sun. This means that it is only 1.2 times the radius of Jupiter. The mass of 122B is also only 10 per cent of the Sun, which makes it about 100 times more than Jupiter. OGLE-TR-122B's mass is close to the lowest possible mass for a hydrogen-fusing star. The average density of the star is approximately 50 times that of the Sun or over 80 times the density of water. The observed transit of OGLE-TR-122B provides the first direct evidence of a star with a radius comparable to Jupiter.

Stars of 123

The primary star for OGLE-TR-123, known as OGLE-TR-123A, is thought to be slightly larger than the Sun. The smaller star, OGLE-TR-123B, is

Solar planets with 122B for scale. 123B is only slightly smaller than 122B in mass, but slightly greater in radius.

estimated to have a radius around 0.13 times that of the Sun. This makes it only 1.3 times the radius of Jupiter. The mass of 123B is also only 8.5 per cent of the Sun, which makes it about 95 times more than that of Jupiter. OGLE-TR-123B's mass is close to the lowest possible mass for a hydrogen-fusing star. The threshold for hydrogen fusion is thought to be around 0.07 or 0.08 of the mass of the Sun. The observed transit of OGLE-TR-123B provides the second evidence for a star with a radius comparable to Jupiter. This allowed us additional data for calculations after 122B was first observed.

An artist's representation of OGLE-TR-123 on the horizon of alternate worlds.

Asterism

An asterism is a pattern of stars that is recognised in Earth's night sky. It may be a part of an official constellation or composed of more than one star. In most cases, asterisms are composed of stars that are visible in the same general direction, but are not physically related. They are at significantly different distances from Earth, like constellations.

Background

Right since the beginning of astronomy, it is common to cluster various stars together into connect-the-dots or stick-figure patterns. Most cultures have recognised forms or groups of stars called constellations. Constellations were informal; anyone could create a figure and call it a constellation. Clarification was necessary to determine which groupings are constellations and which stars belonged to them.

Official naming

In 1930, the IAU divided the sky into 88 official constellations with precise boundaries. Any other grouping is an asterism. However, a true star cluster, whose stars are gravitationally related, is not an asterism.

Examples

There are various prominent examples of seasonal Asterisms (as seen in the northern hemisphere).

● **Spring** — the Great Diamond consisting of Arcturus, Spica, Denebola and Cor Caroli

● **Summer** — the Summer Triangle of Deneb, Altair and Vega

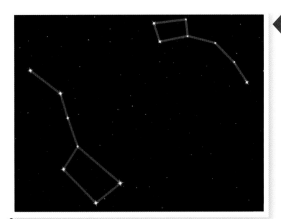

The Big Dipper or The Plough is one of the most recognisable asterisms. It is also a part of Ursa Major.

Brocchi's cluster or "the coat hanger" asterism in the constellation Vulpecula as seen through binoculars.

● **Autumn** — the Great Square of Pegasus is the quadrilateral formed by the stars α Pegasi, β Pegasi, γ Pegasi and α Andromedae

● **Winter** — the Winter Hexagon formed with Sirius, Procyon and Pollux, including 2nd magnitude Castor - Capella, Aldebaran and Rigel on the periphery and Betelgeuse located off-centre

FUN FACT

Asterisms are groups of stars that have not been categorised as something else. Objects that do not fall within the bounds of this definition include the Milky Way, nebulae and open clusters.

Cygnus

Cygnus is a northern constellation lying on the plane of the Milky Way. It derives its name from the Latinised Greek word for swan. In Greek mythology, this constellation represented God Zeus's swan. It may either be the one that was taken to seduce the Spartan queen Leda or the nymph Nemesis. It is one of the most recognisable constellations of the northern summer and autumn, and was among the 48 constellations listed by Ptolemy.

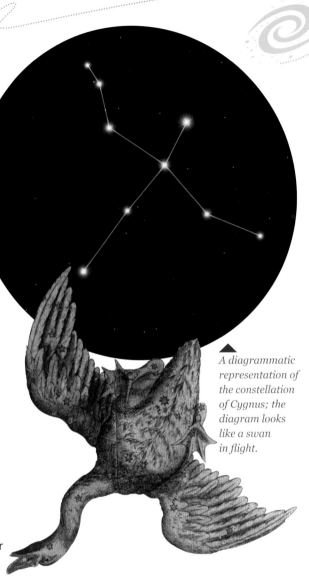

A diagrammatic representation of the constellation of Cygnus; the diagram looks like a swan in flight.

Location of Cygnus

Cygnus is a very large constellation. It is bordered on the east by Lacerta, on the west by Lyra, on the south by Vulpecula, on the north and east by Cepheus, on the north and west by Draco, and on the southeast by Pegasus. A polygon of 28 segments is considered as an official constellation. Belgian astronomer Eugène Delporte set this rule in 1930. Cygnus ranks 16th of the 88 constellations when sorted by size. It covers 804 square degrees and around 1.9 per cent of the night sky.

Constituents of Cygnus

The brightest star in Cygnus is Deneb, which is the 19th brightest star in the sky. Deneb is one of the stars of the prominent asterism, the Summer Triangle along with Vega and Altair. The Milky Way runs through Cygnus.

Cygnus also contains many notable objects such as:

● Cygnus X-1 — the first known black hole

● The Cygnus Loop — a large supernova remnant

Cygnus as visible through a telescope.

● The North American Nebula — a cloud of interstellar gas shaped like a continent

● The star 61 Cygni — 11.4 light years from Earth, it is the 15th nearest star and was the first to have its distance measured and recorded

● Over hundred known planets — Cygnus is a constellation that includes stars that have over 100 known planets. This is more than the planets of the stars of any other constellations. This has been possible because the Kepler satellite had surveyed when it was looking for extrasolar planets. It contains the Kepler-11 system that has six planets all within 1° to each other.

Ursa Major

Ursa Major is a constellation that is visible throughout the year in most of the northern hemisphere. The name comes from the Latin word meaning "larger bear". It is also known as the Great Bear and Charles' Wain. It has been reconstructed as an Indo-European constellation.

Background

The constellation of Ursa Major has been seen as a bear by many distinct civilisations. It dates back to more than 13,000 years and stems from a common oral tradition. Julien d'Huy reconstructed the following Palaeolithic state of the story:

"There is a horned herbivorous animal, especially an elk. One human pursues it in the sky. The animal is alive when it is transformed into a constellation, forming the Big Dipper".

This story was created to support the idea of Ursa Major's origins. It was one of the 48 constellations listed by the second century CE astronomer Ptolemy.

In literature

The Ursa Major is also prominent in literature. Poets such as Homer, Spencer, Shakespeare and Tennyson mention it in their work. The Finnish epic "Kalevala" has references to Ursa Major.

▲ *A star map of Ursa Major.*

Constituents of Ursa Major

The constellation consists of one major asterism and seven distinct stars. They are as follows:

1. The "Big Dipper" (or plough) asterism. It is made up of seven bright stars that together comprise one of the best-known patterns in the sky.

2. Alpha Ursae Majoris, also known by the Arabic name "Dubhe" (the bear). It is the 35th brightest star in the sky and the second brightest of Ursa Major.

3. Beta Ursae Majoris, called "Merak", which is Arabic for "the loins of the bear".

4. Gamma Ursae Majoris or "Phecda" (thigh).

5. Delta Ursae Majoris or "Megrez" (root of the tail).

6. Epsilon Ursae Majoris, known as "Alioth". This name does not refer to a bear, but to a "black horse". Alioth is the brightest star of Ursa Major and the 33rd brightest star in the sky.

7. Zeta Ursae Majoris, "Mizar", is the second star at the end of the handle of the Big Dipper and the constellation's 4th brightest star. Mizar means girdle in Arabic.

8. Eta Ursae Majoris, known as either "Alkaid" or "Benetnash", meaning the "end of the tail". Alkaid is the 3rd brightest star of Ursa Major.

A diagrammatic representation of the constellation of the Great bear; the diagram looks like a bear standing on two legs.

Orion

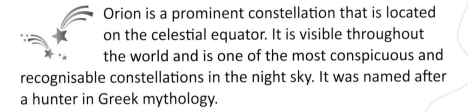

Orion is a prominent constellation that is located on the celestial equator. It is visible throughout the world and is one of the most conspicuous and recognisable constellations in the night sky. It was named after a hunter in Greek mythology.

Background in different cultures

Orion has been observed from antiquity and finds a mention in the astronomy of the following regional cultures:

- Ancient Near East
- Greco-Roman antiquity
- Middle East
- East Asian antiquity
- European folklore
- Americas

Constituents of Orion

The brightest and most important seven stars in Orion are as follows:

1. Betelgeuse, or Alpha Orionis, is a massive M-type red supergiant star nearing the end of its life. It is the second brightest star in Orion, and is a semi-regular variable star and the 8th brightest star in the night sky. It forms the right shoulder of Orion.

2. Rigel, also known as Beta Orionis, is a B-type, blue supergiant that is the 6th brightest star in the night sky. It serves as the left foot of Orion, the hunter.

3. Bellatrix or Gamma Orionis is colloquially known as the "Amazon Star". It is the 27th brightest star in the night sky. Bellatrix is considered to be a B-type blue giant. It serves as Orion's left shoulder.

4. Mintaka, also known as Delta Orionis, is the faintest of the three stars in Orion's Belt. It is a multiple star system, composed of a large B-type blue giant and a more massive O-type white star. It is located in the Orion's Belt.

5. Alnilam is also called Epsilon Orionis. Also called Al Nathin, Alnilam is named for the Arabic phrase meaning "string of pearls". Alnilam is a B-type blue supergiant. Despite being nearly twice as far from the Sun as Mintaka and Alnitak, the other two belt stars, its luminosity makes it nearly equal in magnitude.

6. Alnitak, meaning "the girdle", is also called Zeta Orionis. It is the easternmost star in Orion's Belt. It is a triple star some 800 light years away. The primary star of Alnitak is a blue supergiant and the brightest class O star in the night sky.

7. Saiph is also called Kappa Orionis. It serves as Orion's right foot. Saiph is of a similar distance and size to Rigel, but appears much fainter.

An Orion constellation map with details of the stars and their relative placements.

Nakshatra

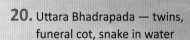

Nakshatra or náksatra is the term for lunar mansion in Hindu astrology. A nakshatra is one of 27 (sometimes also 28) sectors along the ecliptic. These are named after the most prominent asterisms in the respective sectors.

Origin and background

Nakshatras are often referred to as Hindu constellations, though their distinctive name is more commonly used. Originally, in Vedic Sanskrit, the term náksatra may refer to any heavenly body or to "the stars" collectively. The classical sense of "lunar mansion" is first found in the Atharvaveda. This later evolved into the primary meaning of the term in Classical Sanskrit.

The starting point

The starting point for the nakshatras is that on the ecliptic, which is directly opposite to the star Spica, called Chitrā in Sanskrit. The ecliptic is divided into each of the nakshatras eastwards starting from this point. The number of nakshatras reflects the number of days in a lunar month. The modern period of a lunar month is 27.32 days. Thus, the moon traverses the width of a nakshatra in about one day. Each nakshatra is further subdivided into four quarters (or padas).

Nakshatras and their symbols

1. Ashwini — the horse's head
2. Pushya — cow's udder, lotus, arrow and a circle
3. Swati — young sprout swaying in the wind, coral
4. Shravana — ear, three footprints in an uneven row
5. Bharani — Yoni, the female reproductive organ
6. Ashlesha — serpent, a coiled snake
7. Vishaka — triumphant arch, potter's wheel
8. Dhanishta — drum, flute
9. Krittika — Agni, god of fire
10. Magha — royal throne
11. Anurada — triumphant arch, lotus
12. Shatabhishak — empty circle, thousand flowers, stars
13. Rohini — chariot, temple, banyan tree
14. Purva Phalguni — bed, hammock, fig tree
15. Jyeshta — amulet, umbrella, earring
16. Purva Bhadrapada — sword, funeral cot, man with two faces
17. Mrigashira — deer's head
18. Uttara Phalguni — bed, hammock
19. Mula — bunch of roots, elephant god
20. Uttara Bhadrapada — twins, funeral cot, snake in water
21. Ardra — teardrop, diamond, human head
22. Hasta — hand, fist
23. Purva Ashadha — elephant tusk, fan, winnowing basket
24. Revati — pair of fish, drum
25. Punarvasu — bow and quiver
26. Chitra — bright jewel, pearl
27. Uttara Ashadha — elephant tusk, small cot, planks of bed

List of nakshatras with stars

This is a list of the nakshatras with the modern stars that are most commonly associated with them. As we can see, some of the nakshatras are repeated over multiple asterisms.

Position of the Hindu nakshatra "Mandala" as per the co-ordinates specified in Surya Siddhantha. This image shows the nakshatras overlaid on classical Greco-Roman constellations for clarity of position.

No.	Name	Associated stars
1	Ashvini - "wife of the Ashvins"	β and γ Arietis
2; 7	Bharani - "the bearer"	35, 39, and 41 Arietis
3	Krittika - an old name of the Pleiades; personified as the nurses of Kārttikeya, a son of Shiva	Pleiades
4; 9	Rohini - "the red one", a name of Aldebaran, also known asbrāhmī	Aldebaran
5; 3	Mrigashīrsha - "the deer's head", also known as āgrahāyaṇī	λ, φ Orionis
6; 4	Ardra - "the moist one"	Betelgeuse
7; 5	Punarvasu (dual) - "the two restorers of goods", also known as yamakau - "the two chariots"	Castor and Pollux
8; 6	Pushya - "the nourisher", also known as sidhya or tiṣya	γ, δ and θ Cancri
9; 7	Āshleshā - "the embrace"	δ, ε, η, ρ, and σ Hydrae
10; 15	Maghā - "the bountiful"	Regulus
11	PūrvaPhalgunī - "first reddish one"	δ and θ Leonis
12	UttaraPhalgunī - "second reddish one"	Denebola
13	Hasta - "the hand"	α, β, γ, δ and ε Corvi
14	Chitra - "the bright one", a name of Spica	Spica
15	Svāti - "Su-Ati" (sanskrit), Arcturus's name	Arcturus
16; 14	Visakha - "forked, having branches", also known as rādhā "the gift"	α, β, γ and ι Librae
17	Anuradha - "following rādhā"	β, δ and π Scorpionis
18; 16	Jyeshtha - "the eldest, most excellent"	α, σ, and τ Scorpionis
19; 17	Mula - "the root"	ε, ζ, η, θ, ι, κ, λ, μ and ν Scorpionis
20; 18	PurvaAshadha - "first of the aṣādhā", aṣādhā – "the invincible one", the name of a constellation	δ and ε Sagittarii
21	Uttara Ashadha - "second of the aṣādhā"	ζ and σ Sagittarii
22; 20	Abhijit - "victorious"	α, ε and ζ Lyrae - Vega
23; 20	Sravana	α, β and γ Aquilae
24; 21; 23	Dhanishta - "most famous", also Shravishthā "swiftest"	α to δ Delphini
24; 22	Shatabhisha - "Comprising a hundred physicians"	γ Aquarii
25; 3	PurvaBhadrapada - "the first of the blessed feet"	α and β Pegasi
26; 4	UttaraBhādrapadā - "the second of the blessed feet"	γ Pegasi and αAndromedae
27; 5	Revati - "prosperous"	ζ Piscium

Zodiac

The zodiac is a circle having 12 divisions of 30° each that are centred upon the ecliptic. The ecliptic refers to a circle on the celestial sphere that represents the Sun's path during the year. Zodiac is a term that is common in both astrology and historical astronomy.

Construction and significance

These 12 divisions are called signs. The zodiac is essentially a celestial co-ordinate system. Specifically, it is an ecliptic co-ordinate system, as opposed to an equatorial one. In the zodiac, the ecliptic is the origin of latitude. It is also the position of the Sun at vernal equinox as the origin of longitude. The vernal equinox refers to the spring equinox, which is the opposite in each hemisphere of Earth.

Etymology

The term zodiac is derived from the Latin word "zōdiacus". Zodiacus, in turn, comes from the Greek word "zōdiakoskyklos". The term means "circle of animals". It stems from the fact that half the signs of the classical Greek zodiac are represented as animals.

Comparison across cultures

The zodiac constellations have been referred to by different names over the ages. We currently use the Latin names most predominantly. Below is a table that compares the different names of the zodiac:

This circular illustration shows the celestial sphere. The diagram shows the imagery as well as a vector representation of the position of the stars in the particular zodiac. There are 12 zodiacs as can be seen here.

No.	Symbol	Long.	Latin name	English translation	Greek name	Sanskrit name
1	♈	0°	Aries	The ram	Krios	Mesha
2	♉	30°	Taurus	The bull	Tavros	Vrishabha
3	♊	60°	Gemini	The twins	Didymoi	Mithuna
4	♋	90°	Cancer	The crab	Karkinos	Karkata
5	♌	120°	Leo	The lion	Leōn	Simha
6	♍	150°	Virgo	The maiden	Parthenos	Kanyā
7	♎	180°	Libra	The scales	Zygos	Tulā
8	♏	210°	Scorpio	The scorpion	Skorpios	Vrśhchika
9	♐	240°	Sagittarius	The (centaur)archer	Toxotēs	Dhanusha
10	♑	270°	Capricorn	"Goat-horned" (the sea-goat)	Aigokerōs	Makara
11	♒	300°	Aquarius	The water-bearer	Hydrokhoos	Kumbha
12	♓	330°	Pisces	The fish	Ikhthyes	Mīna

Differences from astrology

Unlike the zodiac signs in astrology, which are all 30° in length, the astronomical constellations vary widely in size. Due to the constellations not being evenly distributed according to size, the Sun takes a different amount of time in each constellation.

Sun's relation to the Zodiac

Below is a table that details the Sun and its relation to the various zodiac signs. This is a sample using 2011 as a reference. There are minor changes from year to year, due to the nature of Earth's rotation and orbit.

Zodiac today

The zodiac remains the basis of the ecliptic coordinate system that is used in astronomy. However, the term and names of the 12 signs are today mostly associated with horoscopic astrology. Horoscopic astrology is the belief that the constellation in which the Sun is at the time of one's birth somehow determines the traits and future of a person. Along with the Sun, the position of the moon in the zodiac is also used for both astrology and astronomy. However, the moon moves through the ecliptic very quickly, finishing the 360° arc in a little over 27 days.

Constellation			
Name	IAU boundaries	Solar stay	Brightest star
Aries	19 April – 13 May	25 days	Hamal
Taurus	14 May – 19 June	37 days	Aldebaran
Gemini	20 June – 20 July	31 days	Pollux
Cancer	21 July – 9 August	20 days	Al Tarf
Leo	10 August – 15 September	37 days	Regulus
Virgo	16 September – 30 October	45 days	Spica
Libra	31 October – 22 November	23 days	Zubeneschamali
Scorpius	23 November – 29 November	7 days	Antares
Ophiuchus	30 November – 17 December	18 days	Rasalhague
Sagittarius	18 December – 18 January	32 days	KausAustralis
Capricornus	19 January – 15 February	28 days	DenebAlgedi
Aquarius	16 February – 11 March	24 days	Sadalsuud
Pisces	12 March – 18 April	38 days	Eta Piscium

An ancient artifact marking the 12 animals around a dial at the correct longitudinal degree that they adhere to.

Leo

Leo is one of the constellations of the zodiac, lying between Cancer to the west and Virgo to the east. It is easily recognisable, as it contains many bright stars and a distinctive shape that is reminiscent of the crouching lion. Its name is Latin for lion. It is named after the Nemean lion killed by the mythical Greek hero Heracles.

A lion, the animal that represents the zodiac of Leo.

Leo as seen in the night sky.

Leo's stars

It remains as one of the 88 modern constellations today. It was also one of the 48 constellations described by the second century astronomer, Ptolemy. Leo has many bright stars. The most prominent ones are listed below:

● **Regulus:** It is designated as Alpha Leonis; it is a blue-white, main-sequence star that is located 77.5 light years from Earth. It is a double star, visible through binoculars. The traditional name of the star, Regulus, means "the little king".

● **Beta Leonis:** It is commonly called Denebola and is at the opposite end of the constellation to Regulus. It is a blue-white star that is 36 light years from Earth. Denebola means "the lion's tail".

● **Algieba:** Formally known as Gamma Leonis, it is a binary star with a third optical component. The primary and secondary ones are distinguishable in small telescopes, while the tertiary is visible through binoculars. The primary is a gold-yellow giant star and the secondary is similar, but less bright. They are 126 light years from Earth. The tertiary is unrelated and called 40 Leonis. It is a yellow-tinged star. Its traditional name, Algieba, means "the forehead".

● **Delta Leonis:** It is commonly called "Zosma". It is a blue-white star, 58 light years from Earth.

● **Epsilon Leonis:** It is a yellow giant that is 251 light years from Earth.

● **Zeta Leonis:** It is commonly called Adhafera. It is an optical triple star, the brightest and only star designated as Zeta Leonis. It is a white giant star that is 260 light years from Earth. The second brightest star, named 39 Leonis, is widely spaced to the south. The 35 Leonis is to the north and the third star in the trifecta.

● **Iota Leonis:** It is a binary star that is visible through medium-sized amateur telescopes. To the unaided eye, Iota Leonis appears to be a yellow-tinged star. The binary system is 79 light years from Earth.

● **Tau Leonis:** It is a double star that is visible through binoculars. The primary is a yellow giant star that is 621 light years from Earth.

A diagrammatic representation of the stars that are present in the Leo constellation.

Scorpius

Scorpius is one of the constellations of the zodiac. It is Latin for scorpion and the constellation is sometimes known as Scorpio. It is a large constellation that is located in the southern hemisphere near the centre of the Milky Way. It lies between Libra to the west and Sagittarius to the east.

A scorpion, the reptile that represents the zodiac of Scorpius.

The stars connect to show the shape of a scorpion.

Background and history

The Babylonians called this constellation MUL.GIR.TAB, which is Babylonian for "Scorpion". The name can be literally interpreted as "the (creature with a) burning sting". The Javanese people of Indonesia call this constellation "Banyakangrem", which means "the brooded swan", or Kalapa Doyong, meaning "leaning coconut tree". This is due to the shape similarity. It is astronomically shortened to "Sco" in modern usage.

Constituents of Scorpius

It contains many bright stars. The major ones are listed below:

● Antares is formally known as alpha Scorpio and "rival of Mars". The title was conferred because of its distinct reddish hue.

● Beta 1 Sco is commonly called Graffias or Acrab. It is an optical triple star.

● Delta Sco is commonly called Dschubba that means "the front".

● Theta Sco is commonly called Sargas. The origin of its name is unknown.

● Nu Sco is commonly called Jabbah.

● Epsilon Sco is commonly called Girtab, which means "the scorpion".

● PiSco is commonly called Iclil.

● Sigma Sco is commonly called Alniyat.

● Tau Sco is commonly called and also known as Alniyat. It means "the arteries" and refers to both Tau and Sigma Sco.

● Lambda Sco, commonly called Shaula, Upsilon Sco and Lesath, form the

▲ *A diagrammatic representation of the stars that are present in the Scorpius constellation.*

Scorpion's curved tail. These names have a common origin and mean "sting". λ Sco and υ Sco are sometimes referred to as the cat's eyes due to their close proximity.

▼ *Scorpius as seen in the night sky.*

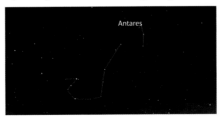

Antares

Taurus

Taurus is one of the constellations of the zodiac. Along with being one of the modern 88 constellations, it is also one of the original 48 defined by Ptolemy. Taurus is a large and prominent constellation in the northern hemisphere's winter sky.

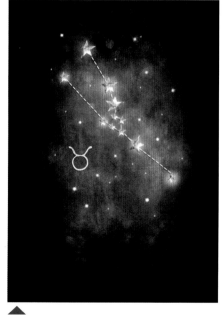

A bull, the animal that represents the zodiac of Taurus.

The stars connect to show the shape of a bull.

Oldest constellation

It dates back to at least the early Bronze Age. At this time, it marked the location of the Sun during the spring equinox. This makes it one of the oldest constellations.

Ring-like structure

It is bordered by Aries in the west and Gemini in the east; in the north by Perseus and Auriga, in the southeast by Orion, in the south by Eridanus and in the southwest by Cetus. It is the only constellation that is crossed by all three equators: galactic equator, celestial equator and ecliptic. The Gould's Belt passes through this constellation. It is a ring-like galactic structure.

Taurus came to symbolise the bull in the mythologies of Ancient Babylon, Egypt and Greece. In Buddhism, legends hold that Gautama Buddha was born when the full moon was in Vaisakha, which is the Hindu name for Taurus.

Constituents of Taurus

Taurus is an extensive constellation that consists of nebulae and supernova remnants as well as stars. Some of the interesting features of the Taurus constellation are listed below:

● Taurus hosts two of the nearest open clusters to Earth. These are the Pleiades and Hyades. Both are visible to the naked eye.

● The red giant Aldebaran is the brightest star in the constellation. Its name is Arabic for "the follower", as Aldebaran appears to follow the Pleiades through the night sky.

● The supernova remnant Messier 1 lies in the northwest part of Taurus. It is more commonly known as the Crab Nebula.

● Part of the Taurus-Auriga complex crosses into the northern part of the constellation. This is one of the closest regions of active star formation.

● The variable star T Tauri that lies in the Taurus constellation is the prototype of a class of pre-main-sequence stars.

Taurus as seen in the night sky.

Taures the Bull · Pleiades

Aldebaran

Orion's Belt

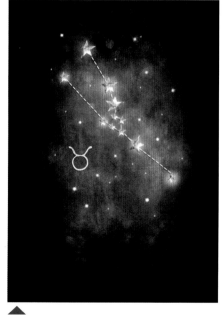

A diagrammatic representation of the stars that are present in the Taurus constellation.

Virgo

Virgo is the second largest constellation in the sky after Hydra. It lies between Leo in the west and Libra in the east. Latin for virgin, Virgo was linked with the harvest in mythology. It symbolises a harvest goddess or the daughter of a goddess. Virgo is connected with harvest because the Sun passed across the constellation during late summer or early autumn, when farmers harvested their crops.

A woman (goddess) represents the zodiac of Virgo.

The stars connect to show the shape of a woman.

Visibility

Virgo is known as a spring constellation because, although you can see some or all of its stars on most nights of the year, the stars put on their best display in the evening sky during spring.

Locating Virgo

Virgo is easily found in the night sky through its brightest star, Spica. Besides Spica, there are many notable features in Virgo. Though Spica is the only bright star in this constellation, it is the 16th brightest star in the night sky. It consists of two other stars, both that are hotter, brighter and heavier than the Sun. "Vir" is the accepted three-letter notation for Virgo.

Constituents of Virgo

1. Bright stars:
   - BetaVirginis, commonly known as Zavijava
   - GammaVir, commonly known as Porrima
   - DeltaVirginis, commonly known as Auva
   - EpsilonVirginis, commonly known as Vindemiatrix

2. Other fainter stars:
   - TauVirginis, commonly known as Heze
   - Eta Virginis, commonly known as Zaniah
   - IotaVirginis, commonly known as Syrma
   - Mu Virginis, commonly known as Rijl al Awwa

3. The star 70 Virginis has one of the first known extra-solar planetary systems. It contains one confirmed planet that has 7.5 times the mass of Jupiter.

4. The star Chi Virginis has one of the most massive planets ever detected. It has a mass that is 11.1 times that of Jupiter.

5. The Sun-like star 61 Virginis has three planets. One is a super-Earth and two are Neptune-mass planets.

6. SS Virginis is a variable star with a noticeable red colour.

7. Virgo also has the distinction of having a very large number of exoplanets. There are 35 verified exoplanets orbiting 29 stars in the constellation of Virgo.

A diagrammatic representation of the stars that are present in the Virgo constellation.

Gemini

Gemini is one of the constellations of the zodiac. It derives its name from a Latin word, meaning "twins". It is associated with the twins Castor and Pollux in Greek mythology. It was one of the 48 constellations described by Ptolemy. It remains one of the 88 modern constellations defined by the IAU today.

Twins, Castor and Pollux represent the zodiac of Gemini.

The stars connect to show the shape of twins.

History and background

In Meteorologica, Aristotle mentions that he observed Jupiter in conjunction with a star, and then occulting one in Gemini. This is the first such recorded observation in human history and probably occurred in 337 BCE. In 1930, Clyde Tombaugh discovered Pluto when he exposed a series of photographic plates centred on Delta Gemini.

Constituents of Gemini

It contains 85 stars that are visible from Earth without a telescope. Pollux is the brightest star in Gemini followed by Castor. Castor's designation as Alpha Gem (Gemini) is, thus, mistaken. The list of stars in Gemini is as follows:

● α Gem (Castor) — Castor is a sextuple star system that is 52 light years from Earth, which appears as a blue-white star to the unaided eye.

● β Gem (Pollux) — The brightest star in Gemini is an orange-hued giant star that is 34 light years from Earth. An extrasolar planet revolves around it.

● γ Gem (Alhena) — It is a blue-white star that is 105 light years from Earth.

● δ Gem (Wasat) — It is a long-period binary star that is 59 light years away from Earth.

● ε Gem (Mebsuta) — A double star, the primary is a yellow supergiant that is 900 light years from Earth. The optical companion is visible through binoculars and small telescopes.

● ζ Gem (Mekbuda) — It is a double star. The primary is a yellow supergiant that is 1200 light years from Earth. It has a radius that is 60 times the Sun, making it approximately 220,000 times the size of the Sun.

● η Gem — A binary star that is 350 light years away is only distinguishable in large amateur telescopes. The primary is a semi-regular red giant.

● κ Gem — Binary star that is 143 light years from Earth. The primary is a yellow giant.

● ν Gem — It is a double star that is visible when using binoculars and small amateur telescopes. The primary is a blue giant.

● 38 Gem — It is a binary star that is 91 light years from Earth. The primary is a white star and the secondary a yellow star.

● U Gem — It is a dwarf nova-type cataclysmic variable.

A diagrammatic representation of the stars that are present in the Gemini constellation.

OBSERVING SPACE

▲ *The silhouette of a telescope against a creatively enhanced sky that shows objects visible through a telescope.*

Astronomy is a natural science that is the study of celestial objects. In short, the observation of space and the theories related to celestial objects and their behaviour fall under the umbrella of Astronomy.

It is one of the oldest sciences. Most of the early civilisations in recorded history performed celestial observations of the night sky. The invention of the telescope helped astronomy develop into a modern science.

Historically, it has included many disciplines as diverse as astrometry, celestial navigation, observational astronomy and calendars creation.

Amateur Astronomy

Amateur astronomy is a hobby that involves observing the sky and an abundance of objects found in it. Even though scientific research is not their main goal, many amateur astronomers make a contribution to astronomy. They monitor variable stars, track asteroids and discover transient objects, such as comets and novae through their observation of the sky. They often use the unaided eye, binoculars or telescopes.

An artist's representation of the night sky as observed by a satellite.

equipment like binoculars or a manually driven telescope. Maps or memory are used to locate known landmark stars. The astronomer then "hops" between them, often with the aid of a finderscope. It is a very common and simple method to find objects in space that are close to the objects in space that are visible to the naked eye.

An amateur skygazer looks through a basic, manual telescope. This needs to be pointed and focussed by hand.

Background

Skygazers observe a variety of celestial objects and phenomena. They commonly view the moon, planets, stars, comets, meteor showers and a variety of deep sky objects such as star clusters, galaxies, and nebulae. Amateur astrophotography involves taking photos of the night sky. This has become more popular with the introduction of equipment such as digital, DSLR and special CCD cameras. A small minority of them experiment with wavelengths outside the visible spectrum. Grote Reber was an amateur astronomer who constructed the first purpose-built radio telescope in the late 1930s.

Common tools

Specialised and experienced amateur astronomers tend to acquire more specialised and powerful equipment over time. However, relatively simple equipment is often preferred for certain tasks. They also use star charts. Depending on the experience and intentions of the astronomer, these may range from simple plan spheres to detailed charts of very specific areas of the night sky.

Star hopping

Star hopping is a method often used by amateur astronomers. It is most preferred by those with low-tech

FUN FACT

Hubble's eight-foot light-collecting mirror had to be polished continuously for a year to achieve an accuracy of 10 nanometers, which is about 1/10,000[th] the width of a human hair.

Setting circles

More advanced methods of locating objects in the sky include telescope mounts with setting circles.

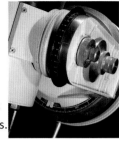

Setting circles are angular measurement scales. These can be placed on the two main rotation axes of telescopes. The widespread adoption of digital setting circles has led to many classical engraved setting circles, now being specifically identified as an "analogue setting circle" or ASC.

A computerised setting circle is called a "digital setting circle" or DSC. By knowing the co-ordinates of an object, the telescope user can use the setting circle to align the telescope in the appropriate direction. He can then look through its eyepiece and locate the desired object.

GOTO telescopes

GOTO telescopes have become more popular since the 1980s. This is due to an improvement in technology and reduction in prices. These are simply computer-driven telescopes. The user typically just enters the name of the object of interest. The computer manipulates the mechanics of the telescope to point it automatically towards that item. They usually have to be calibrated using alignment stars to provide accurate tracking and positioning. Recently developed telescope systems are calibrated with the use of built-in GPS. This allows them to be adjusted more easily.

Remote control telescopes

Remote telescope astronomy is a viable means for amateur astronomers not aligned with major telescope facilities. This enables them to partake in research and deep sky imaging. The development of broadband internet during the late twentieth century and advances in computer controlled telescope mounts and CCD cameras enables anyone to control a telescope that is at a significant distance away in a dark location.

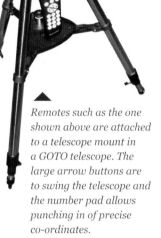

Remotes such as the one shown above are attached to a telescope mount in a GOTO telescope. The large arrow buttons are to swing the telescope and the number pad allows punching in of precise co-ordinates.

Stargazing requires a clear, cloudless night. Areas devoid of air and light pollution are also preferred. On a good night, billions and billions of stars become visible to the naked eye.

Telescopes

A telescope is an instrument that aids in the observation of remote objects. It enhances images by collecting electromagnetic radiation, generally visible light. The first known practical telescopes were invented in the Netherlands at the beginning of the seventeenth century. Hans Lippershey and Zacharias Janssen, who were spectacle makers in Middelburg, as well as Jacob Metius of Alkmaar invented them. They were widely used in terrestrial applications and astronomy.

Origin of name

The word "telescope" comes from the Greek "tele", meaning "far" and "skope", meaning "to look" or "see". Thus, the term "teleskopos" means "far-seeing". Greek mathematician Giovanni Demisiani coined the name for one of Galileo Galilei's devices in 1611. Demisiani saw the instruments presented at a banquet at the Accademia dei Lincei. In the Starry Messenger, Galileo himself had used the term "perspicillum" to refer to telescopes.

History of telescopes

The earliest recorded working telescopes were those mentioned above. Galileo heard about the Dutch telescope in June 1609. Within a month, he built his own and then greatly improved upon the design in the following year. In 1668, Isaac Newton built the first practical reflecting telescope. This used a mirror instead of a lens as the objective and was an impressive leap forward.

Construction

A telescope consists of various elements that receive and focus electromagnetic radiation. Some telescopes also rely on gravity and neutrinos to form images. The simplest telescope has visual elements that are just two lenses. Complex telescopes in observatories can be huge with receiver dishes that are dozens of metres across. A telescope mount is a mechanical structure that supports it. It supports the mass of the telescope and allows for accurate pointing of the instrument. The two main types of tracking mount are:

- Altazimuth mount
- Equatorial mount

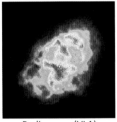
Radio wave (VLA)

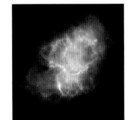
Infrared radiation (Spitzer)

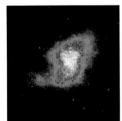
Ultraviolet radiation (Astro-1)

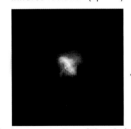
Low-energy X-ray (Chandra)

Visible light (Hubble)

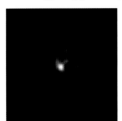
High-energy X-ray (HEFT)

A Keplerian Telescope mounted in an Equatorial Mount.

A 6-foot wide view of the Crab nebula supernova remnant. The different images are viewed at different wavelengths of light by various telescopes.

History of Telescopes

The earliest known working telescopes appeared in 1608. The first is credited to Hans Lippershey. Among the others who claimed to have made the discovery was Zacharias Janssen, a spectacle-maker in Middelburg and Jacob Metius of Alkmaar. Objects were magnified upto three times and were considered to be a great novelty.

Refracting telescopes

The early refracting telescopes consisted of a convex objective lens and a concave eyepiece. Galileo used this design in 1609 and made some of his most famous discoveries. Johannes Kepler described how a telescope could be made with a convex objective lens and convex eyepiece lens in 1611. By 1655, astronomers such as Christiaan Huygens had built powerful but unwieldy telescopes with compound eyepieces following Keplerian designs.

A depiction of an early Dutch telescope. Telescopes such as these were used in many other fields along with astronomy.

Reflecting telescopes

Isaac Newton built the first "practical" reflector in 1668. His design incorporated a small flat diagonal mirror to reflect the light to an eyepiece mounted on the side of the telescope. In 1672, Laurent Cassegrain described the design of a reflector with a small, convex secondary mirror to reflect light through a central hole in the main viewing mirror.

Achromatic lenses and shorter telescopes

The achromatic lens first appeared in a 1733 telescope made by Chester Moore Hall. It greatly reduced colour aberrations in objective lenses. This allowed for shorter and more functional telescopes. Starting 1758, John Dollond produced telescopes using achromatic lenses on a commercial scale.

Important developments in reflecting telescopes

● John Hadley's produced larger paraboloidal mirrors in 1721.

● The process of silvering glass mirrors, which was introduced by Léon Foucault in 1857.

● The adoption of long-lasting aluminised coatings on reflector mirrors that began in 1932.

A replica of Newton's second reflecting telescope in 1672.

Types of Telescopes

The name "telescope" is used to cover a wide range of instruments. Most of these detect electromagnetic radiation. However, there are major differences in how astronomers could go about collecting light in different frequency bands. They are generally classified by the wavelengths of light that they detect.

A very large array (VLT) Auxiliary Telescope and Cerro Armazones.

Major differences and classifications

Although it is possible to make very tiny antennae, it becomes easier to use antenna technology to interact with electromagnetic radiation as wavelengths become longer. They may also be classified by location as ground, space or flying telescopes.

Optical telescopes

An optical telescope gathers and focusses light mainly from the visible part of the electromagnetic spectrum. However, some of these work in the infrared and ultraviolet as well. These telescopes work by employing one or more curved optical elements to

▲ *A refracting Telescope at the observatory in Nice, France.*

gather light and other electromagnetic radiation. It then brings that light or radiation to a focal point. The focussing element is usually made from glass lenses and/or mirrors. There are three main optical types given, as follows:

● The refracting telescope uses lenses to form an image.

● The reflecting telescope uses an arrangement of mirrors to form a reflected image.

● The catadioptric telescope uses mirrors combined with lenses to form an image.

Radio telescopes

These are directional radio antennas that are used for radio astronomy. The antennas are dishes that are constructed from a conductive wire mesh whose openings are smaller than the wavelength being observed. These telescopes are also used to collect microwave radiation. This is mainly used when any visible light is obstructed or faint, such as that from quasars.

X-ray telescopes

X-ray telescopes are instruments created to detect and determine X-rays present outside Earth's atmosphere. Due to atmospheric absorption, these telescopes have to be taken to high altitudes by rockets or balloons or must be placed in orbit beyond the atmosphere. The telescopes carried by balloons can detect the deep penetrating X-rays, whereas those carried by rockets or in satellites detect softer radiation. These telescopes use X-ray optics. An example of this is a Wolter telescope that consists of ring-shaped "glancing" mirrors made using heavy metals. These are able to reflect the rays at just a few degrees.

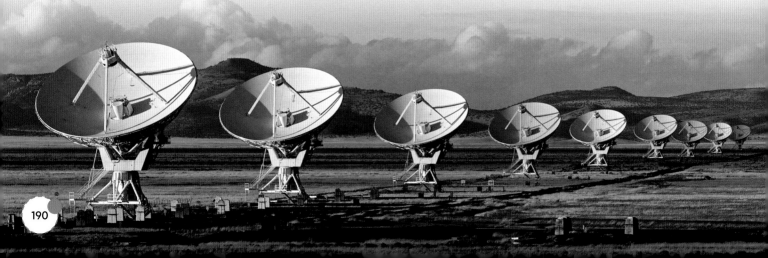

Four VLT Unit Telescopes Working as One.

Antennas of the Atacama Large Millimeter/submillimeter Array (ALMA), on the Chajnantor plateau in the Chilean Andes.

The VLT

The Very Large Telescope (VLT) is an extremely unique facility for ground-based European astronomy, which took off at the beginning of the third millennium. It is the world's most advanced optical instrument, consisting of four unit telescopes with main mirrors of 8.2 m diameter and four movable 1.8 m diameter auxiliary telescopes. These telescopes are put together to form a giant "interferometer". The Very Large Telescope Interferometer allows astronomers to observe details up to 25 time better than the other telescopes. It has made a significant impact on observational astronomy.

Arecibo

The huge dish of the Arecibo is 305 m in diameter and 167 feet deep. It covers an area of about 20 acres. The surface is created using about 40,000 perforated aluminium panels, each measuring about 3 × 6 feet, which is supported by a network of steel cables strung across the underlying karst sinkhole.
It is a spherical reflector. It is the biggest arched-focussing antenna on Earth.

It is the world's most sensitive telescope. Other radio telescopes take several hours to observe a source in order to collect adequate energy for analysis. On the other hand, Arecibo requires only a few minutes of observation.

The Arecibo Radio Telescope, at Arecibo, Puerto Rico.

ALMA

Atacama Large Millimeter/sub-millimeter Array (ALMA) is the world's largest ground-based facility for observations in the millimeter/sub-millimeter regime. It is located on the Chajnantor plateau, which is at a 5000 m altitude in northern Chile. It allows transformational research into the physics of the cold universe, probes the first stars and galaxies, and directly illustrates the formation of planets.

FUN FACT

Gravitational telescopes use the effect of a body's gravitational waves to "see" it.

Hubble Space Telescope

The Hubble space telescope, often abbreviated as HST, is a space telescope. It was launched into low Earth orbit in 1990. With its 2.4 m mirror, Hubble's four main instruments observe in the near ultraviolet, visible and near infrared spectra. The telescope is named after the astronomer Edwin Hubble.

Importance

The HST orbit is outside the distortion of Earth's atmosphere. This allows it to take extremely high-resolution images with almost no background light. As a result, HST has recorded some of the most detailed visible-light images ever. This allows a deep view into space and time. Many HST observations have led to breakthroughs in astrophysics, such as accurately determining the rate of expansion of the universe.

History

Hermann Oberth published *Die Rakete zu den Planetenräumen*, which is German for *The Rocket into Planetary Space*, in 1923. This paper mentioned how a telescope could be propelled into Earth's orbit by a rocket. Astronomer Lyman Spitzer then published a paper,

Astronomical advantages of an extra-terrestrial observatory in 1946. Here, he discussed the two main advantages that a space-based observatory would have over ground-based telescopes. In 1968, NASA developed firm plans for a space-based reflecting telescope with a mirror 3 m in diameter. It was known provisionally as the Large Orbiting Telescope or Large Space Telescope (LST).

Construction and design

Congress approved funding of US $36 million in 1978. The LST began in earnest, aiming for a launch date of 1983. Marshall Space Flight Centre (MSFC) was given responsibility for the design, development and construction of the telescope. Goddard Space Flight Centre was given control of the

scientific instruments and the ground-control centre for the mission. Perkin-Elmer built the Optical Telescope Assembly (OTA) and fine guidance sensors for the space telescope. Lockheed was constructed and integrates the spacecraft, that would house the telescope.

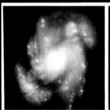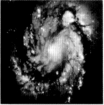

The spiral galaxy M100, shot with HST before and after corrective optics.

The Hubble being deployed from Space Shuttle Discovery in 1990.

FUN FACT

Anyone can apply for time on the HST. There are no restrictions on nationality or academic affiliation. However, the competition for time on the telescope is intense. Only one-fifth of the proposals get accepted.

SETI

The search for extra-terrestrial intelligence or SETI is the collective name for numerous activities undertaken to search for intelligent, extra-terrestrial life. Harvard University, the University of California, Berkeley and the SETI Institute run some of the most well known SETI projects. These projects use scientific methods for research. Most prominently, electromagnetic radiation is monitored for signs of transmissions from civilisations on other worlds.

History

As early as 1896, Nikola Tesla suggested that an extreme, amped up version of his wireless electrical transmission system could be used to contact beings on Mars. Tesla observed repetitive signals, substantially different from the signals noted from storms and Earth noise in 1899. He interpreted these signals as having extra-terrestrial origin. A 1959 paper by Physicists Philip Morrison and Giuseppe Cocconi first noted the possibility of searching the microwave spectrum. They also proposed frequencies and a set of targets.

First experiments

The first modern SETI experiment was done with a 26-m radio telescope in 1960. During the 1960s, Soviet scientists took a strong interest in SETI

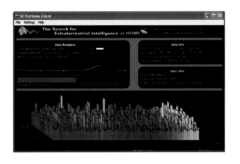

and performed several searches with omnidirectional antennas. In 1979, the University of California, Berkeley, launched a SETI project. They initiated their second SETI effort in 1986.

Funding

In 1978, the NASA SETI programme was heavily criticised by Senator William

A screen shot of the screensaver for SETI@home. This is a distributed computing project, in which volunteers donate idle computer power to analyse radio signals for signs of extra-terrestrial intelligence. It was devised as a low cost method and allowed enthusiasts to donate resources.

Proxmire. As a result, Congress removed funding for SETI research from the NASA budget in 1981. Carl Sagan intervened and funding was restored in 1982.

Hat Creek Allen Telescope Array. These radio-telescope have 6-m antennas used for radio-astronomy and by SETI.

FUN FACT

If the SETI discovers alien life, it may simply not announce it to the world. SETI must follow a procedure called the "post detection disclosure protocol" to avoid mass hysteria.

Rockets

A rocket-powered vehicle is used to transport a spacecraft beyond Earth's atmosphere. This could either be into Earth's orbit or a place in outer space. Such vehicles have been used since the 1950s to send manned spacecraft, unmanned space probes and satellites into space. To reach Earth's orbit, a rocket must accelerate to a minimum velocity of 28,000 km per hour, around 25 times the speed of sound.

▲ A rocket designed for space flight.

How do they work?

Newton's third law of motion, "For every action, there is an equal and opposite reaction" is a suitable example to describe the fundamental working of a rocket. With respect to rockets, the "action" is the gush of exhaust gases from the rear of the vehicle that is produced by the combustion of the vehicle's fuel in its rocket engine. The reaction is the pressure, called thrust, which is applied to the internal structure of the rocket that pushes it in the opposite direction of the exhaust flow. Rockets carry their own oxidising agent so that they can operate in the vacuum beyond the atmosphere.

◄ The two rocket launchers strapped to the spacecraft to enable the launch.

Stages of launch and design

The basic way to launch a rocket into space was first suggested by Konstantin Tsiolkovsky. He suggested that it is best to separate the vehicle into different stages.

First stage: It consists of the largest rocket engines, biggest fuel and oxidiser tanks, and maximum thrust. Its primary function is to impart the initial thrust needed to overcome Earth's gravity and thus to lift the entire weight of the vehicle, and its payload off of Earth. When the first-stage propellants are completely used, it is detached from the other parts of the launch vehicle and falls back to Earth, either into the ocean or onto a scarcely populated area.

Second stage: At the second stage, the rocket engines and propellants continue to speed up the vehicle. Most expendable rocket launchers have only two or three stages. Earlier, they had up to five stages, in order to attain orbital velocity. When the mission of the stage is completed, it either falls back to Earth, enters the orbit itself or breaks apart and evaporates as it comes in contact with atmospheric heating while falling back towards Earth.

FUN FACT

The Chinese were the first to use the principle of a rocket propelled by gunpowder to launch arrows against their enemies the Mongols in 1232 BC.

Upper stages

All launch vehicles employ more than one stage to accelerate spacecraft to orbital velocity. Since the first orbital launch (Sputnik), in 1957, there have been many different upper stages. Most are used as part of only one type of launch vehicle. The evolution of these upper stages is driven by a desire to introduce more modern technology that will increase the overall lift capability of the launch vehicle, lower its costs and increase its reliability — or a combination of these factors.

Energy requirement

Rockets need energy to propel into space. This energy is in the form of fuel. The fuel that is used to power rockets can be divided into two major categories: liquid and solid.

1. Liquid fuels: These fuels range from an easily available one such as kerosene, which can be used at ground temperature, to liquid hydrogen, which must be maintained at the extremely low temperature of 20 K. Liquid hydrogen is known as "cryogenic" fuel. Another type of liquid fuel is called hypergolic. It immediately lights upon contact with an oxidiser. These fuels are tremendously lethal and thus difficult to manage.

2. Solid fuels: These are simple in design, like big fireworks. They have a casing filled with a rubbery mixture of solid compounds that burn quickly once ignited. The fuel is usually some organic material or powdered aluminium; the oxidiser is most often ammonium perchlorate. The rocket propellant is formed when these are mixed. Solid rocket motors, once ignited, burn their fuel until it is exhausted and cannot be turned off. The exhaust from the fuel burning comes out through a nozzle at the bottom of the rocket casing that shapes and accelerates the exhaust to provide a forward thrust.

Space elevator

Chemically fuelled rocket propulsion seems to be the only best means to lift mass out of Earth's gravity. The concept of a space elevator emerged in 1895 by Konstantin Tsiolkovsky. It has an extremely strong cable extending from Earth's surface to the height of geostationary orbit or beyond.

An extremely high amount of heat and pressure is built up under the rocket that enables it to push off from Earth. Once the fuel has been used up, the tank separates from the rocket and becomes space debris.

The forces of gravity towards the lower end and outward centripetal acceleration at the other end keeps the cable under tension and still over a single location on Earth. This concept is subject to serious preliminary research.

The fuel is at a high pressure and when it combusts, it bursts out of the exhaust at the bottom of the rocket, that enables it to liftoff into Earth's orbit or beyond.

Observatories

An observatory consists of telescopes and supporting instruments through which you can observe celestial objects. Observatories are classified based on their electromagnetic spectrum by which they are designed to observe. Many observatories are optical, i.e., they are capable of observing in and around the region of the range visible to the human eye. There are few observatories that are instrumented to discover cosmic emitters of radio waves and others are Earth satellites that carry special telescopes to study celestial sources of energy.

Types of observatories

There are several types of observatories today. Every observatory focusses on different aspects of space such as the Sun, moon and stars among others. Let us take a look at some of these in closer detail.

Kitt Peak National Observatory

The Kitt Peak National Observatory (KPNO) is situated in Tuscon, USA in the Papago Indian Reservation. It is an astronomical observatory at a height of about 2 km. It was established in 1958 by the National Science Foundation (NSF), so that astronomers in East USA could have access to good optical observing facilities in a favourable climate. It is operated by the Association of Universities for Research in Astronomy together with the NSF. It has a collection of two radio and 21 optical telescopes; the largest being the 4 m Mayall Telescope. This observatory also has the biggest telescope designed for solar observation and a smaller vacuum tower telescope, which is used for specifically studying the Sun.

Mount Stromlo

The Mount Stromlo Observatory is located in southeast Australia, operated by the Australian National University. It is one of the important facilities for observation in the Southern Hemisphere. It was established in 1924. Initially, it was a centre for solar studies, but later shifted its focus during the 1940s to stellar astronomy. Here, the main telescope is a 1.9 m reflector. This observatory's viewing capability was endangered during the 1950s by the lights of the growing city of Canberra. Therefore, a new site was established at an elevation of 1,165 m on Siding Spring Mountain, located around 31 km from Coonabarabran, New South Wales. On 18th January, 2003, all five telescopes were destroyed by a bushfire.

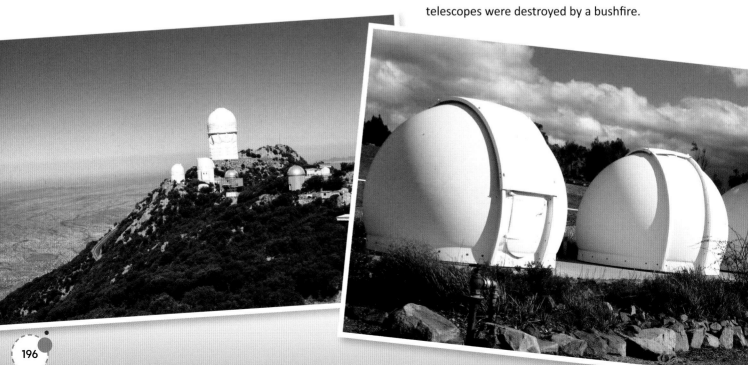

Gemini Observatory

Gemini Observatory is located on the island of Hawaii in the Northern Hemisphere. It is placed on the inactive volcano Mauna Kea. The observatory has two telescopes: the Frederick C. Gillett Gemini Telescope (Gemini North) and Gemini South. The observatory gets its name from the constellation Gemini, which represents the twins Castor and Pollux. One telescope was built in each hemisphere so that the observatory would have a broad range of objects for observation. The two telescopes have been utilised for observations at infrared wavelengths, whereby their primary mirrors were covered with silver, as it does not emit as much thermal infrared radiation as opposed to aluminium coatings that are otherwise used. Construction on the two telescopes began in 1994.

Lick Observatory

The Lick Observatory is situated in east San Jose, California, USA, at Mount Hamilton. It was the first major mountaintop observatory built in USA. In addition, it is the world's first permanently occupied mountaintop observatory. Its construction on Mount Hamilton started in 1880 with funds donated four years earlier by a wealthy Californian, James Lick. Its first major telescope, a 91 cm refractor with optics by Alvan Clark & Sons, began to be used in 1888. It continued to remain the largest in the world until the completion of the 102 cm refractor at Yerkes Observatory in 1897.

IAU

The International Astronomical Union, or IAU, is a collection of professional astronomers. In French, it is called the "Union astronomique international", or UAI. Members of the IAU must have a PhD. and a more advanced degree, as well as be active in professional research and education in astronomy.

Role and significance

It acts as the internationally recognised authority for assigning designations to celestial bodies such as stars, planets, asteroids, etc., and any surface features on them. It is a member of the International Council for Science, abbreviated to ICSU.

History

The IAU was founded in 1919. It was a merger of various international projects such as the Carte du Ciel, the Solar Union and the International Time Bureau or Bureau International de l'Heure. The first appointed President was Benjamin Baillaud.

Composition

The IAU has approximately 10,871 individual members. All of them are professional astronomers and most of them hold PhDs. There are also 73 national members. These represent countries affiliated with the IAU.

The sovereign body of the IAU is its General Assembly, which comprises all members.

Definition of a planet

The 26th General Assembly of the IAU was held from 14th to 25th August, 2006 in Prague, Czech Republic. The Assembly decided on 15th August to restore its individual members the right to vote on scientific matters. This privilege had been taken back at the 25th Assembly in 2003. The business included a proposal to adopt a formal definition of planet.

The dwarf planet controversy

The Assembly passed the final "definition of a planet" resolution on 24th August. It classified Ceres, Eris and Pluto as dwarf planets, and reduced the number of planets in the solar system to eight. Following the closing ceremony, parts of the scientific community did not agree with this ruling and criticised IAU's authority to name celestial bodies.

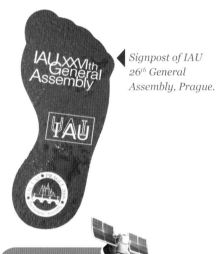

Signpost of IAU 26th General Assembly, Prague.

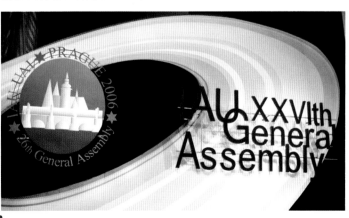

◀ *The IAU 26th General Assembly, Prague.*

FUN FACT

A final decision was made for the acceptance of the term "plutoid" and its official IAU definition: "Plutoids are celestial bodies in orbit around the Sun at a semi-major axis greater than that of Neptune. They have sufficient mass for their self-gravity to overcome rigid body forces so that they assume a hydrostatic equilibrium (near-spherical) shape and they have not cleared the neighbourhood around their orbit. Satellites of plutoids are not plutoids themselves."

PROMINENT SPACE ORGANISATIONS

An artist's rendering of an image of the International Space Station (ISS) with Earth's surface in the background.

Along with the IAU, there are national level bodies that study astronomy. However, the cost of space exploration is prohibitive and also requires access to a very great amount of resources. As a result, most governments have designated a governmental agency that co-ordinates and executes space exploration in the country.

Most space agencies lack the funds and resources to conduct all types of space missions. There are multiple private space agencies also interested in spaceflight. Most of these serve as subcontractors for government agencies. However, some, such as Virgin Galactic and SpaceX aim to offer private spaceflight to tourists as well.

NASA

The National Aeronautics and Space Administration (NASA) is the government agency of USA that is responsible for the civilian space programme as well as the aeronautics and aerospace research of USA.

Station (ISS). It is also overseeing the development of the Orion multi-purpose crew vehicle, space launch system and commercial crew vehicles. It is responsible for the Launch Services Program (LSP). This programme provides an oversight of launch operations and countdown management for unmanned NASA launches.

Other projects

NASA science is focussed on better understanding Earth through the Earth Observing System. It works towards advancing heliophysics through the efforts of the Science Mission Directorate's "Heliophysics Research Program". NASA focusses on exploring bodies throughout the solar system with advanced robotic missions such as New Horizons.

Environmental impact

Space exploration can affect life and environment on Earth. Some rocket propellants, such as hydrazine, are extremely toxic prior to being oxidised. However, it must be noted that NASA addressed environmental concerns with its cancelled constellation programme in accordance with the National Environmental Policy Act.

◀ *NASA's motto is "for the benefit of all". Depicted here is its seal.*

History

President Dwight D. Eisenhower established NASA in 1958. It was founded with a distinctly civilian, non-military orientation, encouraging peaceful applications in space science. The

National Aeronautics and Space Act was passed on 29th July, 1958. It disestablished NASA's predecessor, the National Advisory Committee for Aeronautics (NACA). NASA became operational on 1st October, 1958.

Space exploration

NASA has led most of USA's space exploration efforts. Their famous programme include the Apollo moon-landing missions, the Skylab space station and later the invention of the space shuttle. It is currently supporting the International Space

A part of a rocket designed to travel in space. ▼

ISRO

The Indian Space Research Organisation, or ISRO, is the primary space agency of India. ISRO is among the largest government space agencies in the world by both budget and number of missions launched. ISRO's primary objective is to advance space technology and use its applications for national benefit.

The ISRO logo.

History

ISRO superseded the erstwhile Indian National Committee for Space Research (INCOSPAR) on establishment in 1969. It, thus, institutionalised space activities in India. India's primary spaceport, the Satish Dhawan Space Centre in Sriharikota is run by ISRO.

Early missions and work

ISRO built India's first satellite, Aryabhata. This was launched by the Soviet Union on 19th April, 1975. Rohini became the first satellite to be placed in orbit by an Indian-made launch vehicle, called the SLV-3 in 1980. ISRO subsequently developed two other rockets.

● The Polar Satellite Launch Vehicle (PSLV) for launching satellites into the polar orbits.

● The Geosynchronous Satellite Launch Vehicle (GSLV) for placing satellites into the geostationary orbits.

From the public display held at Kanakakunnu palace at Trivandrum on 29th April, 2015. This is ISROs Space Capsule recovered from the sea.

A miniature model of ISRO's GSLV-D5 situated in College Campus.

FUN FACT

ISRO's Mars Mission team has won the prestigious 2015 Space Pioneer Award in the science and engineering category. This is in recognition of achieving the rare feat of entering Mar's orbit in its very first attempt. ISRO is the first Asian space agency to reach Mar's orbit.

Recent events and future plans

ISRO sent its first mission to the moon, Chandrayaan-1 on 22nd October, 2008. On 5th November, 2013, ISRO launched its Mars Orbiter Mission. The MoM successfully entered the Mars orbit on 24th September, 2014. Future plans include development of GSLV Mk III to be used for the launch of heavier satellites, development of a reusable launch vehicle, human spaceflight, further lunar exploration, launch of interplanetary probes, a satellite to study the Sun, etc.

ESA

The European Space Agency or ESA is an intergovernmental organisation dedicated to the exploration of space. Its French-speaking members know it as "Agence spatiale européenne" or ASE. ESA has 20 member states.

European Space Agency

History

ESA was established in 1975 and headquartered in Paris, France. After WWII, Western European scientists realised that solely national projects would not be able to compete with the two main superpowers. In 1958, Edoardo Amaldi and Pierre Auger, who were two prominent members of the Western European scientific community at the time, met to discuss the foundation of a common Western European space agency. This was only months after the Sputnik shock — the surprise launch of the first satellite by the USSR. As of 2014, ESA has a staff of more than 2000 with an annual budget of about €4.28 billion.

The ESA Logo. ESA is responsible for setting a unified space and related industrial policy, recommending space objectives to the member states and integrating national programme like satellite development, into the European programme as much as possible.

Its objective

The treaty establishing the ESA states, "ESA's purpose shall be to provide for and to promote, for exclusively peaceful purposes, co-operation among European States in space research and technology and their space applications, with a view to their being used for scientific purposes and for operational space applications systems".

This image shows the European Space Agency ESA's Headquarters in Paris, France.

European expendable launch system at the Le Bourget Air show in Paris, France.

Missions and work

ESA's space flight programme includes human spaceflight, mainly through its contribution in the International Space Station programme. It maintains a major spaceport, called the Guiana Space Centre at Kourou, in the French Guiana, and designs launch vehicles. It also works on operations of unmanned exploration missions to other planets and the moon, Earth observation, science and telecommunication.

European Space Expo in Zagreb, Croatia.

FUN FACT

The International Rosetta Mission is supposed to end on 15th December, 2015.

RFSA

The Russian Federal Space Agency (RFSA) is the government agency that is responsible for the Russian space science programme and general aerospace research. It is commonly called "Roscosmos", which is short for the Russian "Russpace" and abbreviated as FKA and RKA. It was previously the Russian Aviation and Space Agency and commonly known as "Rosaviakosmos".

ПОCKOCMOC

The Roscosmos logo. Roscosmos is headquartered at Shchepkin Street 42, Moscow.

Major facilities

The headquarter of Roscosmos is located in Moscow. The Main Mission Control space flight operations centre is located in the nearby city of Korolev. The Cosmonauts Training Centre (GCTC) is in Star City. The Launch facilities used by Roscosmos are the Baikonur Cosmodrome in Kazakhstan and Plesetsk Cosmodrome in northern Russia. Baikonur is mostly civilian with most launches occurring there, both manned and unmanned, while Plesetsk flights are primarily unmanned military.

History

The creation of a central agency after the separation of Russia from the Soviet Union was a new development as the Soviet Union did not have a central space bureau. Yuri Koptev became the agency's first director. This agency was later renamed to Roscosmos.

Crisis years

The 1990s saw serious financial problems in Russia because of decreased cash flow. This encouraged them to improvise and seek other financial sources. As a result, they gained a leading role in commercial satellite launches and tourism. Scientific missions, such as interplanetary probes or astronomy missions played a very small role during these years.

However, Roscosmos managed to operate the space station Mir well past its planned lifespan. It also contributed

The Soyuz TMA-9 spacecraft launches from the Baikonur Cosmodrome in Kazakhstan 18th September, 2006 carrying a new crew to the International Space Station.

to the International Space Station and continued to fly additional Soyuz and Progress missions.

Current programme

Some of Roscosmos's future projects are the Soyuz successor, the Prospective Piloted Transport System, scientific robotic missions to one of the Mars moons as well as an increase in lunar orbit research satellites.

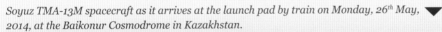

Soyuz TMA-13M spacecraft as it arrives at the launch pad by train on Monday, 26th May, 2014, at the Baikonur Cosmodrome in Kazakhstan.

Japan Aerospace Exploration Agency

Japan Aerospace Exploration Agency (JAXA) is Japan's national aerospace working agency. It was established in 2003 and is headquartered in Chofu (Tokyo). It is responsible for technology development, research works, launching of satellites into the orbit, asteroid data, moon exploration and many other advanced missions. The agency's motto is, "Reaching for the skies, exploring space".

▲ Japan Aerospace Exploration Agency's logo.

JAXA's projects
- Advanced Land Observation Satellite
- Carbon dioxide monitoring
- Rainfall observation
- GCOM series

JAXA's missions
- Hayabusa: Small body exploration
- Lunar explorations
- Solar sail research

Reaching for the stars

Japan has 10 astronauts. Surprisingly, being a technologically advanced nation it has not developed its own manned spacecraft. They tried to develop a potentially manned space shuttle plane called the HOPE-X project. It was launched by the conventional space launcher H-II and was developed for several years. Unfortunately, the project was postponed. Projects for single-stage to orbit, horizontal takeoff, reusable launch vehicle and landing ASSTS and the vertical takeoff and landing Kankoh-maru exist; however, these have not been adopted yet.

▲ A drone developed by JAXA for use during disasters.

Gen-next technology

JAXA is developing technology for a next-generation supersonic transport. If successful, it could become the commercial replacement for the Concorde. The design goal of the project is to develop a jet that can carry 300 passengers at Mach 2. A subscale model of the jet underwent aerodynamic testing in September and October 2005, in Australia. The economic success of such a project is still unclear and as a consequence the project has been met with limited interest from Japanese aerospace companies like Mitsubishi Heavy Industries.

The science museum at Nagoya that has a rocket on display outside it.

FAMOUS COSMOLOGISTS AND ASTRONOMERS

The sculpture of Copernicus on a pedestal holding a heliocentric model of the universe.

Physical cosmology is the study of the largest-scale structures and dynamics of the Universe. The field is concerned with fundamental questions about the origin, structure, evolution and ultimate fate of our Universe.

For most of human history, cosmology was a branch of metaphysics and religion. This changed with science being applied to cosmic phenomena. The first of these was the Copernican Principle, stating that all heavenly bodies follow the same rules as the objects on Earth.

Modern cosmology developed along tandem tracks of theory and observation as the nature of the Universe became clearer with bits of additional data.

Galileo Galilei

Galileo Galilei, often known as Galileo, was an Italian physicist, mathematician, engineer, astronomer and philosopher. He lived in Italy from 15th February, 1564 to 8th January, 1642. Galileo played a major role in the scientific revolution during the Renaissance. Thus, Galileo has been called the "father of modern observational astronomy", "father of modern physics", "father of science" and "the father of modern science".

Early life

Galileo was born in Pisa, Tuscany. His family moved to Florence in the early 1570s, where they lived for generations. In 1581, Galileo matriculated at the University of Pisa, where he studied medicine as physicians earned much more than mathematicians. However, he became enamoured with mathematics and made it his profession.

This is a painting of Galileo showing the Doge of Venice how to use his telescope as depicted in a fresco by Gieuseppe Bertini.

He then became the mathematics chair for Padua until 1610. At this point, he moved to Florence, to join the court of the Medicis.

Telescope

Hans Lippershey, in the Netherlands, made the first practical telescope in 1608. After hearing the descriptions, Galileo made a telescope with about three times the magnification in the following year. He taught himself the art of lens grinding and quickly figured out how to improve the instrument. He, thus, produced increasingly powerful telescopes, reaching one with upto 30 times magnification.

Telescopic discoveries

In December 1609, he drew the moon's phases as seen through the telescope. These show that the moon's surface is not smooth, but is rough and uneven — contrary to popular belief at the time. He discovered four moons revolving around Jupiter in January 1610. This was shocking to most since the Aristotelian theory postulated that everything revolved around Earth.

Galileo quickly produced a little book called Sidereus Nuncius (The Sidereal Messenger), in which he described these discoveries. He named the moons of Jupiter after Cosimo II de Medici, but they were soon after renamed in his honour.

The sculpture of Galileo holding a telescope.

FUN FACT

Galileo was prosecuted for stating that Earth revolves around the Sun. At the end of his trial, Galileo formally recanted his conclusions. Yet, there is an unverifiable rumour that under his breath he whispered "Eppur si muove" or "And yet it moves" — reaffirming that Earth indeed underwent rotational and revolutionary motions.

GALILEO GALILEI

Ptolemy

Claudius was a Greco-Egyptian writer of Alexandria from CE 90 to CE 168. He was known as a mathematician, astronomer, geographer, astrologer and poet of a single epigram in the Greek Anthology. Ptolemy is of interest as the author of several scientific treatises, three of which were of continuing importance to later Islamic and European science. He wrote the astronomical treatise now known as the Almagest.

▲ *An artist's rendition of Ptolemy.*

The almagest

The Almagest is the only surviving comprehensive ancient treatise on astronomy. Ptolemy claimed to have derived his geometrical models from selected astronomical observations by his predecessors spanning more than 800 years, which would make it unique in those days. The Almagest also contains a star catalogue and a list of 48 constellations.

Ptolemy's planetary hypotheses

These hypotheses went beyond the mathematical model of the Almagest. It attempted to present a physical realisation of the universe as a set of nested spheres. He estimated that the Sun was at an average distance of 1,210 Earth radii, while the radius of the sphere of the fixed stars was 20,000 times the radius of Earth. Ptolemy's model was geocentric like those of his predecessors. It was almost universally accepted until the appearance of simpler heliocentric models.

A sixteenth century Latin ▶
edition of the Almagest
or Almagestum as it was
called in Latin.

Ptolemy's almanac

In his Handy Tables, he presented a useful tool for astronomical calculations. It tabulated all the data needed to compute the positions of the Sun, moon and planets, the rising and setting of the stars and eclipses of the Sun and moon. These also provided the model for later astronomical tables or zījes as they were known by Islamic astronomers.

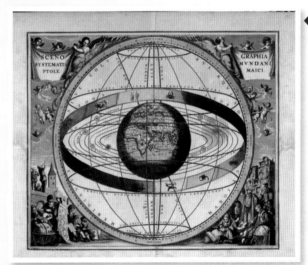

◀ *Cellarius ptolemaic*
system: from Andreas
Cellarius Harmonia
Macrocosmica, 1660/61.
This chart shows signs of
the zodiac and the solar
system with the world at
its centre.

FUN FACT

The Latin name of Claudius in Claudius Ptolemy refers to the Roman who granted Ptolemy Roman citizenship. Considering the timeline, this was most probably the Roman Emperor Claudius.

Nicolaus Copernicus

Nicolaus Copernicus was a Renaissance mathematician and astronomer. He lived from 19th February, 1473 to 24th May, 1543. He is famous for a model of the universe that placed the Sun rather than Earth at its centre. This is called "heliocentricity" and is the currently accepted model of the solar system.

Heliocentricity

Copernicus based his model on seven basic assumptions. They are reproduced as below:

1. There is no one centre of all the celestial circles or spheres.

2. The centre of Earth is not the centre of the universe, but only of gravity and the lunar sphere.

3. All the spheres revolve about the Sun as their mid-point and therefore the Sun is the centre of the universe.

4. The ratio of Earth's distance from the Sun to the height of the firmament (outermost celestial sphere containing the stars) is so much smaller than the ratio of Earth's radius to its distance from the Sun that the distance from Earth to the Sun is imperceptible in comparison with the height of the firmament.

5. Whatever motion appears in the firmament arises not from any motion of the firmament, but from Earth's motion. Earth, together with its circumjacent elements performs a complete rotation on its fixed poles in a daily motion, while the firmament and the highest heaven abide unchanged.

6. What appears to us as the motion of the Sun arises not from its motion, but from Earth's motion and our spheres. We revolve about the Sun like any other planet. Earth has, therefore, more than one motion.

◄ *Copernicus' model of the solar system as described in "De revolutionibus orbium coelestium" or "On the Revolutions of the Celestial Spheres" in 1543.*

7. The apparent retrograde and direct motion of the planets arise not from their motion, but from Earth's. The motion of Earth alone, therefore, suffices to explain so many apparent inequalities in the heavens.

◄ *A statue of Copernicus.*

FUN FACT

Copernicus was a true "Renaissance man". He was a polyglot and polymath. His numerous accomplishments include obtaining a doctorate in canon law and practicing as a physician, classics scholar, translator, governor, diplomat and economist.

Edwin Hubble

Edwin Powell Hubble was an American astronomer who lived from 20th November, 1889 to 28th September, 1953. He played a crucial role in establishing the field of extragalactic astronomy. Hubble is generally regarded as one of the most important observational cosmologists of the twentieth century.

Early years and education

Edwin Hubble was born to Virginia Lee James and John Powell Hubble in Marshfield, Missouri. He studied at the University of Chicago. He earned a Bachelor of Science degree in 1910 with concentration on mathematics and astronomy. He studied astronomy at the Yerkes Observatory of the University, where he received his PhD on Photographic Investigations of Faint Nebulae in 1917.

Beyond the Milky Way

Edwin Hubble's arrival at Mount Wilson, California with the completion of the 2.5 m Hooker Telescope was the largest in the world. Hubble identified Cepheid variable stars in several spiral nebulae, including the Andromeda Nebula and Triangulum. His observations proved conclusively that these nebulae were much too distant to be part of the Milky Way. They were, in fact, entire galaxies outside our own.

Redshift

In 1929, Hubble formulated the Redshift Distance Law. It is nowadays termed simply as the Hubble's law. The observance of increasing "redshift" in more distant stars proves that the farther galaxies were receding faster. This supported the Big Bang Theory that had been proposed by Georges Lemaître in 1927.

The 2.5 m Hooker telescope at Mount Wilson Observatory that Hubble used to measure galaxy distances. Using this, Hubble determined a value for the rate of expansion of the universe.

The HST when raised above the observatory when in use.

FUN FACT

Hubble discovered the asteroid 1373 Cincinnati.

Edmond Halley

Edmond Halley, FRS was an English astronomer, geophysicist, mathematician, meteorologist and physicist. He lived from 8th November, 1656 to 14th January, 1742. He worked at the University of Oxford's Royal Observatory, in Greenwich.

Predicting a comet that he had not seen or witnessed firsthand made Edmund Halley a pioneer in the use of analytical prediction methods.

It is said of Mark Twain that he had stated in 1909 that he had come (taken birth) with the Halley's comet in 1835 and wanted to leave (die) with it as well, in 1910. He passed away on 21st April, 1910, only one day after the comet had appeared in the sky from around the Sun.

Early life and education

Edmund Halley was born in Haggerston, London. He was named after his father Edmond Halley Sr. Halley Sr came from a Derbyshire family and was a wealthy soap-maker in London. Halley was very interested in mathematics as a child. He initially studied at St Paul's School. From 1673 he studied at The Queen's College, Oxford. While still an undergraduate, Halley published papers on the solar system and sunspots.

Introduction to astronomy

In 1675, Halley became an assistant to John Flamsteed, the Astronomer Royal at the Greenwich Observatory. Interestingly, he had the job of assigning what are now called Flamsteed numbers to stars. In 1676, Halley visited the south Atlantic island of Saint Helena. He set up an observatory with a large sextant with telescopic sights in order to catalogue the stars present in the southern hemisphere.

Size of the solar system

While in St Helena, he observed a transit of Mercury. Halley immediately realised that a similar transit of Venus could be used to determine the absolute size of the solar system. In doing so, he was following the method described by James Gregory in Optica Promota. He may or may not have been aware of this.

Halley's comet

In 1705, he published the *Synopsis Astronomia Cometica*. In this, he stated his belief that the comet sightings of 1456, 1531, 1607 and 1682 related to the same comet and he predicted it would return in 1758. He did this by applying historical astronomy methods. Halley did not live to witness the comet's return. But when it returned, the comet became generally known as Halley's Comet.

Edmund Halley's portrait by Thomas Murray, circa 1687.

FUN FACT

Flamsteed described Halley as a Southern Tycho Brahe for cataloguing the stars in the Southern Hemisphere.

Johannes Kepler

Johannes Kepler was a mathematician, astronomer and astrologer. He was German and lived from 27th December, 1571 to 15th November, 1630 in what is now Austria, but was then part of the Holy Roman Empire.

Early years and education

Johannes Kepler was born on 27th December, 1571 at the Free Imperial City of Weil der Stadt, which is now part of the Stuttgart Region in Germany. His father, Heinrich Kepler, was a mercenary and left the family when Johannes was five years old. At age six, Johannes observed the Great Comet of 1577 and developed a love for astronomy that would span his entire life. He attended Tübinger Stift at the University of Tübingen. Under the instruction of Michael Maestlin, he learned both the Ptolemaic system and the Copernican systems and became a Copernican.

Mysterium Cosmographicum

Johannes Kepler's published his first major astronomical work, *Mysterium Cosmographicum* or *The Cosmographic Mystery* in 1596. It was the first published defence of the Copernican system. Mysterium, is seen as an important first step in modernising the theory proposed by Nicolaus Copernicus in his "De Revolutionibus". Copernicus resorted to Ptolemaic devices like epicycles and eccentric circles in his work. Mysterium paved way for newer mathematical models.

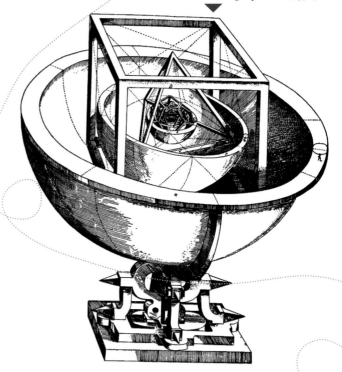

Kepler's Platonic solid model of the solar system from Mysterium Cosmographicum (1596).

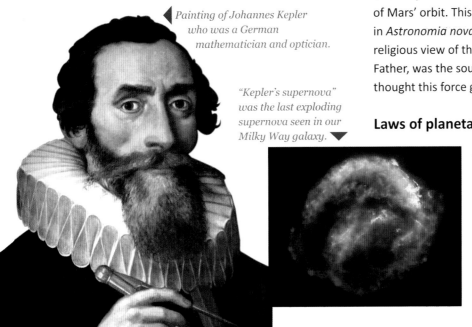

◄ Painting of Johannes Kepler who was a German mathematician and optician.

"Kepler's supernova" was the last exploding supernova seen in our Milky Way galaxy. ▼

Astronomia nova

Under Tycho Brahe's direction, Kepler began the analysis of Mars' orbit. This extended line of research culminated in *Astronomia nova* or *A New Astronomy*. Within Kepler's religious view of the cosmos, the Sun, as a symbol of God the Father, was the source of motive force in the solar system. He thought this force got weaker with distance.

Laws of planetary motion

Kepler is most famous for his three laws of planetary motion. Through these, he explained various phenomena like the seasons, the different speeds of movement and the fact that orbits are actually ellipses and not circles.

Albert Einstein

Albert Einstein was a German-born theoretical physicist and philosopher of science. He is best known in popular culture for his mass – energy equivalence formula $E = mc^2$, which is thought to be the most famous equation in history. He also developed the general theory of relativity. In 1921, he received the Nobel Prize in Physics for his discovery of the law of the photoelectric effect. This was a basis for modern quantum mechanics.

Summary of accomplishments

Einstein published more than 300 scientific papers and over 150 non-scientific works. Universities and archives announced the release of Einstein's papers, comprising more than 30,000 unique documents on 5th December, 2014. Einstein's intellectual achievements and originality have made the word "Einstein" synonymous with genius. Thus, he is often regarded as the greatest genius who ever lived.

◄ Albert Einstein pictured in his office in 1920.

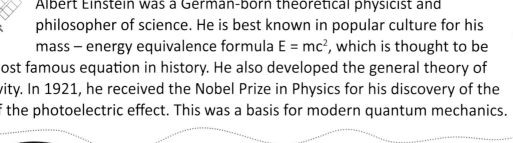

◄ Einstein's formula of mass-energy equivalence that made history.

Cosmological constant

Einstein apprehended that his equations predicted the universe to be either contracting or expanding. To reconcile this with his view of a static universe, Einstein modified the general theory by introducing a new notion. This was the cosmological constant, which he called "Lambda". However, Edwin Hubble confirmed that the universe is expanding in 1929 and Einstein supposedly reconsidered and discarded the cosmological constant.

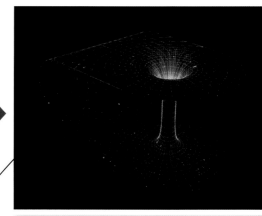

A diagrammatic representation of the working of a wormhole. ▶

Theory of relativity

Einstein thought that Newtonian mechanics was not enough to reconcile the laws of classical mechanics with the laws of the electromagnetic field. He, thus, developed the special theory of relativity. He later realised that the principle of relativity could also be extended to gravitational fields. He, thus, published a paper on the general theory of relativity.

Wormholes

Einstein collaborated with others as outlined in his paper, *Do Gravitational Fields play an Important Role in the Constitution of the Elementary Particles?* In fact, a hypothetical traversable wormhole or one that we can travel through is known as an Einstein-Rosen Bridge.

FUN FACT

Einstein advocated the development of nuclear bombs to the US President FD Roosevelt. After Hiroshima and Nagasaki, he regretted this stance.

Stephen Hawking

Stephen William Hawking CH CBE FRS FRSA is an English theoretical physicist, cosmologist, author and Director of Research at the Centre for Theoretical Cosmology within the University of Cambridge. He was born on 8th January, 1942 in Oxford and currently resides at Cambridge in the UK.

▲ *Stephen Hawking introduces the public to the Corpus Clock, at the Taylor Library, Corpus Christi College, Cambridge.*

Family

Hawking was born to Frank and Isobel Hawking. Despite their financial constraints, both his parents attended Oxford. Hawking has two younger sisters, Philippa and Mary, and an adopted brother, Edward. He has also been married twice and is father to three children.

Medical condition

Hawking suffers from a rare, early-onset, slow-progressing form of amyotrophic lateral sclerosis (ALS), or motor neurone disease. This has gradually paralysed him over the decades. He initially used crutches, but was confined to a wheelchair by the end of the 1960s. He also lost the use of his vocal chords due to a tracheotomy that was performed when he contracted a life-threatening case of pneumonia.

He currently communicates by using a single cheek muscle attached to a speech-generating device.

Awards and accolades

Hawking is an Honorary Fellow of the Royal Society of Arts, as well as a lifetime member of the Pontifical Academy of Sciences. He is also a recipient of the Presidential Medal of Freedom, which is the highest civilian award in the USA. He also served as the Lucasian Professor of Mathematics at the University of Cambridge between 1979 and 2009. He also has a list of awards including the Dirac award, Einstein award and the fundamental physics prize.

Significant works

Hawking collaborated with Roger Penrose on gravitational singularity theorems in the framework of general relativity. He made the theoretical prediction that black holes emit radiation. This is often called Hawking radiation. Hawking was the first to set forth a cosmology explained by a combination of the general theory of relativity and quantum mechanics. He is also a vigorous supporter of the many-worlds interpretation of quantum mechanics.

◀ *Professor Stephen Hawking with David Fleming, manager of the Intel Innovation Open Lab in Ireland (centre) and Martin Curley, vice president of Intel Labs Europe.*

FUN FACT

Hawking writes many non-academic works. His "A brief history of time" was a NY bestseller for 237 weeks.

Neil DeGrasse Tyson

Neil De Grasse Tyson is an American astrophysicist, cosmologist, author and science communicator. He was born on 5th October, 1958 as the second of three children in Manhattan and raised in the Bronx. Tyson obsessively studied astronomy in his teens. He gained some fame in the astronomy community because of his lectures on the subject at the age of 15. Astronomer Carl Sagan tried to recruit Tyson to Cornell for undergraduate studies while he was a faculty member there.

Popularisation of science in media, work as a science communicator

From 2006 to 2011, Tyson hosted the educational science television show ''NOVA Science Now'' on PBS. He was a frequent guest on The Daily Show, The Colbert Report and Real Time with Bill Maher. From 2009, he hosted the weekly radio show Star Talk. Tyson hosted Cosmos: A Spacetime Odyssey, which was a sequel to Carl Sagan's Cosmos: A Personal Voyage (1980) television series in 2014.

Career

Tyson has held numerous positions at both academic and scientific institutions such as the University of Maryland, Princeton University, the American Museum of Natural History and Hayden Planetarium. He served on the Commission on the Future of the United States Aerospace Industry in 2001. In 2004, he served on the President's Commission on the implementation of United States Space Exploration Policy. This is better known as the "Moon, Mars, and Beyond" commission.

Specialisations

Tyson's research focusses on observations in cosmology, stellar evolution, galactic astronomy, bulges and stellar formation.

A picture of Neil De Grasse Tyson on the extreme right, with US President Barack Obama in the centre and TV Presenter Bill Nye, who is clicking the "selfie".

Dr Neil De Grasse Tyson visited Director Chris Scolese of Goddard's Space Flight Center.

FUN FACT

Neil De Grasse Tyson is a published author and also very popular on social media. His tweets often focus on urban myths and religious mythology in the context of science.

Neil De Grasse Tyson at the "1,000 days since launch" party for Kepler.

HUMANS IN SPACE

▲ Astronauts in outer space leave their shuttle for repairs or experimentation during a spacewalk.

The idea of humans in space refers to human spaceflight, but is not limited to it. Over the past century, humans have made vast progress in various fields of science. As a result, we have not only been able to observe space but actually leave Earth's atmosphere and enter space.

Over the past 50 years, hundreds of artificial satellites have been sent into space. Humans have also entered space to a previously unheard of extent. However, the field of space exploration is still in its infancy.

Space Launch

Space launch is the earliest part of any flight that reaches space. It involves liftoff. This is when a rocket or any other space launch vehicle leaves the ground at the start of a flight. Liftoff is of two main types:

- Rocket launch - the current, conventional method
- Non-rocket space launch - other forms of propulsion are employed, such as air breathing jet engines.

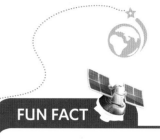

FUN FACT

At Earth's surface, escape velocity occurs at a speed of 11.2 km per second. This is the speed required to overcome Earth's gravity.

Reaching "Space"

Space has no physical edge. There is no sharply defined boundary to space. Space is experienced as the atmospheric pressure gradually reduces with altitude. The edge of space is defined by convention. The Kármán line of 100 km is most popular. Other definitions have been created as well. For example, in USA, space has been defined as 80—81 km from Earth.

Energy required

Sufficient altitude is necessary for spaceflight to occur. For 100 km, at least the gravitational potential energy, i.e., the energy caused by the presence of "weight" must be overcome. In practice, a higher energy than this is expended due to losses such as air drag, propulsive efficiency, cycle efficiency of engines that are employed and gravity drag.

Usable G-forces

Humans cannot stand forces more than three to six times those of gravity. As a result, some launchers such as gun launchers are completely unsuitable. These would cause accelerations that are hundreds or thousand times the force of gravity.

▲ *An image of the Russian Spaceport of Baikonur as a craft launches.*

Trajectory optimisation

Trajectory optimisation is the process of "designing a trajectory that minimises or maximises some measures of performance within prescribed constraint boundaries". This problem was first studied by Robert H. Goddard. It is also known as the Goddard problem.

Artificial Satellites

A satellite is an artificial object that has been intentionally placed into orbit. More specifically, such objects are called artificial satellites to distinguish them from natural satellites such as the moon.

Launch and functioning

Satellites are propelled to their orbits by rockets. Usually, the launch vehicle itself is a rocket lifting off from a launch pad that is based on land. However, in a few cases, satellites are launched at sea. This is usually from a submarine or mobile maritime platform. Some launches can be from aboard a plane as well.

History and background

The world's first artificial satellite, the Sputnik 1, was launched by the Soviet Union in 1957. After that, thousands of satellites have been launched into orbit around Earth or into deep space. Some satellites, most notably space stations, have been launched in parts and then assembled in orbit. Artificial satellites originate from more than 40 countries. However, they have all used the satellite launching capabilities of only 10 nations.

Current status

A few hundred satellites are currently operational. Most of the thousands of unused satellites and satellite fragments orbit Earth as space debris. Also, a few space probes have been placed into orbit around other bodies. These become artificial satellites to the moon, Mercury, Venus, Mars, Jupiter, Saturn, Vesta, Eros and the Sun.

Uses

Satellites are currently used for a rather large number of purposes. Common classifications include military and civilian Earth observation satellites, communications satellites, navigation satellites, weather satellites and research satellites. Space stations and

Pictured here is a full-size model of Earth observation satellite ERS 2.

human spacecraft in orbit also fall under the category of satellites. Their orbits vary greatly. Depending on the purpose of the satellite, an orbit is chosen. Orbits are classified in several ways. Well-known classes include low Earth orbit, polar orbit and geostationary orbit. Sometimes, these overlap.

The first artificial satellite displayed in the exhibition in GUM, 2011, at the State Central Museum of Contemporary History of Russia.

Space satellite orbiting Earth with the Sun in the background.

FUN FACT

The name of the first satellite, "Sputnik", means wanderer.

Human Spaceflight

Human spaceflight is space travel with a crew aboard the spacecraft. It is often termed as manned spaceflight. When a spacecraft is crewed, it can be operated directly, as opposed to being remotely operated or autonomous.

History and background

The Soviet Union launched the first human spaceflight on 12th April, 1961. It was launched as a part of the Vostok programme. The flight had cosmonaut Yuri Gagarin aboard. Since then, numerous missions have gone into space. Humans have been continually present in space for 15 years and 67 days on the International Space Station (ISS) as of 2015.

Current flight capabilities

The retirement of the US Space Shuttle was carried out in 2011. Since then, only Russia and China have maintained domestic human spaceflight capability, with the Soyuz programme and Shenzhou programme respectively. Currently, all crewed flights to the International Space Station use Soyuz vehicles. These remain attached to the station to allow quick return if needed. USA is also developing commercial crew transportation to facilitate domestic access to ISS and low Earth orbit. It is also developing the Orion vehicle for beyond-low Earth orbit applications.

Commercial spaceflight

Spaceflight has typically been a government-directed activity. However, commercial spaceflight has gradually been taking on a greater role. The first private human spaceflight took place on 21st June, 2004. A private company, Space Ship One, conducted a suborbital flight. Since then, a number of non-governmental companies have been working to develop a space tourism industry. NASA has also played a role to stimulate private spaceflight through programmes such as Commercial Orbital Transportation Services (COTS) and Commercial Crew Development (CCDev).

The "Semyorka" - the Rocket R7 by Sergei Korolyov in VDNH, Ostankino, Moscow.

Pictured here is Astronaut Bruce McCandless floating free in space with the help of a space suit and Manned Manoeuvring Unit.

Future plans

Commercial resupply of ISS began two years after the retirement of the Shuttle in 2013. Commercial crew launches are slated for 2017.

Effects of Spaceflight on Humans

Humans are physiologically well adapted to life on Earth. Consequently, spaceflight has many negative effects on the body. Space medicine is a developing medical practice. The main purpose of this academic pursuit is to discover how well and for how long people can survive the extreme conditions in space. Also, it checks how fast they can re-adapt to Earth's environment after returning from space.

Direct exposure to the extreme environment of space

The environment of space is lethal without appropriate protection. The greatest threat in the vacuum of space is from the lack of oxygen and pressure. However, extremes of temperature and radiation also pose ample risks.

The vacuum of space

A certain amount of oxygen is required in the air for us to breathe. The minimum concentration, called partial pressure, of oxygen that can be tolerated is 16 k/Pa. In the vacuum of space, gas exchange in the lungs continues as normal. However, it results in the removal of all gases, including oxygen, from the bloodstream. After nine to 12 seconds, deoxygenated blood reaches the brain and results in a loss of consciousness. Death would gradually follow after two minutes of exposure.

Astronaut Frank De Winne is attached to a treadmill with bungee cords aboard the International Space Station. Regular exercise is necessary to maintain muscle mass in space.

Increased radiation levels

Without the protection of Earth's atmosphere and magnetosphere, astronauts are exposed to high levels of radiation. This can damage lymphocytes – cells heavily involved in maintaining the immune system. This damage contributes to lower immunity. Solar flare events are rare, but can administer a fatal radiation dose in minutes.

The effects of weightlessness

Following the advent of space stations, exposure to weightlessness has been demonstrated to have some harmful effects on human health. In response to weightlessness, various physiological systems begin

An astronaut using a space simulation capsule to get used to the loss of gravity.

to change, and in some cases, cause atrophy. In the absence of gravity, fluids tend to build up in the upper half of the body. Redistributed fluids around the body cause balance disorders, distorted vision and a loss of taste and smell.

Astronaut in outer space against the backdrop of Earth.

First Man in Space

Yuri Alekseyevich Gagarin was a Russian-Soviet pilot and cosmonaut. He lived from 9th March, 1934, to 27th March, 1968. Gagarin became the first human to journey into outer space when his Vostok spacecraft completed an orbit of Earth on 12th April, 1961.

Early years and history

Yuri Gagarin was born in the village of Klushino near Gzhatsk on 9th March, 1934. He was the third of four children. In 1946, the family moved to Gzhatsk. Gagarin continued his secondary education there. After graduating in 1951 from both the seventh grade and vocational school, he was selected for further training at the Saratov Industrial Technical School. It was in Saratov that Gagarin volunteered for weekend training as a Soviet air cadet at a local flying club. He learned to fly here— first in a biplane and later in a Yak-18 trainer.

Military career

In 1955, the Soviet Army drafted Gagarin. He was sent to the First Chkalov Air Force Pilot's School in Orenburg. Here, he solo piloted a MiG-15 in 1957.

Post-graduation, he was assigned to the Luostari airbase in Murmansk Oblast.

Soviet space programme

In 1960, Yuri Gagarin was chosen with 19 other pilots for the Soviet space programme. After further testing, Gagarin was selected for an elite training group known as the Sochi Six. The first cosmonauts of the Vostok programme would be chosen from the Sochi Six. Space was limited in the small Vostok cockpit and Gagarin was rather short at 1.57 m. This was an important factor in his selection.

Vostok 1

On 12th April, 1961, Gagarin became the first human to travel into space, as well as the first to orbit Earth. His call sign was Kedr. His post flight report

The Vostok 1 capsule on display at the RKK Energiya museum.

On 27th March, 1968, Gagarin died in a MiG-15 UTI crash near the town of Kirzhach.

stated: "The feeling of weightlessness was somewhat unfamiliar compared to Earth conditions. Here, you feel as if you were hanging in a horizontal position in straps. You feel as if you are suspended".

FUN FACT

In Gagarin's honour, his village of Klushino was renamed Gagarin in 1968 after his death.

Famous Astronauts

Human spaceflight records are extensive and saw a lot of competition to establish during the "space race" of the Cold War. As a result, many astronauts achieved great fame. They were seen similar in status to the Air Aces of World War I and World War II.

● **Valentina Tereshkova** — The first woman in space was Soviet Valentina Tereshkova. She was launched on 16ᵗʰ June, 1963, aboard Vostok 6 and orbited Earth for almost three days.

● **Alan Shepard** — He was the first American and second person in space. He was launched on 5ᵗʰ May, 1961, on a 15-minute sub-orbital flight.

● **Sally Ride** — She was the first American woman in space during the Space Shuttle Challenger's mission STS-7, on 18ᵗʰ June, 1983.

● **Alexei Leonov** — He was the first person to conduct an extravehicular activity (EVA), on 18ᵗʰ March, 1965, on the Soviet Union's Voskhod 2 mission.

● **Pham Tuan** — He was the first Asian (Vietnamese) in space, aboard Soyuz 37 on 23ʳᵈ July, 1980.

● **Neil Armstrong** — He was the first human to walk on the moon in 1969.

● **Buzz Aldrin** — He was the second human to walk on the moon in 1969.

● **Yang Liwei** — He was the first person sent into space by China.

● **Dennis Tito** — He was the first self-funded space tourist on board the Russian spacecraft Soyuz TM-3 on 28ᵗʰ April, 2001.

Valentina Tereshkova ▶

Alan Shepard ▼

Sally Ride ▲

◀ *Dennis Tito*

Alexei Lenov ▲

▼ *Yang Liwei*

Buzz Aldrin ▼

Pham Tuan ▲

◀ *Neil Armstrong*

Moon Landing

A moon landing is the arrival of a spacecraft on the surface of the moon. Moon landings include both manned and unmanned, i.e., robotic missions. The first human-made object to reach the surface of the moon was the Soviet Union's Luna 2 mission on 13th September, 1959.

Escaping Earth

In order to go to the Moon, a spacecraft must first leave the "gravity well" of Earth. This requires it to attain "escape velocity". The only practical way of accomplishing this is with a rocket. Other airborne vehicles such as balloons or jets lose thrust as they go higher due to the thinning of the atmosphere. A rocket is the only known form of propulsion that can continue to increase its speed in the vacuum outside Earth's atmosphere.

Landing on the moon

Upon approaching the moon, a spacecraft gets drawn ever closer to its surface at increasing speeds due to its gravity. In order to land intact, the spacecraft must decelerate to less than about 160 km per hour and toughened to withstand what is called a "hard landing" impact. It may also decelerate to a negligible speed at contact for a "soft landing". A soft landing is the only viable option with human occupants. The Soviets first achieved the milestone of a hard lunar landing with a ruggedised camera in 1966. Only months later, the US managed the first unmanned soft lunar landing.

On 14th September, 1959, Luna 2 successfully landed east of Mare Imbrium near the craters Aristides, Archimedes and Autolycus.

Returning to Earth

To return to Earth, the escape velocity of the moon must be attained for the spacecraft to escape the gravity well of the moon. Here again, rockets must be used to leave the moon and return to space. Upon reaching Earth, however, rockets are not needed for deceleration. Atmospheric entry techniques are used to absorb the kinetic energy of a returning spacecraft and thus reduce its speed for a safe landing.

Neil Armstrong's footstep imprinted in the soil on the moon.

FUN FACT

Armstrong maintains that he said, "One small step for a man, one giant leap for mankind", but the "a" was lost on radio. One small step for man would mean the same thing as one small step for mankind!

Technical difficulties

The return and landing functions greatly complicate a moon-landing mission. They lead to many additional, operational considerations. Some of these are noted in sequence below:

● Any moon departure rocket must first be carried to the moon's surface by a moon-landing rocket. This increases the latter's required size.

● The moon departure rocket, larger moon landing rocket and any Earth atmosphere entry equipment such as heat shields and parachutes must in turn be lifted by the original launch vehicle. This greatly increases the size of the original launch vehicle by a significant amount. In fact, it is this factor that makes moon missions expensive and difficult to an almost prohibitive degree.

Luna 2

Luna 2 of the E-1A series was the second of the Soviet Union's Luna programme spacecraft launched to the moon. It became the first spacecraft to reach the surface of the moon and also the first artificial object to land on another celestial body.

Luna 2 construction

The instrumentation of Luna 2 was similar to Luna 1. It contained scintillation counters, geiger counters, a magnetometer, Cherenkov detectors and micrometeorite detectors. The Luna 2 had external boosters as there were no propulsion systems on it.

A copy of the Soviet Pennant carried aboard the Luna 2. ▼

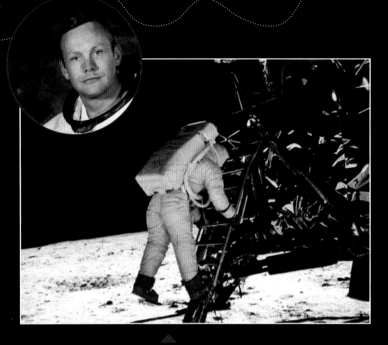

Neil Armstrong descends a ladder to become the first human to step onto the surface of the moon. His words on radio have gone on to become some of the most famous in human history.

Apollo 11

Apollo 11 was the spaceflight that landed the first humans on the moon. Americans Neil Armstrong and Buzz Aldrin landed on the surface of the moon on 20th July, 1969. The third member of the mission, Astronaut Michael Collins, piloted the command spacecraft alone in lunar orbit until Armstrong and Aldrin returned to it for the trip back to Earth.

Moon launch, the liftoff of Apollo 11 on a Saturn V missile started the Moon mission of astronauts Neil Armstrong, Michael Collins and Edwin Aldrin. 16th July, 1969.

Astronaut Training

Human spaceflight is almost as old as space exploration. Due to the challenge and novelty of the environment, extensive screening and testing of candidates is required.

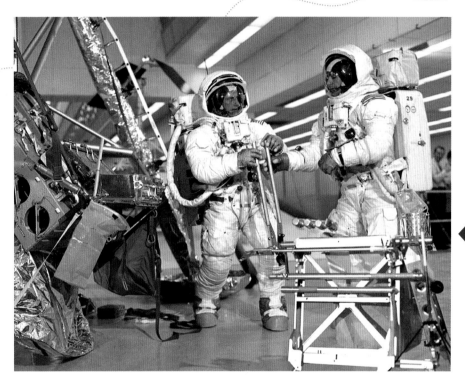

Astronauts in simulated weightless flight in C-131 aircraft flying "zero-g" trajectory at Wright Air Development Center.

The Apollo 12 lunar Extravehicular Activity (EVA) crew members, Pete Conrad and Al Bean, conduct a simulation of the lunar surface activity.

The beginning

Those accepted to become an astronaut, report to Houston, Texas. It is the NASA's primary astronaut training facility. Today, it is known as the Johnson Space Center (JSC). It was established in 1961 as the Manned Spacecraft Center. In 1973, its name was changed to honour former president and Texas native Lyndon B. Johnson, who died that January. The JSC played an important role in the Gemini, Apollo, Skylab, space shuttle and International Space Station programmes. Over the course of its history, JSC has trained more than 300 US astronauts and 50 astronauts from other countries. The training process used today is the result of this significant experience.

Major players

In the 1960s, the space club only included Russia and then USA. Later, the pool of human space flight faring nations grew. Today, it still includes USA (NASA) and Russia (Roscosmos). However, it has grown to also include Europe (ESA), Japan (JAXA), China (CNSA) and India (ISRO). Outside government agencies, this list will also soon include passengers of Space Tourism.

Selection process

The selection process for candidates has become more and more detailed and targeted as human spaceflight capabilities have grown. Spaceflight began as the selection of military fighters and test pilots in the 1960s. There was a considerable focus on physical capability. It has now evolved into a search for aptitude in engineering, sciences, life sciences and mathematics. These will also continue to evolve in stride with human spaceflight capabilities as well as each nation's individual objective.

Current training modules

Currently, astronauts are only trained to fly in the Soyuz and live on the board ISS as these are the only space shuttle and station available.

FUN FACT

Soyuz is the only space shuttle that can transport astronauts to and from the International Space Station.

Training in space

On the ISS, astronauts are involved in assembly and orbit operations. This includes, but is not limited to, EVAs, robotics operations using the remote manipulators, experiment operations and ISS maintenance tasks. They are, thus, trained in simulated microgravity environments to prepare them for these tasks in space.

Theoretical training

It is essential for astronauts to have an in depth knowledge about ISS and its sub systems. They must know operational characteristics, mission requirements and objectives, and supporting systems and equipment for each experiment on their assigned missions. As a result, the long duration missions aboard the ISS that last from three to six months take about two to three years of increment specific training.

Training facilities

Astronauts have to be prepared for general space travel and for their specific mission. In order to prepare them for the same, NASA has several locations for astronaut training. These are some of the training facilities:

● The Jake Garn Training Facility: This facility at JSC houses a functional space station simulator, which makes astronauts familiar with the in-orbit laboratory systems of the International Space Station before they go there in person.

NASA astronaut Elliot See, pilot of the Gemini 5 backup crew, inside the Gemini Static Article 5 spacecraft prior to water egress training in the Gulf of Mexico.

● The Space Vehicle Mockup Facility (SVMF): This facility consists of components that prepare astronauts for station operations. The Space Station Mockup and Training Facility (SSMTF) is a complete imitation of the ISS, providing as much realism as possible to match conditions that will be experienced upon the orbiting space station.

● The Virtual Reality (VR) Laboratory: Here, astronauts preparing for spacewalks or robotic arm operations test their skills. In a simulated microgravity environment generated by powerful computers, astronauts — each wearing special gloves, video display helmet, chest pack and a controller — learn how to orient themselves in outer space, where up and down are vague, and even negligible corrections with a thruster can send someone spinning off into space.

Astronauts pictured during water egress training in a large indoor pool at Ellington Air Force Base, Texas.

Spacesuits

A spacesuit serves the purpose of protecting an astronaut in an environment where his/her body cannot sustain itself. The outer space environment calls for a special suit to protect people going into the deep realms of a territory that one cannot survive in without special protection. It is here that spacesuits come into action.

The need for spacesuits

Spacesuits help astronauts in several ways. They protect the people entering into space from getting very hot or cold. They also give astronauts oxygen to breathe, while they are working in space. They hold water to drink and also prevent astronauts from being harmed by space dust. Space dust may not sound very dangerous but when it moves at a very high speed, it can hurt someone. The suits even have special gold-lined visors to protect the eyes from bright sunlight.

Parts of a spacesuit

It is made up of several parts. One part covers the astronaut's chest and the other connects to the gloves. There is a helmet that protects the head. The third part covers the legs and feet. Some parts of the suit are made of various layers of material. Each layer serves a different purpose. Some keep oxygen in the suit whereas others protect from space dust. Below the suit, astronauts wear another piece of clothing that covers their body except for the head, hands and feet. Tubes are woven into it and water flows through these tubes to keep the astronaut cool.

On the back, there is a backpack. It holds oxygen for the purpose of breathing. It eliminates the carbon dioxide that is breathed out. It also supplies electricity for the suit. A fan moves the oxygen through the spacesuit and a water tank holds the cooling water. The back of the suit also has a tool called SAFER. It has several small thruster jets. If an astronaut drifts away from the space station, he or she could use the SAFER to fly back.

Mobility in the suit

It is difficult to move within an inflated space suit. It is like trying to move your fingers in a rubber glove blown up with air; it doesn't ensure much movement. To counter this difficulty, these suits are equipped with special joints or tapers in the fabric to help the astronauts bend their hands, arms, legs, knees and ankles.

Communications

Space suits have radio transmitters/receivers so that spacewalking astronauts can talk with ground controllers and/or other astronauts.

Modern space suit – EMU

Today's Extravehicular Mobility Unit (EMU) is made up of a combination of soft and hard components to provide support, mobility and comfort. The suit has 13 layers of material, including an inner cooling garment (two layers), pressure garment (two layers), thermal micrometeoroid garment (eight layers) and outer cover (one layer). The materials used include: nylon tricot, spandex, urethane-coated nylon, dacron, neoprene-coated nylon, mylar, gortex, kevlar (materials used in bullet-proof vests) and nomex. All these layers are sewn and joined together to form the suit. In contrast to early space suits, which were individually tailored for each astronaut, the EMU has component pieces of varying sizes that can be put together to fit the size of any given astronaut.

Extravehicular Visor Assembly (EVA)

The EVA fits over the helmet. It has the following pieces:

● A metallic-gold-covered visor to filter the sunlight

● A clear, impact resistant cover for thermal and impact protection

● Adjustable blinders to block sunlight

● Four head lamps

● A TV camera

● In-suit Drink Bag (IDB)

Astronauts working in a space suit for up to seven hours need water. Therefore, it has the IDB, which is a plastic pouch mounted inside the HUT.

Helmet:
The helmet is made of clear, impact-resistant, polycarbonate plastic and fits to the HUT by a quick-connect ring. It is padded at the back for comfort, because it remains secure rather than rotating with the astronaut's head. There is a purge valve to eliminate carbon dioxide if the backup oxygen supply needs to be used. Oxygen flows from behind the astronaut's head, over the head and down his/her face. Inside, the helmet has an anti-fog compound used prior to the spacewalk.

Arms:
Arm units contain shoulder, upper arm and elbow joint bearings so that the astronaut can move his/her arms in many directions. The arm units come in various sizes so that the EMU can be fitted to different astronauts. The arm units fit into the HUT by quick connect rings.

Hard Upper Torso (HUT):
It is a hard fiberglass shell, shaped like a vest. It supports several structures including the arms, lower torso, helmet, life-support backpack and control module. It can also hold a mini-tool carrier. Pieces click into the HUT through quick-connect rings.

Gloves:
The gloves have wrist bearings for stress-free movement. They fit into the arms by quick-connect rings. They have rubberised fingertips to help astronauts grip things. Astronauts also wear fine-fabric gloves inside the outer glove units for comfort. The outer gloves have loops on them to tether tools.

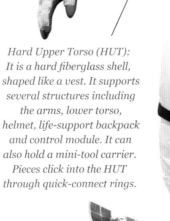

FUN FACT

The IDB can hold 1.9 l of water and has a small tube, a straw, that is positioned next to the astronaut's mouth.

International Space Station

The International Space Station (ISS) is a space station in low Earth orbit. Scientifically, the ISS is a habitable artificial satellite. It is a modular structure, i.e., it is built of pieces that can be joined together. Its first component was launched in 1998.

The International Space Station in Earth's orbit. This can be reached only by the Russian spacecraft, Soyuz. Astronauts are trained in simulations that mimic the conditions of the ISS and the Soyuz to prepare them for space missions.

The structure of the ISS has been picturised against a background of Earth's horizon and space full of stars.

Purpose

According to the original Memorandum of Understanding between NASA and Roscosmos, the ISS was, "intended to be a laboratory, observatory and factory in low Earth orbit".

It was also planned to provide transportation, maintenance and act as a staging base for any future missions to the moon, Mars and/or asteroids. Through the 2010 United States National Space Policy, the ISS was given additional roles of serving commercial, diplomatic and educational purposes.

Importance

Small, unmanned spacecrafts can provide platforms for zero gravity and exposure to space. However, space stations offer a long-term environment, where studies can be performed for decades. The ISS simplifies individual experiments. It eliminates the need for separate rocket launches and research staff. Scientists on Earth have access to the crew's data and can modify experiments or launch new ones. These benefits are generally unavailable on unmanned spacecraft.

Also, it forms a base for all the astronauts to conduct their experiments and make their observations as well as conduct research. It becomes the one point of contact in space where people from Earth can reach and get information or carry out instructions as soon as possible.

FUN FACT

The ISS was built piece by piece in space. The first module did not have long-term life support. Missions were based out of the nearby Mir station for two years. Today, the ISS has been assembled through over 1000 hours of work in space and carried out over 127 spacewalks.

Microgravity

Researchers are investigating the effect of the station's near-weightless environment on the evolution, development, growth and internal processes of plants and animals. NASA wants to investigate microgravity's effects on the growth of three-dimensional human tissues, as well as the unusual protein crystals that can be formed in space. Both these may provide breakthroughs in cloning and stem cell research.

Education

The ISS crew provides opportunities for students on Earth in the following ways:

● By running student-developed experiments

● Making educational demonstrations

● Allowing for student participation in classroom versions of ISS experiments, directly engaging students using radio, video link and email.

The construction of ISS

As we already know, the ISS was not built at one go and then placed in space. A small part of it was made first and elevated in space. Next, as astronauts went to the ISS and came back, they continued construction on it. There were parts that were made on Earth, then elevated to the station and attached to the main body. They had begun the construction in November 1998. The components of the ISS are pressurised modules that provide an environment for the astronauts, nodes that connect the separate modules, docking ports where the Soyuz can be landed, a framework where all the modules attach to the mainframe, external research accommodation that allow for experimentation in full space exposure and the spacecraft itself, such as the Soyuz that carries astronauts to and from the space station.

NASA astronauts and STS-128 mission specialists are busy with various tasks in the Destiny laboratory of the ISS while Space Shuttle Discovery remains docked with the station.

Expedition 20 crew members view a monitor in the ISS's Unity node as they celebrate Father's Day and the birthday of cosmonaut Gennady Padalka (centre), commander.

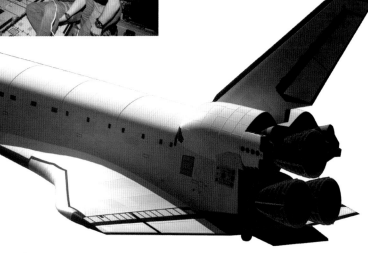

▲ *Space Shuttle orbiting Earth.*

A Day in Space

We take our planet for granted. It is difficult for us to imagine what life would be like if this planet would cease to exist. There are many astronauts who have lived in space for a considerable amount of time. Let's find out what a day in space is like.

Time

Since the space shuttle is in space and at a high velocity, there is no way for the astronauts to tell the time of the day. Hence, all the astronauts follow a standard time and that is of the Mission Control Centres at Houston, Texas, or Moscow. This becomes convenient as it becomes easier for the astronauts to take directions from them. This centre plans the day and time of astronauts in space and advises what they have to do every day in space.

The day begins

For the astronauts living at the ISS, the day begins with a wake-up call from the control centre. They have 12-hour working shifts. Since water is not available in space, they have to use it very sparsely. That is why, they do not have showers or proper baths in space. The astronauts simply use a cloth dipped in soapy water to clean themselves. Then the mission control tells them what has been planned for the day ahead.

Schedule

From the time that an astronaut gets sent into space, the mission control directs them on what has to be done on a daily basis. Most of their time is spent conducting experiments and making observations from space.

At other times, regular maintenance has to be carried out at the space station or shuttle. Also, they have to clean up after themselves, so a part of their time is also spent doing mundane, daily household chores.

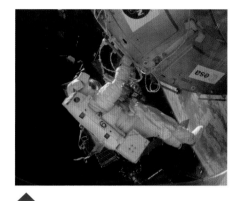

During the almost eight-hour spacewalk, Walheim and astronaut Stanley Love (out of frame), mission specialist, installed a grapple fixture on the Columbus laboratory and prepared electrical and data connections on the module while it rested inside Space Shuttle Atlantis' payload bay. The crew members also began work to replace a large nitrogen tank used for pressurising the station's ammonia cooling system.

Silence

Space is made up of vacuum. On Earth, even when it is silent, we hear many other sounds that we are used to. But in space, it is silent and becomes uncomfortable for astronauts. Hence, they often carry sound recordings of mundane sounds from Earth to keep them company.

Astronaut in space around the solar batteries.

FUN FACT

In space, astronauts do not do laundry. To preserve water, they end up discarding their dirty clothes instead of washing them.

Food

In space, the astronauts are given three meals a day; breakfast, lunch and dinner. At other times of the day, snacks and drinks are also available to them. Since the amount of food that can be carried with them is limited, space food needs to be compact and crammed with all the nutrients that are required for a balanced diet. Some space food is specially made so it can be cooked in a low-gravity environment and machinery.

▲ *An astronaut goes through the hatch into space. This hatch is air tight and made to be able to withstand high amount of pressure.*

◀ *The Expedition Four and STS-110 crewmembers share a meal in the Zvezda Service Module on the ISS. In zero-gravity, everyday tasks like having a meal become difficult too.*

Exercise

We already know about the weightlessness in space. Because of it, astronauts do not need to use their muscles a lot. However, this leads to wastage of muscle. This means that if an astronaut is to return to Earth after a long time in space, his/her muscles would not work as they have been inactive for such a long time. The astronaut would have to retrain his/her muscles for gravity. This is why, they have a rigorous exercising programme that they have to strictly follow when in space. They use treadmills to run on and since they keep floating away, there are bungee cords that are used to hold them to the treadmill.

Other activities

On Earth, we have a lot of ways to pass time, like go for a walk, go on a long drive or observe nature. In space, all these options are not available and hence astronauts find some indoor options to pass their time. They read or even watch the TV to spend their leisure time. Occasionally, if the mission control schedules it, robotic activities and space walks also become possible.

Dreams

We dream of things that we see around us. Every once in a while we will dream of our memories or something surreal. Astronauts report that the first few days, they dream a lot about their life on Earth but as time passes by, these dreams become rarer and rarer. They begin to dream more about their life in space. Every once in a while, a memory of Earth pops up in their subconscious, that the astronauts see as a dream.

European Space Agency (ESA) astronaut Paolo Nespoli, STS-120 mission specialist, rests in his/her sleeping bag in the Harmony node of the ISS while space shuttle Discovery is docked with the station. ▶

Spaceflight Accidents

Since the advent of spaceflight, there have been many accidents in space or during space missions. In particular, there have been over 20 astronaut and cosmonaut fatalities till date. There have been some astronaut fatalities during training for space missions. An example of this is the Apollo 1 launchpad fire that killed all three crew members.

Soyuz 1, 24th April, 1967

This one-day mission had been plagued by a series of mishaps. The Soyuz 1 in question was a new spacecraft type. This culminated with its parachute not opening properly after atmospheric re-entry.

Fatalities: Vladimir Komarov was killed when the capsule hit the ground at high speed while landing.

Cause: Parachute failure

Soyuz 11, 30th June, 1971

The crew of Soyuz 11 were killed after undocking from space station Salyut 1. They were departing after a three-week stay. A cabin vent valve accidentally opened at service module separation. The recovery team found the crew dead. These are the only fatalities in space, i.e., ones to have died above the Karman Line, thus far.

Space shuttle Challenger disaster. Space shuttle exhaust plumes entwined around a ball of gas after a few seconds after the explosion caused by ruptured O-rings.

Fatalities: Georgi Dobrovolski, Viktor Patsayev and Vladislav Volkov

Cause: Decompression

Challenger, 28th January, 1986

The Space Shuttle Challenger was destroyed 73 seconds after liftoff.

The strut at the rear end of the tank failed, allowing the top of the SRB to rotate into the top of the tank. Challenger was thrown sideways into the Mach 1.8 wind stream and broke up with the loss of all seven crewmembers. Any survivors of the breakup were killed when the largely intact cockpit hit the water at 320 km per hour.

Fatalities: Greg Jarvis, Christa McAuliffe, Ronald McNair, Ellison Onizuka, Judith Resnik, Michael Smith and Dick Scobee

Cause: Vehicle disintegration on launch

Columbia, 1st February, 2003

Damage to the shuttle's thermal protection system (TPS) led to structural failure of the shuttle's left wing and the spacecraft ultimately broke apart during re-entry into Earth's atmosphere. Investigation revealed damage to the reinforced carbon leading edge wing panel. This had likely resulted from the impact of a piece of foam insulation that broke away from the external tank during the launch.

Fatalities: Rick D. Husband, William McCool, Michael P. Anderson, David M. Brown, Kalpana Chawla, Laurel B. Clark, Ilan Ramon

Cause: Vehicle disintegration during re-entry

An artist's representation of what an accident in outer space could be like.

EXPLORING SPACE

From rockets to satellites, a probe into space exploration has reached another level since the last decade. The "Kármán" line is conventionally used as the starting point of outer space in space treaties and for aerospace records keeping. It starts at an altitude of 100 km above sea level.

Outer space represents a challenging environment for human exploration because of the combined hazards of vacuum and radiation. Microgravity also has a negative effect on human physiology. Besides solving all these health and environmental issues, humans will also need to find a way to significantly reduce the cost of getting into space.

Space Mining

Minerals could be mined from an asteroid or spent comet, then taken back to Earth or used in space for construction materials. This includes iron, nickel and titanium for construction. The idea is important because Earth might run out of phosphorus, antimony, zinc, tin, silver, lead, indium, gold and copper in as little as 60 years.

Asteroids used for mining

Multiple types of asteroids have been identified as suitable for mining. The three main types include the C-type, S-type and M-type asteroids.

● C-type asteroids have a high abundance of water. By using the available water from the asteroid rather than carrying it, we could reduce costs. C-type asteroids also have a lot of organic carbon, phosphorus and other key ingredients for fertiliser; thus, they could be used to grow food.

● S-type asteroids carry little water, but contain numerous metals that include nickel, cobalt and more valuable metals such as gold, platinum and rhodium. A small, 10 m, S-type asteroid is thought to contain about 650,000 kg of metal with 50 kg of rare metals like platinum and gold.

● M-type asteroids are very rare, but contain up to 10 times more metal than S-type asteroids.

Extraction of metal

Surface mining

On some types of asteroids, material may be scraped off the surface using a scoop. There is fairly strong evidence that many asteroids consist of rubble piles. This would make it possible.

Shaft mining

A mine can be dug into the asteroid and the material extracted through the shaft. This would require precise knowledge about the accuracy of the astro location under the surface regolith. We would also need a transportation system to carry the desired ore to the processing facility.

Magnetic rakes

Asteroids with a high metal content may be covered in loose grains that can be simply scooped up using a magnet.

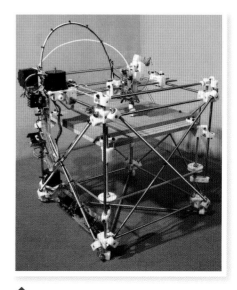

The RepRap 1.0 "Darwin" is a self-replicating machine. It is theorised that these could be used for space mining as they can create an entire complex of themselves.

Heating

For volatile materials in extinct comets, heat can be used to melt and vaporise the matrix, and then extract the resulting vapour.

FUN FACT

All the gold, cobalt, iron, manganese, molybdenum, nickel, osmium, palladium, platinum, rhenium, rhodium, ruthenium and tungsten mined from Earth's crust, originally came from the rain of asteroids that hit Earth after the crust cooled.

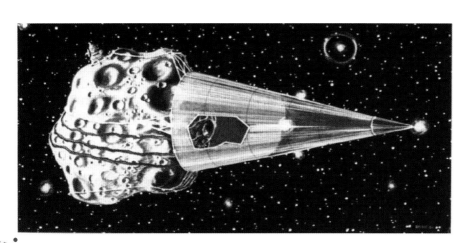

Space Manufacturing

Space manufacturing is the production of manufactured goods in an environment outside a planetary atmosphere. This includes conditions of both microgravity and hard vacuum. Space manufacturing could either be conducted in deep space or on space objects.

Benefits of space manufacturing

● The unique environment allows for industrial processes that cannot be readily reproduced on Earth due to gravity and the presence of an atmosphere.

● Raw materials could be lifted to orbit from other bodies within the solar system. These can then be processed at a low expense compared to the cost of lifting materials into orbit from Earth.

● Potentially hazardous processes can be performed in space with minimal risk to the environment of Earth or other planets.

● Items that are too large to launch on a rocket can be assembled in orbit for use.

Barriers of space manufacturing

Heavy capitalisation costs of assembling the mining and manufacturing facilities would be incurred in space. The most significant cost is overcoming the energy hurdle for boosting materials into orbit. There would also be a need to collect the requisite raw materials at a minimum energy cost.

Examples of the benefits of space manufacturing

● The microgravity environment allows control of convection in liquids or gases and eliminates sedimentation. Diffusion becomes the primary means of material mixing. This allows otherwise immiscible materials to be intermixed. The environment also allows enhanced growth of larger, higher-quality crystals in solution.

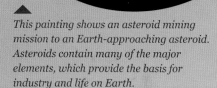

This painting shows an asteroid mining mission to an Earth-approaching asteroid. Asteroids contain many of the major elements, which provide the basis for industry and life on Earth.

● Space vacuum allows the creation of extremely pure materials and objects by using vapour deposition.

● Surface tension causes liquids in microgravity to form perfectly round spheres that are useful when perfect spheres of consistent sizes are needed.

● Space can provide readily available extremes of heat and cold due to the lack of an atmosphere.

A NASA image of insulin crystal growth in outer space (left) as opposed to on Earth. Microgravity allows crystal formation of a better quality.

FUN FACT

The absence of gravity, rotational forces and atmospheric pressure means that we can build mega structures such as space elevators.

Communications Satellites

A communications satellite, often abbreviated to "comsat", is an artificial satellite that is sent into space for the purpose of telecommunications. Communications satellites provide a microwave radio relay technology that supplements communication cables. They are used for mobile applications such as communications to ships, vehicles, planes and handheld terminals, as well as for TV and radio broadcasting.

This satellite, called the AEHF, is used for secure radio communications.

Satellite telephones

Long distance telephony is the first and historically most important application for communication satellites. The fixed Public Switched Telephone Network relays telephone calls from landline telephones to an Earth station. From here, they are then transmitted to a geostationary satellite. Satellite communications provide connections to the edges of Antarctica and Greenland, rigs at sea, aeroplanes, serve as a backup for hospitals, the military, and are used for recreation.

Television

Television demands for simultaneous delivery of relatively few signals of large bandwidth to many receivers. This made it a very precise match for the capabilities of geosynchronous comsats. Two satellite types are used for North American television and radio. They are termed as Direct broadcast satellite (DBS) and Fixed Service Satellite (FSS). On 29th October, 2001, the first digital cinema was transmitted by a satellite in Europe. It was a feature film by Bernard Pauchon and Philippe Binant.

Radio

A satellite radio or subscription radio (SR) is a digital radio signal that is broadcast by a communications satellite. It covers a much wider geographical range than terrestrial radio signals. Radio services are usually provided by commercial ventures and are subscription-based. Amateur radio operators also have access to the amateur radio satellites. These have been designed specifically to carry amateur radio traffic.

A life-size, cut-away model of a Venera type Venus communication lander on display.

Internet

After the 1990s, satellite communication technology has been used to connect to the Internet via broadband data connections. This is very useful for users located in remote areas who cannot access a cable-based broadband connection, or for those who require high availability of services. Thus, satellite internet is very popular today.

FUN FACT

Satellites follow several orbits like geostationary, low-Earth and Molniya.

Planetariums

A planetarium is a theatre that demonstrates the various aspects of astronomy and the night sky. It is also used for training in celestial navigation. The concept has existed since antiquity as Archimedes was believed to own an ordinary planetarium device that could predict the movements of the Sun, moon and planets. Most planetaria are characterised by the large dome-shaped projection screen. Here, scenes of stars, planets and other celestial objects can be made to appear and move.

Elements of a planetarium show

Most planetariums host shows for the general public. Themes such as "What's in the sky tonight?" or shows relating to topical issues such as religious festivals are traditionally popular. Since the early 1990s, fully featured 3D digital planetaria allow simulation of the view from any point in space. Music is an important element to complete the experience of a good planetarium show. Space-themed music or music from the genres of space music, space rock or classical music is often used as the background score for a show.

Here, you see the room where the Planetarium Zuylenburgh is situated.

Working of the projection mechanism

The traditional planetarium projection apparatus uses a hollow ball with a light inside and a pinhole for each star. This has led to the rise of the name "star ball". In modern planetarium star balls, the individual bright stars often have individual projectors, which are shaped like small hand-held torches with focussing lenses.

Rise of digital technology

An increasing number of planetaria are using digital technology to replace the entire system of interlinked projectors that were traditionally employed around a star ball. Compared to traditional "star balls", these employ few moving parts and generally do not require synchronisation of movement across the dome between separate systems.

The Mark I projector pictured here was the world's first planetarium projector. It was installed in the Deutsches Museum in 1923.

Image of the ExploraDome presentation.

Geodesy

Geodesy is a branch of applied mathematics and Earth sciences. It is rarely also known as geodetics or geodetics engineering. It is the scientific discipline that deals with the measurement and representation of Earth. Geodesists study gravitational field and also geodynamical phenomena such as crustal motion, tides and polar motion.

> **FUN FACT**
>
> Geodesy comes from the Greek word "geodaisia", which literally means, "division of Earth".

Evolution of Geodesy

The shape of Earth is, to a large extent, due to its rotation. This causes its equatorial bulge and the difference in gravity in different parts of Earth. Earth's gravitational field actively resists the competition of geological processes such as the collision of plates and volcanism. Earth's gravitational field also greatly affects the solid and liquid surface as well as Earth's atmosphere. To study the effects of these, geodesy evolved as a science.

Techniques to study Geodynamic phenomena

● Satellite positioning by GPS and other such locating systems

● Very Long Baseline Interferometry (VLBI) – using the difference in radio signals at different telescopes from the same radio star

● Satellite and lunar laser ranging

● Precise levelling, regionally and locally

● Precise tachometers

● Monitoring changes in gravity

● Interferometric synthetic aperture radar (InSAR) – uses two waves reflected back from Earth's surface to digitally map the deformations using satellite images

▲ GPS satellites discovered that the coasts of Croatia and Italy are nearing each other at 4 mm per year and in 50—70 million years there will be no seawater boundary between them.

Prominent phenomena in Geodynamics

The study of deformations and motions of Earth's crust and solid Earth as a whole is called geodynamics. It involves the following:

● Continental plate motion, plate tectonics.

● Episodic (i.e., due to a single instance), motion of tectonic origin, such as those close to fault lines.

● Periodic effects due to Earth tides.

● Postglacial land uplift due to isostatic adjustment.

● Various movements due to human activities. These include, for instance, petroleum or water extraction or reservoir construction.

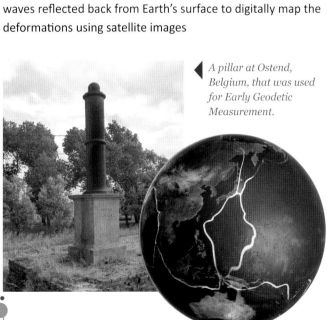

◀ A pillar at Ostend, Belgium, that was used for Early Geodetic Measurement.

Space and Military

The early exploration of space in the mid-twentieth century had, in part, a military motivation. The USA and the USSR used space exploration as an opportunity to demonstrate ballistic missile technology and other technologies that had the potential for military application. However, currently there is an accepted moratorium on putting weapons in space and a treaty that bans weapons of mass destruction being deployed in orbit.

Outer Space Treaty

Because of the Outer Space Treaty, weapons have not been stationed in space. However, outer space has been used as an operating location for military spacecraft such as imaging and communications satellites. Also, some ballistic missiles pass through outer space during their flight.

During the Cold War, the world's two great superpowers, namely the USSR and the USA, spent large proportions of their GDP on developing military technologies. In 1957, the USSR launched the first artificial satellite, Sputnik 1. Spy satellites were used by militaries to take accurate pictures of their rivals' military installations. Thus, the USA and the USSR began to develop anti-satellite weapons designed to either blind or destroy each other's satellites.

Weapons in space

Currently, there are no weapons in space with the exception of small handguns carried by Russian Cosmonauts. Even these are for use after they have landed on Earth, but have not been retrieved from the landing place. The different technologies with military applications currently in space are:

▲ *An artist's concept of Soviet land, air and space-based lasers. (Soviet Military Power, 1987).*

● Spy satellites – used for taking pictures from orbit.

● Communication satellites – used for secure military communications.

● GPS – the Global Positioning System used for location.

● Military space planes – certain spacecraft like NASA's X-37 shuttle are controlled by the military of their respective country.

An artist's concept of the interception and destruction of nuclear-armed re-entry vehicles by a space-based electromagnetic railgun. The LTV Aerospace and Defense Co. has demonstrated hypervelocity launch technology in the laboratory that is applicable to a ballistic missile defence system. ▼

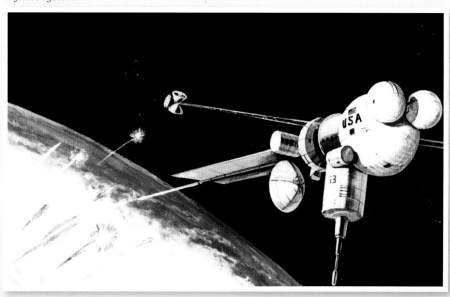

FUN FACT

Laser weapons, kamikaze style satellites, kinetic energy weapons and orbital nuclear explosions were researched with varying levels of success during the space weaponisation phase of research.

Military Communications Systems

From the earliest days of warfare, communication between the different elements of a military force have been considered critical. The uncertainty in "situational awareness" or lack of knowledge of what is currently experienced in military operations is a well-known fact. It is often described by the term "Fog of War". Military communications systems have greatly evolved with the advent of satellites, with the goal of dispelling this fog of war.

Doctrine for military communications

The emerging military doctrine of near instantaneous communication is termed as network-centric warfare relying on high-speed communications. This allows all the soldiers and branches of the military to view the battlefield in real-time and receive instantaneous instructions and updates.

Working of communication satellites

Communication satellites are commonly used to co-ordinate military action and receive intelligence. For example, a soldier in the battle zone can access satellite imagery of enemy positions two blocks away. He can then, if necessary, e-mail the coordinates to a bomber or weapon platform hovering overhead. The entire time, his commander, who is hundreds of miles away, watches as the events unfold on a monitor. He can, thus, countermand the orders or change them.

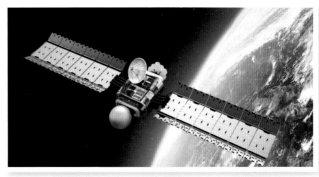

▲ *A file photo of a military satellite taken by another in space.*

Support system

This high-speed communication is facilitated by a separate Internet created by the military for the military. Communication satellites hold this system together. They create an informational grid over the given theatre of operations.

Other uses

Satellite phones enable a person to make calls anywhere on Earth; Internet facilities are outcomes of this technology.

◀ *Futuristic anti satellite weapon (ASAT) that will apparently destroy other artificial satellites by the process of "circular saw".*

◀ *An artists' representation of a directed military high power laser in space destroying a terrestrial target.*

FUN FACT

Communications satellites also allow military personnel to video chat with their family members thousands of km away. This has drastically improved the quality of life for the people in armed services.

Spy Satellites

A spy satellite is an Earth observation satellite or communications satellite deployed for military or intelligence applications. They are formally referred to as reconnaissance (recon) satellites. The first generation type of recon satellites took photographs on film. These were then ejected into the atmosphere and retrieved mid air. Current satellites use radio communication to transmit data.

Types of recon satellites

Recon satellites are classified mainly according to their functions. The major groups are early warning, nuclear explosion, photo surveillance, electronic interceptor and radar imaging.

Early warning satellites — These form a net that warns of an attack by detecting ballistic missile launches. Earliest known examples are satellites of the Missile Defence Alarm System.

Nuclear explosion detection — These identify and characterise nuclear explosions in space. The Vela satellite is the earliest known example of this type.

Photo surveillance — These provide imaging of Earth from space. Images can be a survey image or a close-look telephoto. The Corona satellite is the earliest known example of this type. Spectral imaging is also commonplace today. Many civilian satellites provide this functionality to a reduced degree.

Electronic-reconnaissance - These are used to carry out intelligence signals. They intercept stray radio waves and decrypt encoded ones for intelligence.

Radar imaging — Most space-based radars use synthetic aperture radar. Thus, they can be used during the nights or through cloud cover, as these don't impede microwave radiation as they impede light. The earliest known examples are the US-A series satellites.

Space Expo Resurs Spy Satellite: This seems to be Russian made and is at the moment on display at a Netherland museum.

An aerial view of Osama bin Laden's compound in the Pakistani city of Abbottabad released by the CIA. Satellite surveillance played a critical role in the operation that resulted in Osama's capture.

FUN FACT

On 17th February, 2014, a Russian Kosmos-1220 that was originally launched in 1980 made an uncontrolled atmospheric entry. It is a scientific way of saying that it crashed. It was used for naval missile targeting until 1982.

Space Law

Since humans are now capable of entering space and have access to it, it becomes necessary that some rules and laws are put in place to protect space as well as themselves. Care needs to be taken that this access is not misused.

How it began

The conduct in the area above Earth as well as the lower atmosphere is regulated by the international law and is known as the space law. In 1957, US President Eisenhower proposed this concept to the UN with regards to the disarmament negotiation. After the launch of the Russian satellite Sputnik in 1957 and the US satellite Explorer 1, both the countries took the initiative to put these international space laws in place.

Peaceful exploration

As the world stands right now, if any country is to find any unexplored, uninhabited land, they can legally claim it as a part of their country. However, when it comes to space, this rule cannot be applied. The space right above a particular country cannot be considered as a part of that country, neither can any unexplored space territory can be claimed by that country. All the countries have the permission to peacefully explore space.

Ban of nuclear testing

A permanent Outer Space Committee was formed in 1959. When the intention to carry out nuclear tests in space became evident, this committee signed a treaty to prohibit it. The Nuclear Test Ban Treaty was signed in 1963.

FUN FACT

There is a Moon Treaty that prohibits countries from exploiting its and other celestial bodies' resources. However, this treaty has not been ratified yet.

Space Treaties

As seen, the presence of weapons in space gives a sizable tactical and strategic advantage to the party that holds them. Mutually Assured Destruction (MAD) would then trigger an arms race in space. So, as MAD became the deterrent strategy between the two superpowers during the Cold War, many countries worked together to avoid extending the threat of nuclear weapons to space based launchers to prevent this catastrophe.

The Outer Space Treaty

The Outer Space Treaty is currently agreed to by a majority of the World's Nation states. The Legal Subcommittee of the United Nations General Assembly (UNGA) originally formed it in 1966. Later that year, the UNGA voted to accept the treaty through a majority.

Provisions of the Outer Space Treaty

The principles of the Outer Space Treaty are given below:

● The exploration and use of outer space shall be carried out for the benefit and in the interests of all countries and shall be the province of all humankind.

● Outer space shall be free for exploration and use by all states.

● Outer space is not subject to national appropriation by claim of sovereignty, by means of use or occupation or by any other means.

● States shall not place nuclear weapons or other weapons of mass destruction in orbit or on celestial bodies or station them in outer space in any other manner.

● The moon and other celestial bodies shall be used exclusively for peaceful and non-military purposes.

● Astronauts shall be regarded as the envoys of humankind.

● States shall be responsible for national space activities whether carried out by governmental or non-governmental activities.

● States shall be liable for damage caused by their space objects.

● States shall avoid harmful contamination of space and celestial bodies.

Shortcomings of this treaty

The outer space treaty does not ban the placement of weapons in space in general, but only nuclear weapons and weapons of mass destruction. Thus, in 2006, the UN General Assembly proposed The Space Preservation Treaty against all weapons.

An artists' representation of ▶
Earth and the space in future.

Strategic Defence Initiative

US President Ronald Reagan proposed The Strategic Defence Initiative (SDI) on 23rd March, 1983. It aimed to use ground and space-based systems to protect the USA from attack by strategic nuclear ballistic missiles. This was a huge transformation from the regular policy as it focussed on strategic defence rather than on the prior strategic offense doctrine of MAD.

Formation of the SDI and use of space based weapons

During the early phases of the Cold War, the necessity for anti-ballistic missile systems was realised. Ground based missiles were found to be too large and cumbersome to use against Intercontinental Ballistic Missiles, (ICBM) as each missile would have deployed multiple warheads before it could be reliably shot down. However, if the interceptor missiles were placed in orbit, some of them could be positioned over the opposing country at all times. These would fly "downhill" to attack the missiles. Therefore, they could be considerably smaller and cheaper than an interceptor that needed to launch up from the ground and could target an ICBM in its vulnerable launch phase.

SDI weapons and their designs

The weapons that were considered can be broadly classified as follows:

1. Ground-based programmes
- Extended Range Interceptor (ERINT)
- Homing Overlay Experiment (HOE)
- wExoatmospheric Re-entry-vehicle Interceptor Subsystem (ERIS)

A payload launch vehicle carrying a prototype exoatmospheric kill vehicle is launched from Meck Island at the Kwajalein Missile Range on 3rd December, 2001, for a planned intercept of a ballistic missile target over the central Pacific Ocean.

2. Directed-energy weapon (DEW) programmes such as:
- X-ray laser
- Chemical laser
- Neutral Particle Beam
- Laser and mirror systems, which remained only experimental
- Hypervelocity Rail Gun in form of the CHECMATE system

3. Space-based programmes such as:
- Space-Based Interceptor or SBI
- Brilliant Pebbles

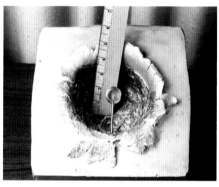

▲ *The SDI tested a Kinetic Energy Weapon by firing a 7 g projectile at an Aluminium test block at 7000 m per second.*

Result of the SDI

Due to the SDI, the US now holds a significant advantage in the field of comprehensive advanced missile defence systems. Under the Bill Clinton administration, the SDI was changed to the Ballistic Missile Defence Organization (BMDO). The current patriot missile defence system would have been impossible without the SDI.

FUN FACT

The SDI was very poorly received, both by the masses and scientific community. It was popularly referred to as the Star Wars programme.

Space Warfare

Space warfare refers to combat that occurs in outer space. This includes ground-to-space warfare, such as attacking satellites from Earth, and space-to-space warfare, such as satellites attacking satellites or spacecraft attacking each other. Technically, this does not include space-to-ground warfare, i.e., where orbital objects directly attack ground, sea or air targets. However, common usage often mixes the two terms.

Existence of satellite weaponry

Currently, some anti-satellite weaponry does exist. This is usually launched from planes or from Earth's surface. No satellite weaponry currently exists. The People's Republic of China successfully tested a ballistic missile by launching an anti-satellite weapon on 11th January, 2007. On 21st February, 2008, the USA used a SM-3 missile to destroy a satellite USA-193, which is a spy satellite, while it was 247 km above the Pacific Ocean. Japan also uses the SM-3 missile system.

Space weaponry

Space warfare can use a large variety of weapons. Some are currently in existence while others are in the realm of science fiction.

Ballistic Warfare — Systems proposed for ballistic warfare range from measures as simple as ground and space-based anti-missiles to rail guns, space-based lasers, orbital mines and other futuristic weaponry.

▲ An image created to show a missile destroying a satellite in space.

Electronic Warfare – Since spacecraft and satellite rely very heavily on electronics, these systems are designed to jam, sabotage and outright destroy enemy electronics.

Kinetic bombardment — The energy that a projectile would gain while falling from orbit would make it rival all except the most powerful explosives. Thus, simply dropping objects from orbit is a viable weapons system.

Directed-energy weapons — Lasers, linear particle accelerators or particle-beam based weaponry, microwaves and plasma-based weaponry all rely upon imparting high energy density to various particles and targeting the enemy with them.

◀ An artists's representation of the future of the USA Space Command in 2020.

FUN FACT

Rail guns and lasers in space, work in most aspects. Currently, the only problem is that the batteries in space aren't big enough to power them.

Space Tourism

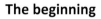

Space tourism refers to recreational space travel. It can be either on established government-owned vehicles such as the Russian Soyuz and the ISS or on the growing number of vehicles that are fielded by private companies.

The beginning

Space tourism began at the end of the 1990s. It occurred due to a deal between a Russian company MirCorp and an American company Space Adventures Ltd. MirCorp was a private venture responsible for the Russian space station Mir. MirCorp decided to sell a trip to Mir to generate income for maintenance of the aging space station.

First space tourist

American businessman Dennis Tito was the world's first space tourist on 28th April, 2001. Tito paid $20 million for his flight on the Russian spacecraft Soyuz TM-32. However, before Tito could make his trip, the decision was made to de-orbit Mir. Fortunately, after the intervention of Space Adventures Ltd.,

the mission was diverted to the ISS and Tito spent seven days on board.

South African computer millionaire Mark Shuttleworth (2002) and American businessman Gregory Olsen (2005) visited the ISS. Iranian-born American entrepreneur Anousheh Ansari became the first female fee-paying space traveller and visited the ISS in September 2006.

The future of space tourism as digitally rendered by an artist. ▼

Cost of a spaceflight

Most space tourists spend about US $20-30 million for a trip to the ISS. However, since 2007, Space Adventures has offered a spaceflight around the moon on a Soyuz spacecraft for a fee of US $100 million. As of 2015, Virgin Galactic has seats for tourists at US $200,000 to go into sub-orbital space.

▲ *Dennis Tito, pictured above, is the world's first space tourist.*

FUN FACT

Tito objected to the use of the word "tourist" due to the arduous training required for his mission. Since his flight, the term "spaceflight participant" is used to distinguish commercial space travellers from astronauts.

Space Colonisation

Space colonisation is permanent human habitation off planet Earth. The concept is also called space settlement or extra-terrestrial colonisation. The two most common reasons of its popularity is as follows:

- The survival of human civilisation and the biosphere in case of a planetary-scale disaster.
- The vast resources in space for expansion of human society and the possibilities of development and evolution.

Space colonies

The building of a space colony presents a set of prohibitive challenges that are both technological and economic in nature. Space settlements would have to provide for all the material needs of hundreds or thousands of humans. This is extremely difficult in an environment that is very hostile to human life.

Space technologies

Technologies such as controlled ecological life support systems have yet to be developed in a meaningful manner. These would be essential to any long-term settlement. Colonies would have to deal with the issue of how humans would behave and thrive in such places. We have absolutely no data on the long-term effects of space on either our bodies or minds.

The cost of sending anything from Earth's surface into orbit is colossal – it would cost roughly about US $20,000 per kg. Thus, a space colony would be an extremely expensive project.

▲ *A digitally created image of what space settlements would look like.*

▲ *Goldman Award winner and noted environmentalist Terri Swearingen famously said, "We are living on this planet like we have another one to go to". Her comment highlights the fact that Earth is rapidly running out of resources.*

Planetary Habitability

Planetary habitability is the measure of a planet or a natural satellite's potential to develop and sustain life. Habitability applies to life developed directly on a planet or satellite or that transferred to it from another body.

What makes a planet habitable?

There are many necessary conditions for planetary habitability. These range from the planet itself to the star system in which it resides. They are briefly outlined here.

Kinds of star with a habitable object around it

Spectral class – These stars should be sufficiently big to give off the necessary temperature and flare conditions, but small enough to have an adequately long life span to sustain life. The shaped area around a star, where water can exist and the condition is sufficiently moderate for life to thrive. This must be stable for evolution.

Low stellar variation – Some stars fluctuate greatly with respect to brightness. This must be sufficiently low so that the planet does not experience any extreme conditions of heat or cold.

High metallicity – The star should contain a sufficient amount of heavier elements (all heavier than Helium and Hydrogen) that will support life.

Requirements for a planet to support life

Mass – This must be adequately large to hold an atmosphere, but small enough to have significant landmasses.

Orbit and rotation – It must have an orbit and rotation that is both moderate and stable. Seasons must occur regularly and not be extreme so that they won't be hostile to life.

Geochemistry – The planet must have sufficient amounts of heavier elements for life to evolve and sustain.

Microenvironments – The environment on the planet should contain micro pockets. The idea is that diversity encourages the evolution of life.

▲ *Moons of certain gas giants satisfy most of these criteria and may be habitable. This is more likely since moons are more numerous than planets.*

▼ *The Atacama Desert is very analogous to Mars' surface. As we can see, it is one of the most lifeless areas on Earth due to a miniscule change in conditions on a cosmic scale.*

Terraforming

Terraforming is the theoretical process of deliberately modifying its atmosphere, temperature, surface topography or ecology to be similar to the biosphere of Earth. This may be done to a planet, moon or any other body to make it habitable to Earth-like life. Terraforming literally means "Earth shaping" or creating something like Earth.

Planetary engineering

The term "terraforming" is rarely used in a general sense. It is used as a synonym for planetary engineering. However, this isn't true. All terraforming is planetary engineering, but the reverse isn't true. The concept of terraforming developed from both science fiction and actual science. Jack Williamson is credited with the idea from a science-fiction story called *Collision Orbit* published in Astounding Science Fiction in 1942. However, it is possible that the concept may pre-date this work.

Possibility of terraforming

Based on experiences with Earth, the environment of a planet can be deliberately altered. However, we're not sure that we can create an unconstrained planetary biosphere on another planet that mimics Earth. Mars is usually considered to be the most likely candidate for terraforming. NASA has even hosted debates on the subject.

An artist's conception of what Mars would look like during various stages of terraforming. ▼

Several potential methods of altering the climate of Mars may fall within humanity's technological capabilities. Much study has been done concerning the possibility of heating the planet and altering its atmosphere. The timescale involved is long, though possible.

An expensive affair

The terraforming of a planet would be an extremely expensive undertaking with undeterminable results.

The economic resources required to do so are far beyond those that any government or society is willing to allocate. The ethics, logistics, economics, politics and methodology of altering the environment of an extra-terrestrial world are barriers to this concept. However, the speeding up of technology means that this may not be true for long.

▼ *The surface of Mars being explored by an astronaut to contemplate terraforming possibilities.*

INDEX

T